BIHAR

History and Archaeology of Incredible Madhepura

BIHAR

History and Archaeology of Incredible Madhepura

Raman Kumar Soni
Gunjan Kumari

Kaveri Books
New Delhi-110002

First Published in 2014
ISBN 978-81-7479-151-1

Published by
Kaveri Books
4832/24, Ansari Road
New Delhi - 110 002 (India)
Tel.: 011-2328 8140, 2324 5799
E-mail: kaveribooks@vsnl.com,
kaveribooks@gmail.com
Website: www.kaveribooks.com

Laser Typesetting by : Deep Graphics, Delhi

PRINTED IN INDIA

Dedicated To

My Family

With Lots of Love

Contents

Acknowledgements

In carrying out the work like this, there are many people to whom we owe thanks. We wish to record appreciation and gratitude for the help and assistance received from various quarters in the preparation of this book. First of all, Prof. Ravindra Kumar needs to be thanked. His inspiring and untiring guidance has made major parts of this work possible today. It has been a great privilege and pleasure to be associated with him. Dr. Ravindra deserves warmest appreciation and gratitude.

We are grateful to director, faculties, and other staff members of School of Social Sciences (SOSS) and Research Unit of Indira Gandhi National Open University (IGNOU), faculties and staff members of Department of History and Department of African Studies of University of Delhi for extending all the help needed while doing research work on the present study area. We would also like to thank the staff members of Department of History, College of Arts and Social Sciences, Adi-Keih, Eritrea; Central Reference Library, Arts Library, and D School Library of University of Delhi; Indian Council of Historical Research Library; Library of IGNOU; and Indian Council of World Affairs (Sapru House).

Special appreciation goes to Dr. Ogbaghebriel Berakhi, Dr. Firdos Anwar, Dr. Aruna Sharma, Late Dr. J. P. Sharma, Dr. R. C. Thakran, Dr. Amar Singh, Late Dr. Surajvan, Dr. R. C. P. Yadav, Dr. Suresh Chaudhary, Dr. R. K. K. Rajrajan, Dr. N. K. Pandey,

Dr. P. K. Mohanty, Dr. B. P. Shau, Dr. Tribhuvan Prasad, Dr. K. Krishna Rao, Dr. S. C. Mishra, Dr. Imtiaz Ahmad, Late Dr. Surajvan, Dr. D. N. Jha, Dr. Verma, Dr. M. V. Krishnappa, Dr. Ravindra Bhardwaj, Prof. Rajiv Dubey, Dr. Qamar Hasan, Dr. Ganesh Prasad, Dr. Nagendra Kumar, Dr. K. P. Yadav, Dr. Khagendra, Dr. Woldetinsae Towelde, Dr. Berhane Keletu, Ravish Nagpal, Anil Kumar Singh, Mukesh, Prabhat Kumar, Kumar Amrendar Singh, Sabbir Ahmad, Bachneshwar Paswan, Inder Chandra Bothra, Late Tekeste Melake, Habtai Zerai, Rezene, Kesete Teweldebrahan, Nuguse Bahre, Asmelash Aymut, Michael, Habtom, Aron Andemichael, and Miriam for their help, encouragement, advice, and time.

We extend heartfelt thanks to our friends Ashutosh, Ajay, Jaybardhan, Brajesh, Rakesh, Mahinder, Asif, Madan, Manoj, Dr. Afsar Alam, Ajit, Yoges Babu, Sujeet, Kishore, Amit, Saroj, Sunil, Jay Prakash, Mithilesh Ranjan, Hemant, Shivani, Anil, Rani, Preeti, and Doli for their kind help and encouragement.

Special thanks go to Prof. Tej Dhar, Prof. R. K. Chaudhary, Dr. T. Vijay Kumar, Anto. A. Paul, Dr. Teena, Dr. Mohammad Ehrar Alam, Dr. Manssor, Dr. Minhazul, Dr. Saleem, Dr. Garnayak, Dr. Neeraj Mishra, Dr. Sanober, Vipan Kumar, Manoverdeen, Sudhakar, Akhilesh, Samuel, Gabriel, Isias, and Habteab for their help in editing and giving valuable advice on the present work.

Mr. Praveen Mishra, Dr. Zubair Islam, and Ravi helped in preparing the maps. We are also indebted to Rakesh Goyal and Kaveri Book Service for bringing this work in public domain. We are very grateful to Shiv Shankar, Kundan, Yashpal, Rahul, Ravi, Late Rustam Baba, Manish, Mithilesh, and Gangesh for their valuable contributions to the present work in one or other way.

Lastly, we express humble gratitude to our family members for their continuous help, support, and encouragement. As usual, Chaturanand Singh and Nutan Singh were constant source of inspiration. Koushal Kishor Singh, Ranju Singh, Suman Kumar

Saurabh, Khushaboo Kumari Arya, Mohan Singh, Neeshu, Mannu, Punoom Singh, Neelam Singh, Shyam Singh, Ashok Singh, Bedanand Singh, Sakaldev Singh, Late Ramchandra Singh, Late Bindeshwari Singh, and Late Tirthanand Singh contributed to the present work in their own way. Moreover, daughter Harshita Singh, niece Aanjali Raksha Singh, and nephew Aditya Singh provided delightful distractions. We dedicate this work to all the family members and relatives.

Raman Kumar Soni
Gunjan Kumari

Preface

The present work, ***Bihar: History and Archaeology of Incredible Madhepura*** is a dream come true. It is result of several stimuli. One of them is strong attachment with the homeland (Madhepura, Kosi River region, and Bihar). Secondly, Kosi belt is wanting in systematic and scientific historical and archaeological researches. All these together created a powerful desire to contribute to this area and its people in one's own field of study.

The current book is the result of extensive research work. It involved thorough archaeological cum historical exploration of Madhepura district with special focus on its historical settlement pattern. The latter was specifically aimed as it is relatively new and piquant in South Asian archaeology. Such type of study also helps in understanding the interaction between human beings and environment in the past as well as the present.

The first author believes that he and his academic life has been immensely influenced and shaped by five people namely Dr. Firdos Anwar, Late Dr. J. P. Sharma, Prof. R. C. Thakran, Prof. Ravindra Kumar, Late Dr. Surajvan, and Ram Chandra Guha. So, in a way their contribution to the present work directly or indirectly is very obvious. Moreover, Dr. Raman Kumar Soni strongly feels that his whole life, he has been probably preparing for this work.

The book is divided into twelve chapters. Each of them is further divided into several parts and sub-parts. Besides, there are maps, tables, and figures to facilitate better understanding of the area under study and its history.

The first chapter entitled as "**A Forgotten Land**" provides necessary background as well as justification for the present exercise. It begins by exploring the question as to why Madhepura is a forgotten land. Then the chapter dwells on the location, nomenclature, administrative history, and modern settlement and subsistence systems of the district.

"**Geology and Topography**" forms the second chapter of the book. It gives description on the geological formation and physical features at macro as well as micro level. The chapter begins with tracing out the geology of the great North Indian Plain and then slowly moves on to see the same in case of Bihar, Kosi plain, and Madhepura. Thereafter, the physical features of Middle Gangetic Plain of which Madhepura district forms a part are described.

The third chapter is "**Kosi and Its Plain**". First of all, it traces out the source and course of Kosi. Then it goes to describe its characteristics and physical features. The chapter also discusses the geographical features of several districts constituting the Kosi Plain.

"**Ecological Setting**" constitutes the fourth chapter of the present work. Here, the landscape of Madhepura district and Kosi plain is studied in detail. It includes the study of physical elements such as landforms and soils; living elements of flora and fauna; and abstract elements such as weather conditions etc. It focuses on the study of the relationships between human being and their natural setting. The chapter also takes into account the way people shaped their land, consciously or unconsciously.

The fifth chapter, "**The History**" as the title suggests traces out the general history of Madhepura district from ancient to modern times. The fate of the district and surroundings during phases of *Janapada*, *Mahajanapada*, Maurya, post-Maurya, Gupta, post-Gupta,

Pala, Sena, Sultanate, Mughal, British, and Freedom struggle is explored and analyzed.

The sixth and seventh chapters, "Historical Places in Madhepura Subdivision" and "Historical Places in Udakishunganj Subdivision" are based on intensive archaeological cum historical survey in Madhepura district. They describe the explored sites, their physical condition, cultural sequence, and location in relation to their respective natural background in two administrative subdivisions of the district which divides Madhepura in almost two equal halves.

The eighth chapter is "Historical Places in Kosi Plain". Since Kosi Plain consists of several modern districts of northeastern Bihar besides Madhepura, this chapter tries to explore and reconstruct the past human activities in Saharsa, Purnea, Bhagalpur, and Munger districts in order to better understand the historical developments in the region. It also talks about the sites of historical importance in these districts.

The ninth chapter titled as "Settlement Distribution" dwells on distribution of settlements over the landscape of Madhepura. It explains culture wise distribution of settlements, cultural sequence, areas of frequency, location, and lines of extension of settlements in the district.

The "Settlement Pattern" constitutes the tenth chapter of the book. Here, the emerging settlement pattern in the research area and their catalyst in overall perspective of physiographic features, rainfall, hydrology, landuse pattern, administrative division, functionality, and movement and migration of people etc., are analyzed. It examines regions rather than only individual sites.

"The History of Education" is the eleventh and second last chapter of the present work. Broadly, as the title suggests, it deals with the history of education and its development in the study area and neighbouring region. The chapter moves from general to particular. It talks about the educational development in Bihar from ancient to modern times. Then, it moves on to explore and analyze the history of education in Kosi region and Madhepura district. Finally, the chapter ends up with a discussion on present state of educational affair in Madhepura and the surroundings and suggestions for its further development.

The concluding and the twelfth chapter entitled "**Epilogue: The Incredible Madhepura**" is the crux of the whole study and a statement of the principal idea "Why is Madhepura Incredible" in spite of long neglect and general apathy. It is also an account of conclusions reached through the research work done in Madhepura and Kosi region.

Finally, the task seems to be accomplished with success. This whole exercise has been challenging but interesting. It consumed years; hundreds of working hours; substantial manpower; and good amount of material resources, energy, and intellect. It involved interaction with hundreds of local inhabitants; investigation of topography, flora, fauna, general environment, and climate; collection of data regarding past human settlements and historical developments; and serious discussion with the learned and expert etc.

The whole workout has helped in unraveling dozens of human settlements of immense archaeological and historical importance unknown to the academic world. Enormous amount of data pertaining to settlements, subsistence, and culture has been collected and analyzed including their location, form, condition, size, surface artifacts, soil type, water resources, vegetation, drainage system, depression, and cultural and chronological records etc.

At last, it is hoped that the present work may have filled some gap in relation to historical and archaeological knowledge of Madhepura District and surroundings. It will help us in understanding the interaction and associated dynamics between human beings and their environment in the past and the present. The findings may further enlighten people on the glorious saga of Kosi region. The use of 'he' in the present work is just for the sake of convenience and should not be taken as gender insensitivity. Moreover, the different measuring unit such as miles, kilometer (km), meter, feet, inch, and millimeter (mm) has been used interchangeably for accuracy as well as convenience. Long live Bihar! Long live Madhepura! Glory to their people and culture!

Raman Kumar Soni
Gunjan Kumari

Abbreviations

BCE	-	Before Common Era
C	-	Centigrade
CBSE	-	Central Board of Secondary Education
C. D. Block	-	Community Development Block
CE	-	Common Era
E	-	East
EH	-	Early Historical
IAS	-	Indian Administrative Service
ICSSE	-	Indian Council of Secondary School Education
IIM	-	Indian Institute of Management
IIT	-	Indian Institute of Technology
Km	-	Kilometer
LH	-	Late Historical
Mm	-	millimeter
N	-	North
Sq. km.	-	Square Kilometer
E Med	-	Early Medieval
L Med	-	Late Medieval
Mod	-	Modern
GPS	-	Global Positioning System

List of Maps

List of Tables

Chapter 10: Settlement Pattern

Appendices

List of Figures

1

A Forgotten Land

The history of Madhepura reminds us the great saga of Bihar[1] of which it is one of the districts. The glorious past of Bihar is based on the achievements of its different regions.[2] Most of its regions have been subjected to extensive archaeological and historical researches. But surprisingly, the history of this grand land is relatively silent over the past developments in Kosi River region in general and Madhepura district in particular. Surprisingly, no systematic archaeological or historical research has been carried out in the area. At best, the previous efforts seem sketchy and superficial. Moreover, whatever little is known about its past is hardly disseminated. There could be several reasons to these.

Probably, the remoteness of the area has some role to play. Besides, Madhepura seems to have relatively lagged behind in the race of modern development. As a result, it lacks heavily in basic infrastructure and logistics sufficient enough to attract researchers, history lovers and enthusiasts. The interiors of the district are not well connected with roads and transport facilities. In last few decades, the perception about the general law and order situation in Bihar also seems to have deterred the stakeholders from venturing into the locality.

Moreover, Kosi River's frequent havoc has also added to it's owe. The area being dotted with its numerous *dhar*[3] and channels loomed large over the mind of learned as well as layman. In addition, the vagaries of the Kosi River also seem to have given a feeling to the researchers of the possible destruction of area's archaeological and historical heritage. Moreover, the relative lack of readily available sources also hampers any will to take up the task of Madhepura's historical reconstruction.

Overall, Madhepura seems to be a "forgotten land". The present exercise is an effort to unravel some of its past. Before moving on to discover the district in geographical and historical perspective, it is better to shed some light up on its location, nomenclature, administrative formation, and the living conditions of the people.

LOCATION

Madhepura district is located in northeastern part of Bihar and in the plains of river Kosi. It is situated between 25°34' to 26°07' N Latitude and 86°19' to 87°07' E Longitude. Madhepura is bordered by Araria and Supaul districts in the north, Khagaria and Bhagalpur districts in the south, Purnea district in the east, and Saharsa district in the West. (Map 1).

NOMENCLATURE

There are several theories associated with naming of the district. One of them said that since Madhepura stands at the centre of Kosi River, so called 'Madhyapura', meaning a place centrally situated. Gradually 'Madhyapura' was transformed to 'Madhipura' and then finally into present Madhepura. Another view is as the area have been inhabited by the bulk of 'Madhavas' (clan of Lord Krishna) so the term 'Madhavpur'. Slowly latter changed into Madhepura.[4]

ADMINISTRATIVE HISTORY

The administrative history of Madhepura district is quite interesting. Earlier it constituted a part of Bhagalpur district during British rule. Madhepura became a subdivision on 9th May, 1845 consisting of seven Community Development Blocks (C. D. Blocks).[5]

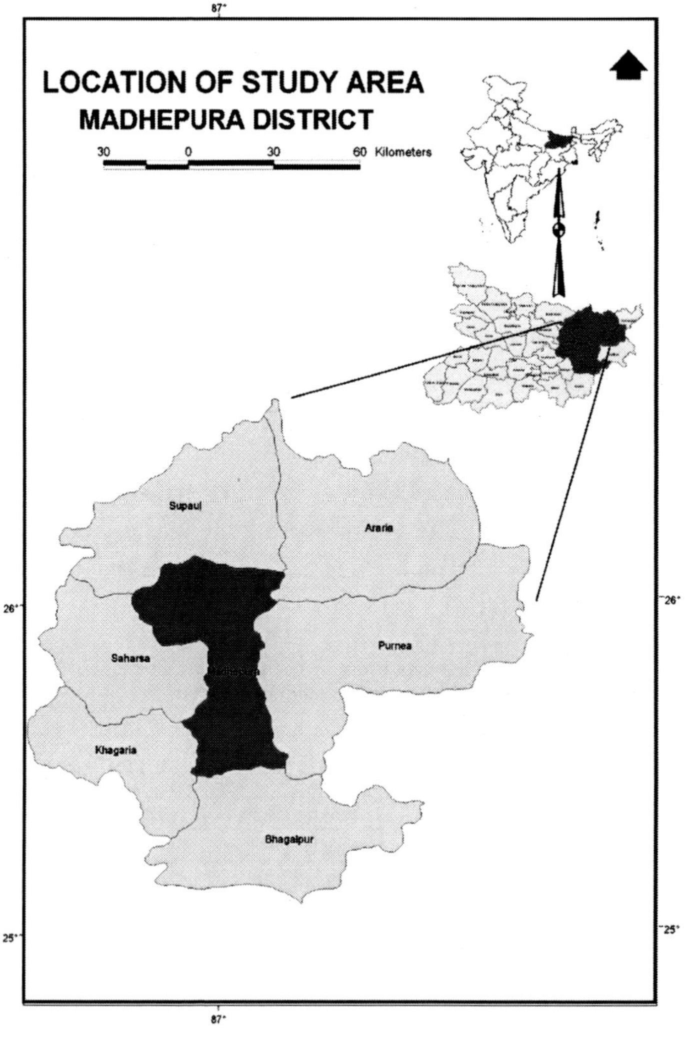

Map 1: Location of Madhepura district

In fact, the present Saharsa district then formed one of its revenue circles. A deputy magistrate was directly responsible for the administrative affair of the subdivision.[6] As far as the judicial administration is concerned, two *munsifs*[7] were stationed at

Madhepura civil court. Curiously, Saharsa got the status of a district on 1st April, 1954 encompassing Madhepura as one of its subdivisions.[8] However, Madhepura got the similar status on 9th May, 1981.[9] On 21st May, 1983, one of its blocks Udakishunganj was upgraded to the level of subdivision. Therefore, the district got bifurcated into two administrative subdivisions such as Madhepura and Udakishunganj.

In the year 1994, besides the exiting seven C. D. Blocks,[10] four new blocks came into existence namely Gwalpara, Puraini, Bihariganj, and Shankarpur. First three of these were put under Udakishunganj subdivision, whereas the last one went with its northern counterpart (Madhepura subdivision). Later on, two more new C. D. Blocks were constituted with the name Ghailarh and Gamharia in 1999. These two were kept under Madhepura subdivision. So, the total numbers of C. D. Blocks reached to thirteen. (Map 1.1) and (Table 1).

Table 1: It shows the number of subdivisions, blocks, and circles in Madhepura district

SL. NO.	SUB-DIVISION	BLOCK	CIRCLE
1	MADHEPURA	Madhepura	Madhepura
2		Singheshwar	Singheshwar
3		Murliganj	Murliganj
4		Gamharia	
5		Ghailarh	
6		Kumarkhand	Kumarkhand
7		Shankarpur	Shankarpur
8	UDAKISHUNGANJ	Chausa	Chausa
9		Puraini	Puraini
10		Gwalpara	Gwalpara
11		Bihariganj	Bihariganj
12		Udakishunganj	Udakishunganj
13		Alamnagar	Alamnagar

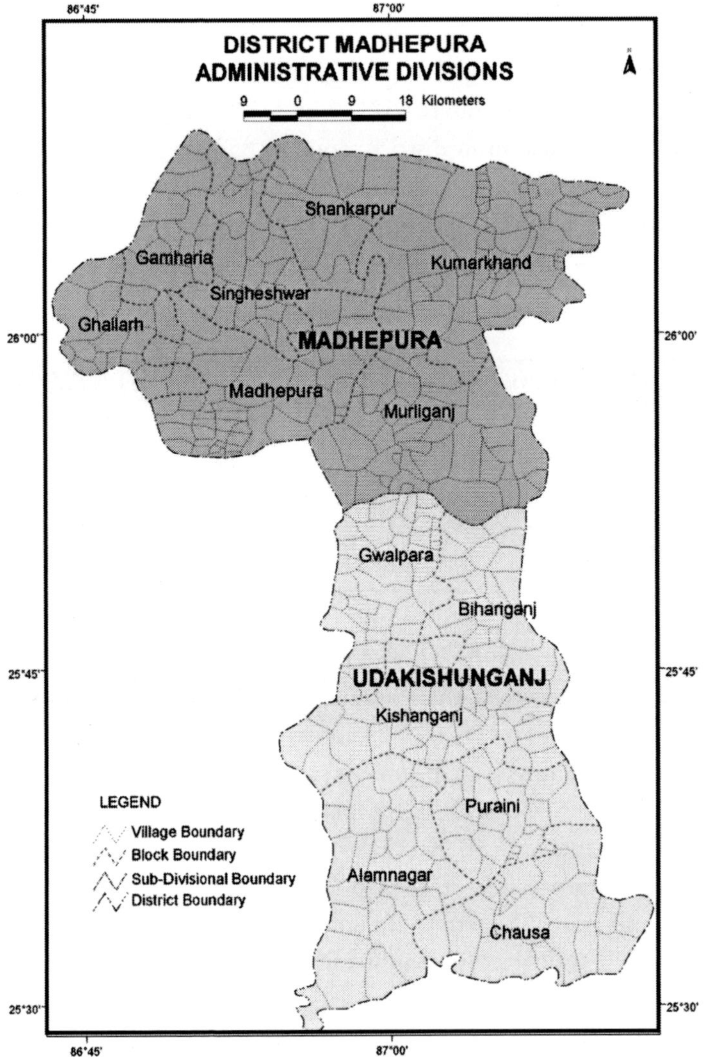

Map 1.1: The district map of Madhepura showing subdivisions, blocks, and villages

MODERN SETTLEMENT AND SUBSISTENCE SYSTEMS[11]

The district consists of 170 *Panchayats*[12] and 449 revenue villages. These villages are almost evenly distributed between two subdivisions in terms of numbers. According to 2001 census, Madhepura has population of 1524596.[13] The population of Udakishunganj and Madhepura subdivisions is 657148 and 799512 respectively. The density of population in district comes to 853 people per sq. km.[14] There are two semi-urban areas in Madhepura district called *nagar panchayat.*[15] (Table 1.1 and Table 1.2).

Table 1.1: The population of two *nagar panchayats* (semi-urban area) in Madhepura district (2001 census)

SL. NO.	NAGAR PANCHAYAT	POPULATION
1.	Madhepura	45015
2.	Murliganj	22921
Total		67936

Madhepura has 36.01 % of main workers.[16] As far as marginal workers[17] are concerned, their percentage is 1.66. The district is having 62.33 % of non-workers. The majority of main workers (92.69 %, 393141) are engaged in primary sector. In the secondary sector, Madhepura has 1.36 % (5804) of total working population. Whereas, a small percentage (5.93 %, 25188), of total working population is engaged in tertiary sector.[18] (Map 1.2). The district is linked with broad gauge rail of Eastern Central Railway. Madhepura is connected with state headquarter (Patna) by rail as well as road.

Agriculture is the main occupation of the people in Madhepura district. Paddy[19] and wheat are grown in alluvial as well as reclaimed soils. People cultivate jute, maize, and sugarcane in large quantities. The oilseed is another favourite. But, the cultivation of indigo has completely stopped.

The total area of land under cultivation is 136646 hectares. There is 1772 hectares of famished land that could be used for

Table 1.2: The number of *panchayats*, villages, and population in each C. D. Blocks of Madhepura district (2001 census)

SL. NO.	BLOCK	PANCHAYAT	VILLAGE	POPULATION
1.	Madhepura	17	49	149667
2.	Ghailarh	9	16	72701
3.	Singheshwar	13	27	101240
4.	Gamharia	8	12	65283
5.	Shankarpur	9	9	82498
6.	Kumarkhand	21	71	187030
7.	Murliganj	17	45	141093
8.	Gwalpara	12	51	95138
9.	Bihariganj	12	22	101662
10.	Udakishunganj	16	44	136842
11.	Puraini	9	31	77757
12.	Alamnagar	14	29	129263
13.	Chausa	13	43	116486
Total		**170**	**449**	**1456660**

agricultural activities. The quantity of barren land is estimated to be 4916 hectares, out of which 1272 hectares are covered with sand. The procurement area of paddy crop is 52165 hectares. Wheat, maize, and sugarcane are grown in 31431, 34098, and 801 hectares of land respectively. The potato is cultivated in 1442 hectares. The Coconut Development Board owned by Central Government is also situated in the district.

At the turn of nineteenth century and in the beginning of the twentieth century, the district's people mainly depended upon the traditional irrigation system.[20] But now, number of canals have been constructed under Kosi project. Apart from this, the irrigational

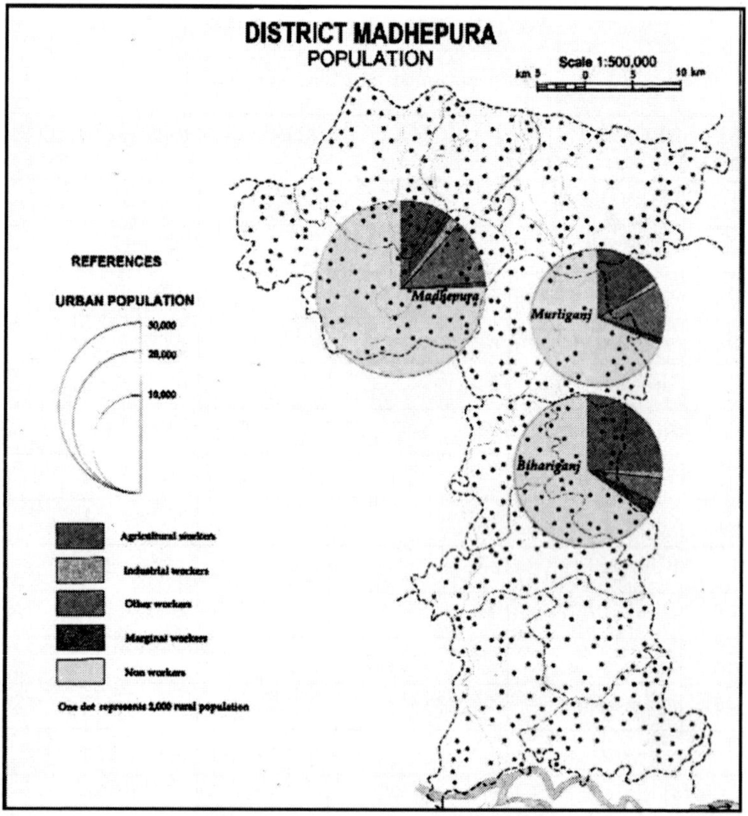

Map 1.2: The population dynamics of Madhepura district

facilities have also been added through number of minor irrigation schemes, surface percolation wells, open wells, and tube wells. In fact, irrigation facilities are available to 77414 hectares of land in Madhepura. The total number of state boring is 3018. On the other hand, 914 borings are owned and operated by other stakeholders. The entire number of state tube wells is 31.

The subsistence pattern of the people of this district also includes domestication of animals. In fact, animal husbandry is intricately attached with the agricultural practices of the people. Cattle, goats, and buffaloes are main livestock apart from the poultry birds. The number of high and general breed buffaloes are 2177 and 109407 respectively. Whereas, there are at least 9285 high breed cows. In contrast, the number of general breed cows is very high, 165429. The people of this district also tame about 222886 goats and 30580 pigs. Under poultry industries, about 110720 cocks and hens are estimated. The Animal Husbandry Department has taken number of measures to improve the quality of animal breed. Moreover, the number of veterinary hospitals and dispensaries has also increased in recent years. There are 16 animal hospitals and 3 artificial breeding centers in the district.

Table 1.3: The number of livestock in Madhepura district

SL. NO.	LIVESTOCK	NUMBER
1.	Buffalo (High breed)	2177
2.	Buffalo (General breed)	109407
3.	Cow (High breed)	9285
4.	Cow (General breed)	165429
5.	Goat	222886
6.	Pig	30580
7.	Cock and Hen	110720

The condition of the industry is very poor. It probably lacks the resources and suitable infrastructure. There are practically no mines as the only known minerals existing in the district are sand and black soil. To some extent, sand-mining is flourishing due to prevalence of Kosi and several *dhar* in the district. Lead ores occurs at Gamharia.

Generally, there is lack of large-scale industry. Recently, a railway sleeper plant was established by the Ministry of Railway at an approximate cost of 7 crores of rupees.[21] Unfortunately, the Railway Ministry's ambitious plan for the establishment of a railway coach factory in the district has become the victim of politics.[22] Some of the other industrial plants are Khandsari Sugar mill at Udakishunganj, Mustard Oil factory at Bihariganj, and Katha Factory at Murliganj (now closed) etc. One electric pole manufacturing plant is being set up in the vicinity of the district town.

Even the condition of small scale industry is not satisfactory. Only eight small scale industries are running in the district. There are 2875 very small industries.[23] But, there are several small scales timber mills (*Aara* machine), brick factories (*chimnee*), and jute mills scattered throughout the district. The registered unit under Factory Act is 323. The numbers of persons employed in these units are 2981.

Madhepura has a rich history of trade and commerce. During eighteenth, nineteenth, and twentieth centuries the area traded with Nepal and eastern Bengal. Madhepura has been an important trade center. The chief items of import were coal, coke, salt, cotton piece goods, gunny bags, gram, pulses, cement, and tobacco (raw). The main export item consisted of rice, paddy, wheat gram, pulses, linseed, mustard seed, jute, and indigo. (Table 1.4).

Table 1.4: The most important manufactured, imported, and exported commodities in Madhepura district

SL. NO.	NAME OF TOWN	MOST IMPORTANT COMMIDITIES		
		Manufactured	Import	Export
1.	Murliganj	-	Cement	Jute
2.	Bihariganj	Sugar and Mustard Oil	Cement	Jute
3.	Madhepura	-	Cement	Jute

At present Murliganj, Bihariganj, and Madhepura are the main centers of jute collection. The collected jutes are sent to other parts of the Bihar state as well as outside.[24] There are 21 markets and 200 marketing societies in the district under market management. The 32 weekly fairs are also held. There are five nationalized banks in the district, giving their services to industrial and commercial areas with their 64 branches. But several private banks are also operating.

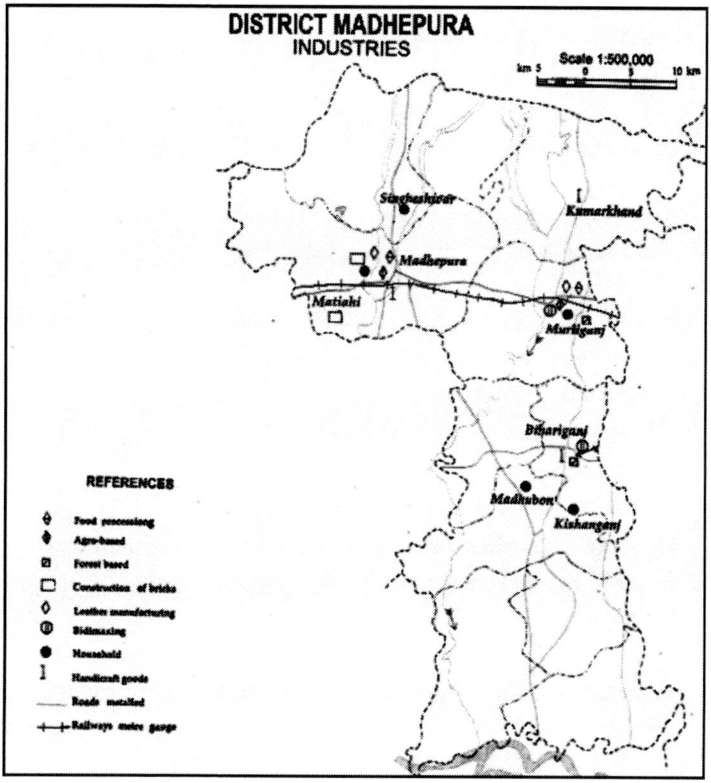

Map 1.3: Industries in Madhepura district

Thus, it can be delineated that Madhepura is situated in the heart of the Kosi land and nearer to international borders of India in eastern sector. It has been made district in early 1980s and so relatively young. The district is administratively divided into two subdivisions and thirteen C. D. Blocks. Madhepura consists of large number of villages but varied in size as well as population. The density of population is high. Its majority of populace is still dependent on agriculture and primary sector for living. In fact, an overwhelming majority of its inhabitants are non-workers. Madhepura is seriously wanting in basic infrastructure and industrial base.

NOTES AND REFERENCES

1. Bihar is one of the 28 provinces of India lying in its eastern portion and sharing the international boundary with Nepal. This state has extremely rich history. The genesis and center of several of early historic *Janapadas*, *Mahajanapadas*, Saisunagas, the Nandas, the great Mauryans, Buddhism, Jainism, the Palas, the grand educational centers like Nalanda and Vikramshila, and the great legendary figure Sher Shah Suri etc, is this land.
2. The archaeological and historical data spread over the different areas of the state have been weaved together to reconstruct a comprehensive history of this province.
3. The water course is locally called *dhar*.
4. *Brihad Hindi Kosh*, 5th edition, p. 887.
5. The total area under it was 3045.82 sq. km.
6. He was usually assisted by a sub-deputy collector. The deputy magistrate assisted the district magistrate in Bhagalpur town (then district headquarter).
7. One of them was permanent. The second was temporary.
8. In private discussions, the elders of Madhepura district feel it to be a political decision which tremendously hampered district's progress for a long period as Madhepura lost its erstwhile administrative prominence. People of the district still believe that Madhepura rather than Saharsa was the natural contender for the status of district in post-independence era.
9. Saharsa was split into two districts- Saharsa and Madhepura- on account of reorganization of districts in Bihar state after 1981 census.
10. The exiting seven C. D. Blocks were Madhepura, Murliganj, Kumarkhand, Singheshwar, Bihariganj, Udakishunganj, Alamnagar, and Chausa.
11. Generally, such kinds of analyses in the present work are based on 2001 census data. In some cases, 1991 census data have also been used. But, wherever the latter is used, it has been indicated. Moreover, wherever it

is possible, some data from 2011 census has also been mentioned against 2001 statistics.

12. *Panchayat* is one of the lowest administrative units consisting of a village or several villages. Generally, it is divided into number of wards. The Mukhia, Sarpanch, Panchayat Samiti, and ward commissioners are the people's representatives elected in *Panchayat* elections.
13. Its population according to 2011 census is 1994618.
14. The density of population according to 2011 census is 1116 people per sq. km.
15. *Nagar Panchayat* is administrative status given to semi-urban area. It is generally divided into several wards. The people of each ward elect their representative and then finally a *Nagarpita* (mayor) is elected out of them.
16. They are the people who have work for major part of the year. These workers are engaged in any economically productive activity for 183 day or six months or more during a year.
17. They are those who had not worked for the major parts of a year. These people worked for less than six months (183 days) in the year.
18. These data are according to census of India 1991. There have been some changes in these categories according to 2001 census. According to latter; the numbers of total workers, main workers, marginal workers, and non-workers are 683976, 498367, 185609, and 842670 respectively.
19. In fact, both the *Bhodoi* and *Aghani* paddies are grown.
20. They used tanks and wells.
21. But interestingly, it is still not operational. The governmental effort to choose a suitable candidate to run the factory has failed till now. The stalemate seemed to be related to the prices on which railway is expecting the sleepers to be delivered.
22. The government failed to acquire the proposed 1200 acres of land and now the whole project is not heard at all.
23. It includes candle making, soap manufacturing, grinding mill, bread, and biscuit factories etc.
24. There is a community locally called Marwari who specializes in this trade. They mainly send the jute from this area to Silleeguree and Kolkata.

2

Geology and Topography

It is necessary to explore and analyze the geographical aspects of Madhepura before actually moving on to reconstruct its archaeological and historical past. The geological analysis tends to precede other aspects in any discourse on natural features. Moreover, since the district constitutes a part of Kosi plain and Bihar state which in turn lay in the great 'North Indian plain,' it is imperative to discuss the geological formation and physical features at macro level first.

GEOLOGY

The 'North Indian plain' was a deep basin in pre Tertiary period. It has been filled by the Tertiary river borne debris from peninsular India and Himalayas[1] known as alluvium. The deposition started during the last phase of Siwalik formation and continued through the Pleistocene up to present. The origin of this basin is a matter of great debate and discussion. Suess argued that it is fore deep in front of the high crustal waves of the Himalayas as they were checked in their southward advance by the inflexible solid landmass of the Indian peninsula. But according to Sydney Burrard, the Indo-Gangetic plain occupies a rift valley.

Like the origin of the basin, the absolute deposit of the alluvium is also debatable. Oldham opined that its thickness might vary from 4,000 to 6,000 meters. One of the recent researches has shown its thickness to be around 1,300 to 1,400 meters on an average south of Bulandshahr.[2] That goes up to 8,000 meters near the foothills of

Himalayas. At Lucknow,[3] a bore well did not strike the bedrock up to 435 meters.[4] This alluvium deposit gradually thins up towards the south until it meets the peninsular blocks.

Wadia believed in the presence of Siwalik and other Tertiary sediments of Himalayan piedmont below these alluviums. He goes further to claim that the more consolidated older formations like Gondwana and Cretaceous rocks exit even below these sediments.

Since Madhepura district is located in Bihar state, a discussion on latter's geological formation is necessary. Bihar's geological structure mainly consists of the Archean rock, the Gondwana rock, and the Gangetic alluvium. The first two rocks are older of the three and entirely concealed by alluvium. This state once formed the part of Gondwana land.

Its main physiographical feature is Ganges and her tributaries such as Kosi. The plain formed by these rivers are extensive and stretches up to the foothills of Himalayas in north. In fact, the southern fringe of Himalayan foothill zone falls within this plain. The area of south of this plain consists of Archean and basement Archean overlaid by sedimentary strata of Vindhyan and Gondwana periods, the lava of Rajmahal hills, and Deccan extending up to the western fringe of the state.

In India, the sedimentary facies of the Archean system of deposits has been loosely grouped under the name Dharwar system of rocks.[5] These rocks are represented in south and south-western part of Bihar. Quartzite, slate, and phyllite form hill ranges along the northern series of Chota Nagpur plateau in Sheikhpura and Rajgir hills lying to the southwest of Madhepura district. The Luckeesarai hill[6] is made up of metamorphosed conglomerate that is overlaid with quartzite.

The Vindhyan rocks occupy a small portion of the extreme southwestern part of Bihar between Sasaram and Son Valley which form the eastern end of the Kaimur plateau. The top of the Kaimur plateau is built up of sandstone, shale, and quartzite of the Kaimur series which is the lowest division of upper Vindhyan. The lower Vindhyan strata known as Semri series[7] is exposed in Kaimur scarps. But south of the Son, the lower stages of this series from low hills merge into the gneisses of Gaya district. The lowermost bed of the Semri series consists of limestone with basal conglomerate. Its thickness is more than 600 meters. This is followed by a thick series of alternating limestone and shale known as the Rohtas stage.

As far as Siwalik system of formation is concerned, Pashchim and Purba Champaran districts[8] encroach upon this type of deposits.[9] Here, the Someshwar range consists entirely of Siwalik sandstones and conglomerates.

The alluvial deposits of Ganges and her tributaries like Kosi constitute the last chapter of the geological history of Bihar and Madhepura. They conceal under them northern extensions of the Chota Nagpur plateau and the Peninsular India. Their formation is interesting. When the sediments accumulated in the Tethys Sea began to be compressed, folded, and raised up by the northerly movement of Peninsular India; its frontal portion sagged down owing to the pressure of advancing and rising earth-waves of the Himalayas. Thus, the depression began to be formed with the Himalayan uplift.

This wide trough between the Vindhyan-Kaimur highlands and the northern proto Himalaya was then occupied by an arm of the sea. It was deposited with the lower Tertiary nummulitic limestone. As the sea retreated after the middle Miocene, it was gradually filled by Tertiary fresh water deposits of India known as Muree and Siwalik systems.

Beyond the Siwalik front, the depression was converted into low flat plain over which Ganges and its tributaries began to meander. The depression is deepest in the north and gradually slopes upward towards the peninsular foreland of the south. This depression[10] must have been further accentuated by the load of deposits. Not surprisingly, the fluviatile borne deposits have been found at great depth. In fact, subsidence allowed further deposition.

A boring for tube well in Patna has shown that alluvial deposits in this area persist below 2000 feet. According to one research,[11] the depth of the alluvium varies from 6000 to 10000 feet.[12] This alluvium could be divided into two forms such as *Bhangar* (older alluvium) and *Khadar* (new alluvium). The former occupies the place above the exiting floodplain and belongs to middle Pleistocene epoch. It is generally 3 to 4 meters and 15 to 20 meters above the highest and lowest levels of the Gangetic bed respectively.

Bhangar is yellowish in colour. It is rich in *kankar*[13] up to the depth of 10 to 15 meters from the surface bed.[14] *Bhangar* is a source for salt-petre as well as sodium sulphate.[15] This older alluvium is suffering erosion due to relative elevation of plain and the resultant steepening of the river ingredients. *Khadar* is blackish in colour and characterized by relative absence of *kankar* and *reys.*[16] This newer alluvium provides materials for brick and pottery. It is still under formation. *Khadar* occupies the present flood plains. Its source lies in the erosion of *Bhangar* as well as the fresh sediments.

As far as the importance of geological formations from economic point of view is concerned, undoubtedly Archean sedimentary rocks with their deposits of iron ore, manganese ore, limestone, dolomite, china clay, kyanite, steatite, and building and other stones rank first. Among the igneous rocks of Archean period; chromites, asbestos, pot stones, magnetites, mica, atomic minerals, copper, and gold are found. The next important geological formation is Gondwana system with its deposits of coal, fire clay, china clay, sandstones, and glass sand. The Vindhyan system of strata is rich in limestone, sandstone, shale, glass, sand, and pyrite. The laterite formation yields bauxite, manganese ore, iron ore, and building stone.

Generally speaking, Bihar is not so rich in mineral resources.[17] But, it is known for its excellent quality of mica called Ruby.[18] Mica is found in Gaya, Munger, and Bhagalpur districts (south and southwest of Madhepura district). Bihar possesses variety of clays. White clay is found in and around Rajmahal hills.

The state is also endowed with springs.[19] There are two main areas of mineral springs such as Munger and Rajgir belts. The springs of Munger belt[20] appear in a line extending over a distance of 30 miles or more along the strike of the Kharagpur hills. Whereas the simple thermal springs of Rajgir group occur in Patna and Gaya districts.[21] They emerge out of Archean quartzite rocks.

As far as Madhepura district is concerned, it has no specific mines, minerals, and mineral springs. But, it is very rich in soil and water resources. In Kosi-Mahananda *doab*,[22] the water is normally struck at 15 cubits[23] and sometimes even at 5-10 cubits.[24] During the annual flood, Kosi brings large quantity of sand and *kankar*.

PHYSICAL FEATURES

Before moving on to reconstruct the physical features of Madhepura district and Kosi plain, it would be better to analyze it on macro level in terms of physical features of 'Indo-Gangetic plain.' The duo ultimately constitutes the part of this great plain. 'Indo-Gangetic plain' is the largest alluvium plain in the world. Not surprisingly, it supports almost half of the South Asia's population. Ganges has been the cradle of Indian culture and civilization. Sir Mortimer Wheeler puts his observation about it in the following ways:

> "If the Indus gave India a name, it may almost be said that the Ganges gave India a faith and is at least as worthy as her sister of solicitude."

The Gangetic plain is a peripheral foreland basin that came into existence in early Miocene, expanded in the middle Miocene, and attained its present form in the late Quaternary Period. The stage wise evolution took place in response to the thrust-fold belt loading events in the Himalayas and the consequent southward expansion of the basin. Presently, this foreland basin is in mature stage of evolution, with an oversupply of sediments, and undefiled condition, building up to 300 to 350 meters above sea level, exclusively by fluvial processes.

Dudley Stamp observed that this plain of northern India forms a great curve from the Arabian Sea to the Bay of Bengal. It is more than 3,200 kilometers long and 240 to 480 kilometers broad. Stamp also opined about the general features of this area:

> "One is the dead flatness of the plain- not a hill, scarcely a mound to break the monotony of the level surface... So gentle is the seaward slope that it is imperceptible to the eye. Nearly thousand miles from its mouth, the Ganga is only 900 feet above sea-level. Another feature is the sudden rise of the Himalayas from the level plain... But otherwise the uniformity is amazing. Not even a rock, not even a pebble is present, to alter the uniform character of the alluvium."[25]

The Gangetic plain is divided into three parts such as the upper Gangetic plain, the middle Gangetic plain, and the lower Gangetic plain. Madhepura falls in the middle Gangetic plain that stretches almost 300 kilometers from Himalayan foothills in north and Vindhyan Ranges in south. The middle Gangetic plain reached its present form in post Tertiary period, when this deep trough was filled by fine alluvium brought down by the Himalayas. Its average thickness is 1,300 to 1,400 meters.[26]

In the prehistoric times, Ganges watered by its tributaries like Kosi flowed sluggishly in the meandering fashion. It formed ox-bow lakes in the process. Some of these lakes are perennial. Once upon a time, they were rich in aquatic fauna. Generally, the land around them was covered with wild grasses.[27] This marshy grassland turned into quality grassland during the Holocene period.[28] As a result, animals were attracted in these areas.[29]

The main rivers of Gangetic plain such as Ganges, Yamuna, Gomati, Ghaghara, Gandak, and Kosi, etc., show very wide river valleys in which the present day active channels and its flood plain is entrenched. They are the areas of sand deposition. The residence time of these rivers in their valleys is in the order of 1,000 to 10, 0000 years.[30]

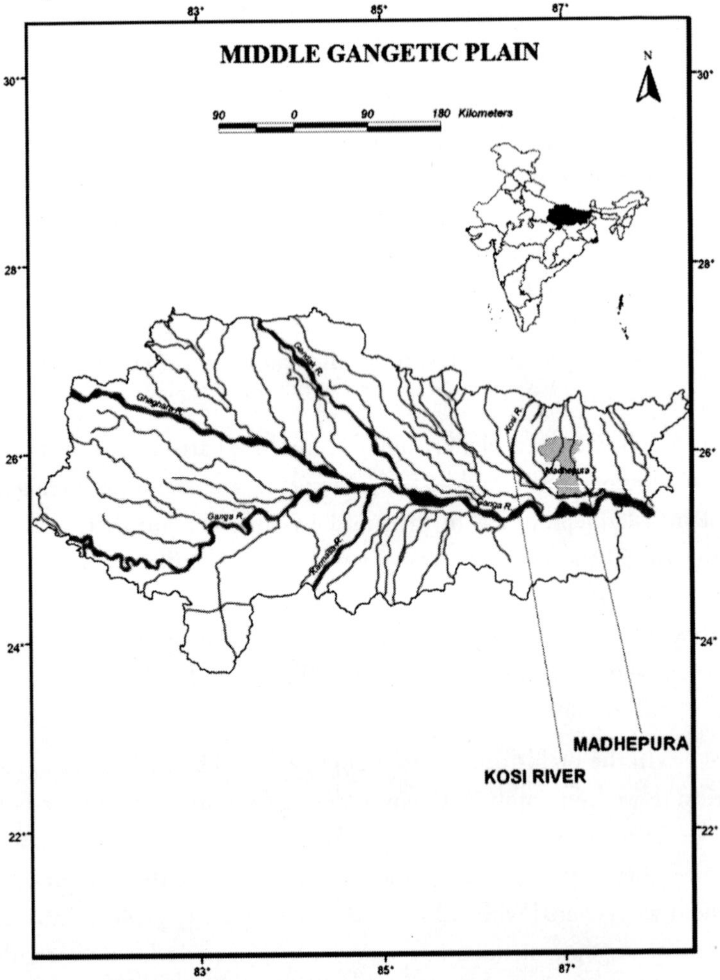

Map 2: Drainage system of the middle Gangetic plain and location of Kosi plain and Madhepura district within it

The middle Gangetic plain is bounded by the Gangetic-Yamuna confluence in the west and the Bihar and West Bengal border in the east, Himalayas in the north, and Vindhyan in the south. The area includes modern Uttar Pradesh and most of Bihar. On the basis of river-system, the middle Gangetic plain could be divided into Gangetic plain in north and Gangetic plain in south. The former could be further sub-divided into the Gangetic-Ghaghara *doab*, the Ghaghara-Gandak interfluves, the Gandak-Kosi *doab*, and the Kosi-Mahananda interfluves. The Gangetic plain south could be divided into the region west of Karmnasa, Karmnasa east interfluves, the lower Son valley, and the Magadha-Anga plain. (Map 2).

The Middle Gangetic plain, particularly its western part is characterized by horseshoe lakes.[31] It might indicate the southward

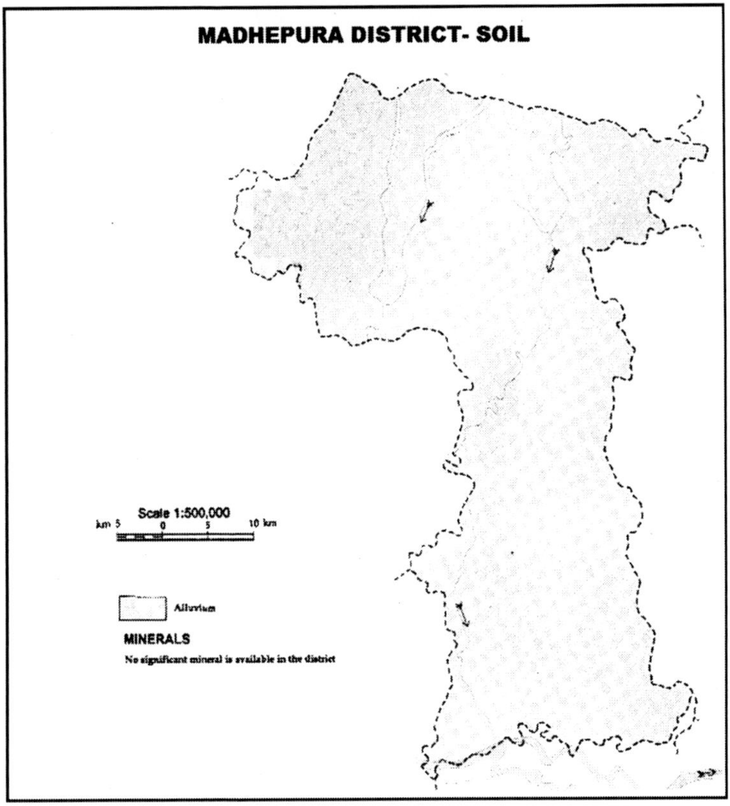

Map 2.1: Rocks and minerals in Madhepura district

shifting of the Ganges. Some researches on these lakes have shown that in the beginning, there was very arid climate followed by arid, semi-arid, and semi-humid conditions. The plain area was mainly grassland at least for last 15,000 years with local forest thickets. The region experienced anthropogenic activities throughout this period.[32] It especially increased during last 5,000 years.

It is clear from the aforesaid discourse that the topmost layer of Madhepura district is made up of fine alluvium deposited by Ganges, Kosi, and other rivers over thousands of years. Besides this alluvium, the other important geological formations are Achaean and Gondwana rocks. Moreover, the alluvium layer is gently sitting upon the northern extension of Chota Nagpur plateau and the great Indian Peninsula. It is also evident that Madhepura district is very fertile and abounds in water resources. But nevertheless, it is lacking in other mineral resources (Map 2.1).

NOTES AND REFERENCES

1. The debris from Himalayas was deposited in later, upper, and late Tertiary period.
2. Bulandshahr is located in Uttar Pradesh state of India. It is situated in the great 'North Indian plain.'
3. Presently, Lucknow is the capital city of Uttar Pradesh state in India and situated in the Gangetic valley.
4. M. Lal, *Settlement History and Rise of Civilization in the Gang-Yamuna Doab* (Delhi, 1984), p. 9.
5. It has been named after the Dharwar district of Karnataka, where these rocks were first recognized. These were the earliest formed sediments to be deposited in the depressions and hollows of the primeval crust.
6. This lies southwest of the Madhepura district and south of Ganges.
7. It extends westward from Sasaram to the watershed between Son and Narmada for a distance of 386 kilometers. The scarps overlook the Son valley from the north.
8. They are also known as West and East Champaran districts respectively. These two districts lie in extreme northwest of Bihar state.

9. It is of Tertiary fresh water formation that is found along the entire length of the Himalaya.
10. As aforesaid, it was earlier formed by the down warping of the crust in front of the rising mountain.
11. This was revealed in a gravity survey with the help of an oscillation of a pendulum.
12. R. R. Diwakar, *Bihar through the Ages* (Calcutta: Orient Longmans, 1958), p. 13.
13. *Kankar* refers to calcium carbonate nodules.
14. Lal, *Settlement History and Rise of Civilization in the Gang-Yamuna Doab*, p. 10.
15. It belongs to Pleistocene epoch.
16. *Reys* means an alkaline soil.
17. But, erstwhile Bihar consisting of present Jharkhand state was extremely rich in mineral resources.
18. It is a muscovite minerollogically.
19. The presence of spring has its own significance. When a group of springs occur more or less along a line; it indicates a line of fault or dislocation. Incase of thermal springs, source of water is deeper than the cold springs.
20. People of the region believe that these springs cure skin diseases, rheumatism, gout, and digestive disorders; and induce appetite.
21. They occur in three distinct series such as the Rajgir springs in Patna district, the Tapoban spring, and the Agnikund springs of Gaya district.
22. *Doab* refers to a land between two rivers. In this case, it is an area exiting between two great rivers such as Kosi and Mahananda in northeastern Bihar. The districts like Saharsa, Supaul, Madhepura, Araria, Kishanganj, Katihar, and Purnea lies in this *doab* region.
23. Cubit is an ancient unit of length, equal to the distance from the elbow to the tip of the middle finger. It is approximately 43 to 56 cm or 17 to 22 inches. Accordingly 15, 5, and 10 cubits are equivalent to 6.45 to 8.40 meters, 2.15 to 2.80 meters, and 4.30 to 5.60 meters respectively.
24. Mohammed Eharar Alam, 'Socio-Economic Profile of Muslims in the Kosi-Mahananda Doab: A Geographical Analysis', unpublished Ph.D. thesis, Department of Geography, Jamia Milia Islamia University, New Delhi, 2002, p. 34.

25. L. D. Stamp, *India, Pakistan, Ceylon and Burma* (London: Metheun & Co. Ltd., 1957).
26. Purshottam Singh and Ashok Kumar Singh, *The Archaeology of Middle Ganga Plain- New Perspective* (New Delhi: Aryan Books International, 2004), p. 1.
27. Many of these grasses were eatables grains.
28. It was due to milder climatic conditions.
29. Singh and Singh, *The Archaeology of Middle Ganga Plain- New Perspective*, p. 2.
30. Not surprisingly, during this long period, several climatic and base-level changes have also transformed the character of these river-channels and the nature of their sediments.
31. These might have been formed due to the meander of shifting Ganges.
32. It has been revealed by the study of cultural pollens collected from the area.

3

Kosi and its Plain

Since Madhepura district lays exactly in the plain of river Kosi, it becomes necessary to explore and analyze this mighty river and its extensive plain. First of all, Kosi's sources, tributaries, and distributaries are studied. Thereafter, the chief characteristics of this great river are analyzed. Since, several districts together constitute Kosi belt, a micro analysis of them is not out of bounds. No discussion on an area could be complete without examining its physical features.

Kosi occupies pivotal position in northeastern Bihar.[1] It is the most important and ancient river in the area. Kosi has been referred as *Kausika* in ancient Sanskrit literatures. This is the third largest river at its debouching in the plains, next only to the Indus and the Brahmaputra River.

Seven Himalayan streams[2] join together in eastern Nepal to form this grand river. Kosi along with its several tributaries such as Balgon and Dhasandhar rises in the Himalayas in Nepal and enters the middle Gangetic plain in Supaul district of Bihar. It drains the Himalayan snows between Gosainthan and Kanchenjunga. Here, this river has three tributaries such as the Sun Kosi, Arun Kosi, and Jaunar Kosi. Kosi leaves its mountain home near Chatra[3] and arrives in Bihar as mighty river heavily laden with sand debris.[4] The river meets with some of its other branches at Tribeniganj[5] and forms the famous 'Sapt Kosi.' Kosi's other arms are Bhotia Kosi, Tambar Kosi, Liku Kosi, and Dudh Kosi.[6]

Thereafter, it runs into a sandy alluvial plain and moves southward into Madhepura and Saharsa districts.[7] Kosi flows from north to south. Overall, it traverses several districts of northeastern Bihar with numerous bifurcations and interlacing. Kosi receives the water of Kamla-Tilguja as well as old Bagmati in the area. Then the river takes a bend towards east and runs into the bed of its old tributary Ghugri and meets Ganges south of Kursela (this junction occurred almost 200 years ago).[8] From then on, it assumes the characteristics of a deltaic river. (Map 3).

The total catchment area of Kosi at Chatra is 23,000 square miles. Interestingly, out of this about 2,200 square miles lie above snowline. The contributions of Sun Kosi and Sapt Kosi (below Tribeniganj) are 7,330 and 112 square miles respectively. In contrast, the total catchment area of its tributaries joining below Chatra is 10,000 square miles.[9]

Kosi has two important characteristics such as shifting of course and frequent flooding. As far as former is concerned, it has been steadily moving towards west and also lengthening its channel in the process. The length of its course from gorge to junction has increased from 161 kilometers in 1870 to 258 kilometers in 1941. In fact, during the last two and quarter centuries, Kosi has marched almost 120 kilometers from near the city of Purnea to Tiljuga (in Darbhanga district).[10]

In 1736, it flowed one mile west to Purnea city and met Ganges opposite Sahibganj. But during 1807-39, Kosi flowed east of Dhamdaha and joined Ganges at Kursela. In between 1840-73, it shifted west of Dhamdaha; and Hiran was the main Kosi during 1840-47.[11] In 1850, its channel lay some miles east of then large trading village at Nathpur.[12] Between 1870-92, it moved further west and since then kept on shifting in westward directions towards Darbhanga at an average rate of almost 1 mile per year.[13] (Table 2).

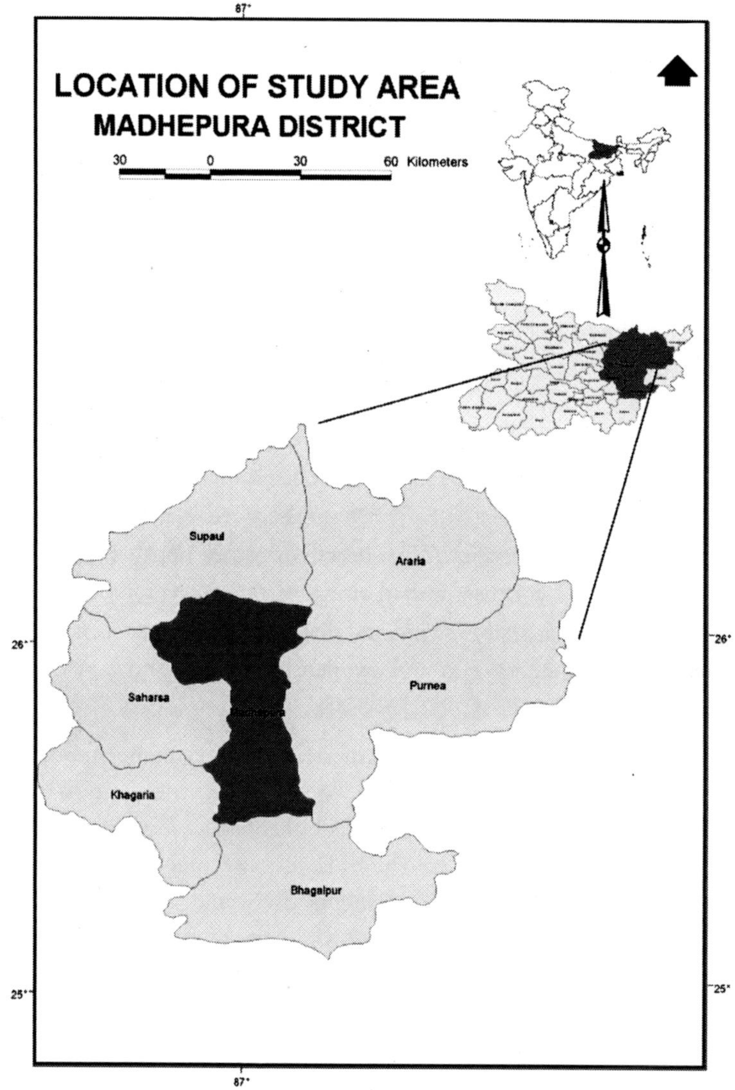

Map 3: Kosi River basin and Madhepura district within that

Kosi is not only notorious for changing its course quite often but also annually inundating a large part of northeastern Bihar. This river is so well known for its flood havoc that people prefer to call it,

Table 2: The shift of Kosi River during 18th, 19th, and 20th centuries[14]

S. No.	Period	Years	Distance moved (km)	Average distance moved in a year (km)
1.	1736-1770	34	6.7	0.2
2.	1770-1823	53	5.8	0.1
3.	1823-1850	33	3.8	0.1
4.	1850-1883	27	8.1	0.3
5.	1883-1907	24	11.5	0.5
6.	1907-1922	15	6.8	0.45
7.	1922-1933	11	18	1.60
8.	1933-1950	17	11	6.65

"The Sorrow of North Bihar."[15] These unique natures of Kosi are really intriguing. In fact, this river has raised bed.[16] It does not have any permanent deep course. Kosi flows with small depth over a wide stretch of a flat country and tears it through several capricious channels. The river assumes wild and devastative character[17] especially when it receives heavy rain and swollen by melting snow. As R. R. Diwakar has remarked:

> "It dashes impetuously down in a tremendous volume of tortured and turbid water, overtops and bursts through its banks, inundating large areas, making fresh channels for itself, and turning fertile fields into arid waste of sands; sweeping away factories, farms, and villages; and changing the whole face of a country from a fruitful landscape into a wilderness of sand and swamp."[18]

Arthur Geddes has tried to explain the violent nature of Kosi in the following way:

> "There is no sufficient space for the river to pass gradually through the stages of grading, maturity, and aggrading old age. Here, after the impetuosity of youth, there is sudden constriction of advanced age, a sudden leap from the degraded to aggraded stage with not graded interval- a sudden change from the young valley in the mountains to the deltaic stage of building and uncertain shuffle

in the plains. This is the most critical feature in the (peculiar) character of Kosi."[19]

Another distinctive feature of Kosi is it's being dangerous for navigation. This is because of strong current in the river especially during rainy season and the possibility of unpredictable changes in its course. Unfortunately, even today people are forced to use unsafe means of transport[20] to cross the river due to lack of proper infrastructural development particularly the bridges and roads across Kosi. As a result, people have developed their own mechanisms to cope up with the problem. They have created certain *ghat*[21] from where one could get some boats, ferries, and even steamers to cross the river.[22] There was a ferry across Kosi at Khanwa *ghat* even in nineteenth and twentieth centuries.[23] One of the very recent instances of Kosi's flood could be seen in Figure 1.

Figure 1: A village flooded by Kosi River in July-August 2007

Kosi floodplain is very interesting. It consists of a part of Madhepura district besides huge portion of northeastern Bihar.[24] Kosi brings a good amount of alluvium to the area. The western part of the tract has sandy soil. The topography and the people of Kosi belt are immensely affected by the ravages of Kosi flood.[25] The westward advancement of Kosi washed away a number of estates during nineteenth and early twentieth centuries. Their proprietors allowed them to be sold for arrears of revenue. The number of *Khas Mahal* was increasing.[26] There was upsurge in the trend of subdivision of estates. In fact, the number of estates and proprietors proliferated by 30 and 80 folds respectively in the whole Bhagalpur district of which Madhepura was a subdivision.[27]

In the meantime, government has built two embankments in western and eastern part of northeastern Bihar to confine Kosi within fixed courses and protect the area from annual flood devastation. Both the governments of India and Nepal came together to build an ambitious project of Kosi barrage that is not far from its mountainous sources. The effort was intended to utilize its water for irrigation and hydro-electricity projects. So, after the construction of this Kosi barrage and embankments, only three C. D. Blocks of Madhepura district namely Alamnagar, Chausa, and Puraini remains flood affected.[28]

Figure 1.1: A signboard indicating one of the canals (Janakinagar branch canal) dug out of Kosi River

In the post Kosi Project phase, a number of irrigational canals has been constructed. (Figure 1.1 and Figure 1.2). As a result, the sandy tracts are being slowly reclaimed. Unfortunately, in recent years, these canals have not been functioning properly due to their bad conditions and poor maintenance.[29]

The physical features of Kosi region and Madhepura district are provoking. They are actually low-lying plain between the

Figure 1.2: One of the narrow channels (locally called *chchahree*) taken out of River Kosi for irrigation purpose

Himalayas in the north and the elevated limestone belt along the bank of Ganges in the south. The two forms a continuation of the great alluvial plain of Tirhut, being intersected by many rivers which are connected with each other by numerous *dhar*.[30]

The Kosi plain mainly consists of gently inclined alluvial plains. Since the Kosi area is prone to annual flood, it is mainly having *Khadar* soil. In the valley of Kosi, some of the older alluvium surface have been removed and re-distributed down the stream. The bank of Kosi is not very high. There is slope from north to the south. The height of the region is 65 meters in the north and 39 meters in the south from the mean sea level.[31] The slope as pointed out by O' Malley doubles as one comes to south. This is due to the *kankar* clay of the older alluvium being in juxtaposition to the sands and silt of the newer alluvium. And in fact, this elevation may even be visualized.

The Kosi area is liable to inundation not only by the flooding of Kosi and its tributaries, but also due to overflow of Ganges on the northern bank. In the extreme north where there are mainly hilly streams, the floods do not leave much sand or silt as their course is very narrow. But coming to the plains, the rivers become wider, though not very deep. It forms one of the most fertile regions in the sub *Tarai* rice tract.[32] The greater part of Kosi belt and Madhepura district consists of fertile land. But Kosi basin does contain sandy area that possesses wild grasses.

There are numerous shallow marshes. Some of the places are covered with the deposits of sand left over by the Kosi during its annual inundation and change of the course, where nothing grows except high jungle grass. Therefore, it has converted thousands of square kilometers of fertile land into sandy flats and grassy marshes.[33] It deposits vast infertile sediments of micaceous sands on arable land.[34] Generally, humidity is also high. Hunter gave a fitting description of Kosi plain falling in Purnea district:

> "In the western division,[35] the most noticeable feature is the extent of the country not under cultivation, which spreads out from the vicinity of the town of Purniah [sic], chiefly to north and west, in the form of radiating stretches of land, opening out occasionally into fine, grassy, prairie-like plains. These afford sustenance everywhere to great herds of cattle, and towards the south, to numerous flocks of sheep. Along the Ganges there is little vegetation, but the newly formed Kusi [sic] *chars*, or sandbanks, are covered with a dense and high jungle of coarse grass, forming the best covert in the district for wild animals."[36]

The traces of such courses go under the name of *Kala Kosi* or black Kosi and touch the Purnea town.[37]

Like most of the Kosi plain, Madhepura district is also largely a level plain. It is really difficult to delineate regional differences in this area. One finds a plain area of which the slope is hardly discernible from the naked eye. For hundreds of kilometers one see the exiting river, dead arm of the river, the old course, numerous *dhar*, certain number of trees and plants, and cropped farmlands, etc. The monotony is broken by the site of villages and groves of mango, litchi, and bamboos.[38] We also find some *chauk*,[39] markets, and even few urban areas in between. The area is highly cultivated and hardly seen bare except in the post-harvesting months succeeding *Rabi* and *Kharif* crops.[40]

Interestingly, during these periods the study area show the most desolate appearance with hardly any greenery in the field except some vegetable gardens and groves near the settlement areas. But, the *Dhak* trees with its scarlet flowers are eye soothing. But the scenario changes with onset of monsoon in the month of June. The land gets rejuvenated and the area again wears a green mantle. That is followed by *Rabi* crops of rice and maize during autumn. These crops are harvested by the end of the year which are followed by the plantation of *Kharif* crops like wheat and gram. Latter get harvested in the months of March and April. And the fields again bear a desolate look.

Another district forming the part of Kosi plain is Saharsa (Map 3.1). This district has an average elevation of 41 meters. Saharsa and its surrounding areas are a flat alluvial plain forming part of the Kosi (Dudh Kosi) river basin. This makes the land very fertile. However, frequent changes in the course of the Kosi have led to soil erosions. It almost suffers from major flooding annually. The major crops cultivated in the district are paddy, *makhana*[41] and jute. The place surrounded on the west by the river Kosi boasts an abundance of fish, milk, and *makhana*.

One of the districts constituting Kosi region is Purnea (Map 3.2). It is 3229 sq. km. Purnea is situated between 25°13' N to 27°7' N Latitude and 86°59' E to 87°52' E Longitude. It is the northwestern

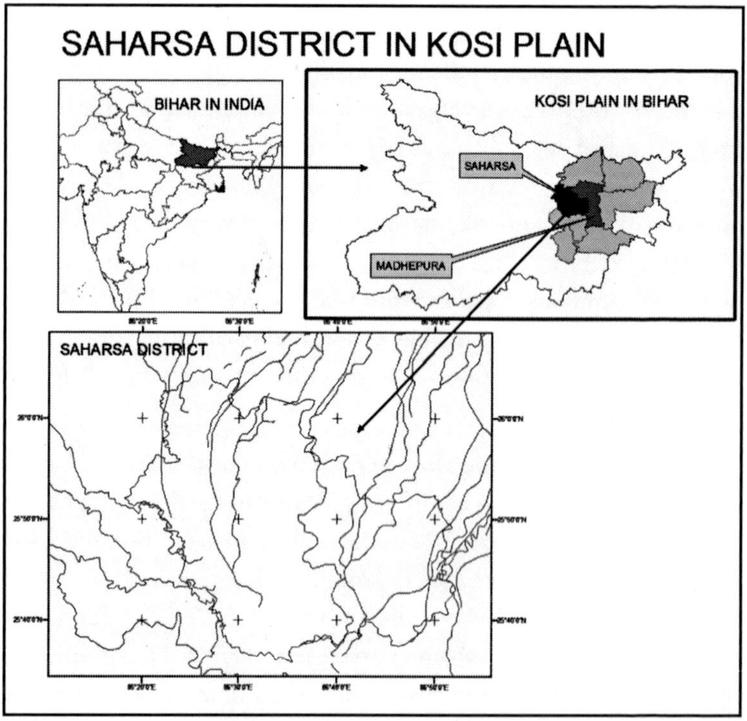

Map 3.1: Map of Saharsa district

extension of the Bengal delta proper.[42] The soil of the district can be called alluvial or sandy loam. These soils are of recent alleviation. Purnea can be divided equally between an eastern section of rich loamy soil and a western segment thickly overlaid with sand deposited by the Kosi in the course of its western movements. The eastern part is dominated by rivers and natural canals. There are large perennial marshes. It is, however, the Kosi dominated western segment which gives it its special character.[43]

The district has a moist humid climate. The temperature is highest in May, when mercury shoots up to 45.5° C and lowest in January, when it is only 8.8° C. The wettest months of the year are July and August. The average annual rainfall in the district is 1411.5

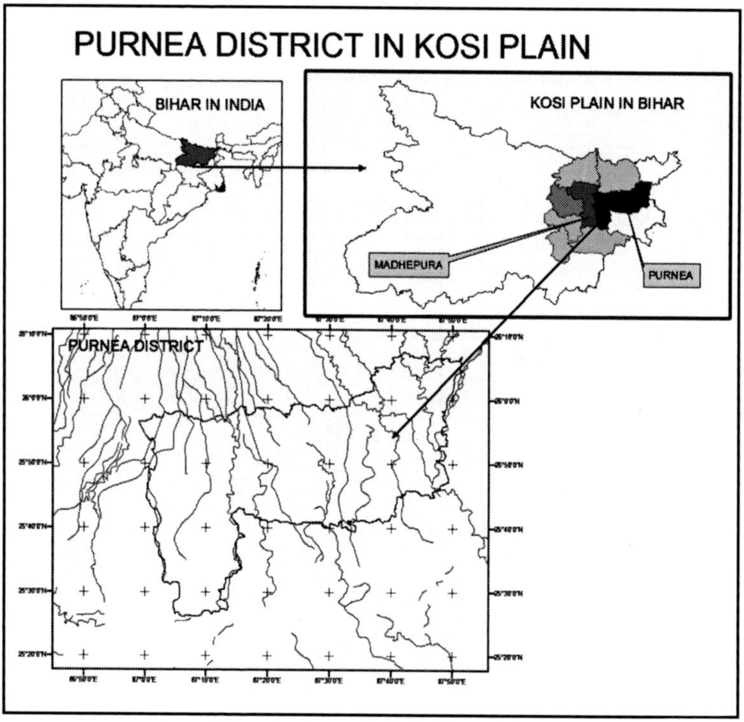

Map 3.2: Map of Purnea district

mm, which is the highest rainfall in the state of Bihar. An average of 65 inches of annual rainfall and a generally high summer temperature exceeding 100° F sum up the climate of the area. The principal crops grown are paddy, jute, wheat, maize, moong, masoor, mustard linseed, sugarcane, and potato etc.[44]

The area of modern Bhagalpur district is 2570 sq. km (Map 3.3). Its population is around 3032226.[45] The major rivers flowing are Ganges, Kosi, and Chanan. The district is divided into two unequal parts by the Ganges. The northern part of the district forms the continuation of great alluvium plains of Tirhut being intersected by many rivers, which are interconnected with each other through numerous watercourses and *dhar*. The two most important rivers

Ganges and Kosi, have changed their courses and liable to change it in future. There are no lakes. But numerous shallow marshes are there. The large tract of land gets flooded every year.

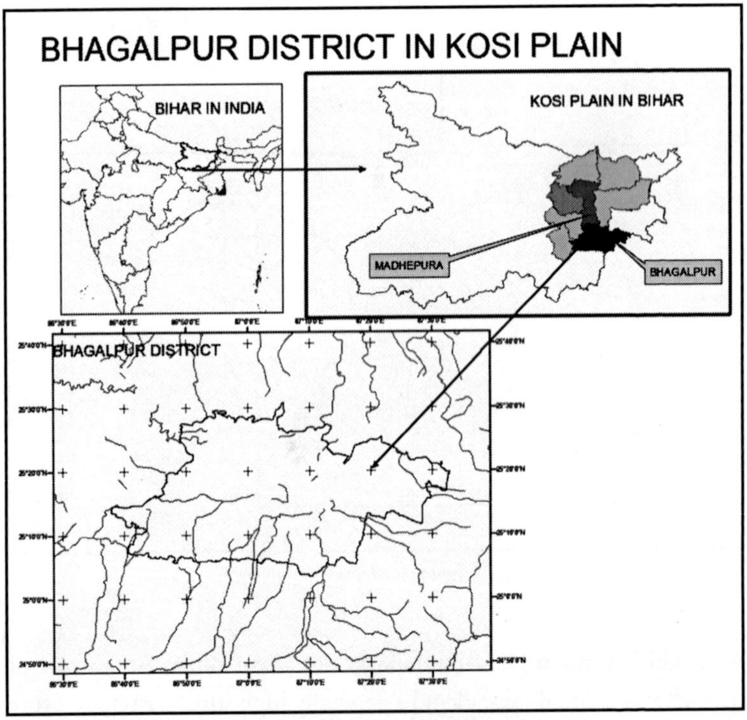

Map 3.3: Map of Bhagalpur district

The geological formations represented are the Archean, the Gondwana, and Gangetic alluvium. Throughout the greater part of the district older rocks are covered with the alluvium. Along the southern banks of the Ganges, the rocks are exposed as detached spurs and outlying prolongations of Rajmahal hills. Some small islands of exceptionally granitoid genesis occur in the Ganges at Kahalgaon. The remaining exposure belongs to Gondwana series. The hills at Pirpainti consist of basic volcanic rocks of Rajmahal groups of upper Gondwana and those at Patarghat of Damodar rocks belonging to the lower coal bearing series. The latter contain siliceous clay suitable for manufacturing of many articles of pottery.

The climate is pleasant and healthy. In the south, summer months are very hot, but in the extreme north, its bit cooler. The major crops cultivated are wheat, rice, maize, gram, potato, sugarcane, and chili etc. There are four principal formations in the district- Alluvium, new and old; the Rajmahal Trappean formation; the Damuda series; and the Gneissic series.[46] The principal mineral products are mica, fire clay, and China clay.[47]

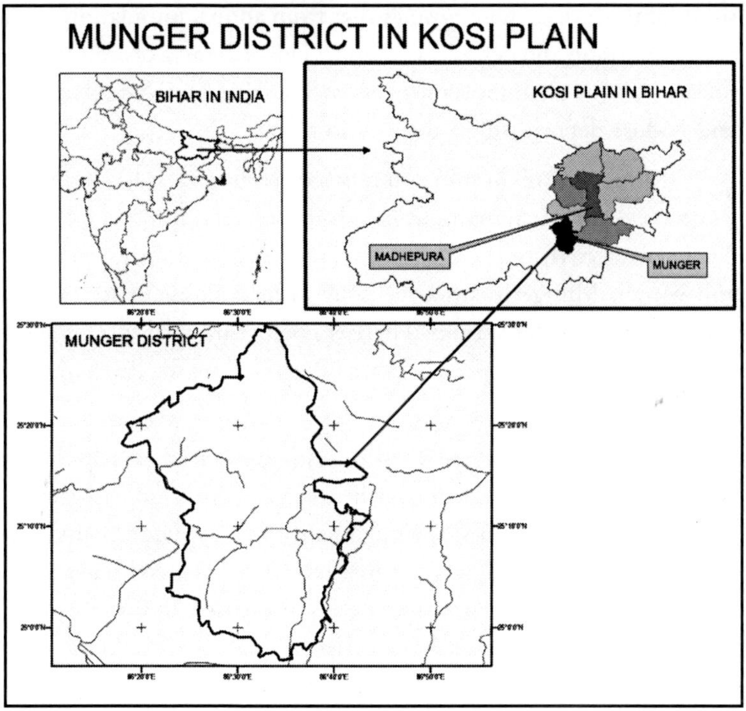

Map 3.4: Map of Munger district

The southwest of Kosi plain is Munger district. It is located in the southern part of Bihar. The district headquarter is located on the southern bank of river Ganges. Munger is spread over

1419.7 sq. km, accounting for 3.3% of the area of Bihar. It lies between 24°22' N to 25°30' N Latitude and 85°30' E to 87°3' E Longitude. The Munger district is situated on an average of 30 to 65 meters above sea level. The average annual rainfall is 1231 mm. The district of Munger is hemmed by the Ganges in the north, Bhagalpur district in the east, Barh district in the west, and the district of Jamui in the south.

The Northern plain of Munger district has two facets of landscape i.e. *diyara*[48] north of the Gangetic levee and *tal*[49] lands south of the levee. These *diyara* suffer from annual inundation along with the erosion and deposition of soils. This is the area of sedimentary rocks. Some of the important rivers such as Kiul Harohar, Dakranal, and Baduar deposit soil in their flood plains.

Munger is sub humid and much drier district. It has monsoon subtropical climate ranging from sub-dry to sub-humid conditions. There are three distinct seasons in this zone viz., summer, monsoon, and winter. Munger district has long been famous for its mineral waters and hot water springs. There is a belt of thermal springs along a zone from the Kharagpur hills to the Rajgir hills of the Patna district.

The soil of Munger district is grey to dark grey in color, medium to heavy in texture, moderately alkaline in reaction, and cracks during summer.[50] It becomes shallow with onset of monsoon, with clay content nearly 40% to 50% throughout the profile. The clay minerals found are smectite followed by hydrous mica. The soil has a good fertility status. *Diyara* land soils are light textured and well drained with free calcium carbonate that varies from 3% to 8%, but seldom exceeds 10%. Minerals found are hydrous mica, smectite, kaolonite, and chloride. The nature of sediments deposited in *diyara* land can be generally stated as those near the streams and are coarser in texture.[51]

Supaul district is one of the 36 districts of Bihar. It is bounded by Nepal in the north and Bihar districts of Araria to the east, Madhepura and Saharsa in the south, and Madhubani to the west.

According to 2011 census, its population and population density are 2228397 and 920 per sq. km respectively. The literacy rate (59.65) and sex ratio (925) are low. The district occupies an area of 2410 sq. km. Its headquarter lies at 25°93' N Latitude and 86°25' E Longitude. Supaul district has an average elevation of 34 meters. It is a part of Kosi division. The Kosi River flows through Supaul causing flood. But, after the construction of Kosi embankment, the flood situation has been improved. The East-West Corridor National Highway 57 passes through the district. It comprises of four subdivisions such as Supaul, Birpur, Tribeniganj, and Nirmali. Supaul has been one of the important centers during India's freedom struggle.

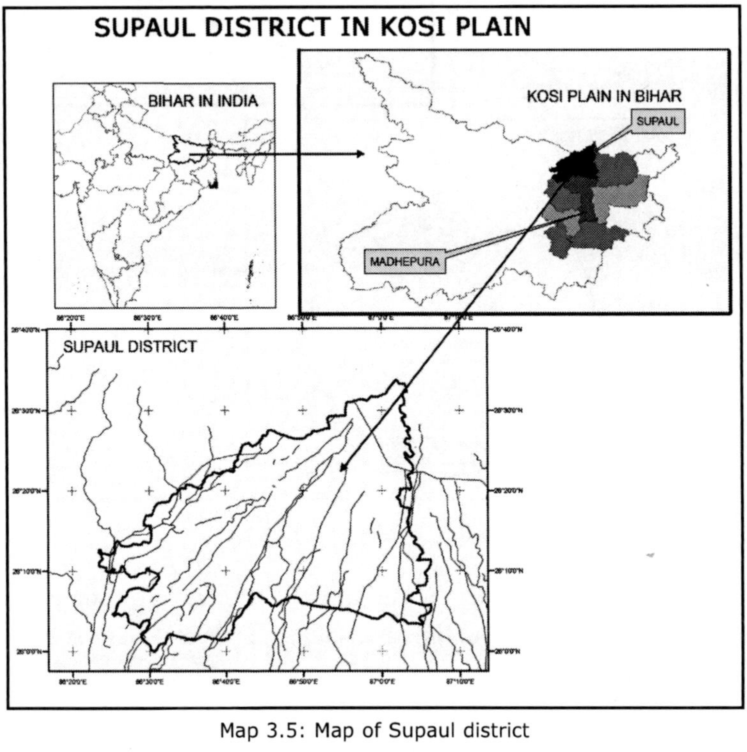

Map 3.5: Map of Supaul district

Araria district occupies an area of 2,830 sq. km. According to 2011 census, the population of the district is 2806200. And the population density is 992 inhabitants per sq. km. Araria has sex ratio of 921 females for every 1000 males and a literacy rate of 55.1%. The major rivers of this district are Kosi, Suwara, Kali, and Koli. Its populace mainly produces paddy, maize, and jute. This district has a number of jute mills. Araria district comprises of two subdivisions such as Araria and Forbesganj.

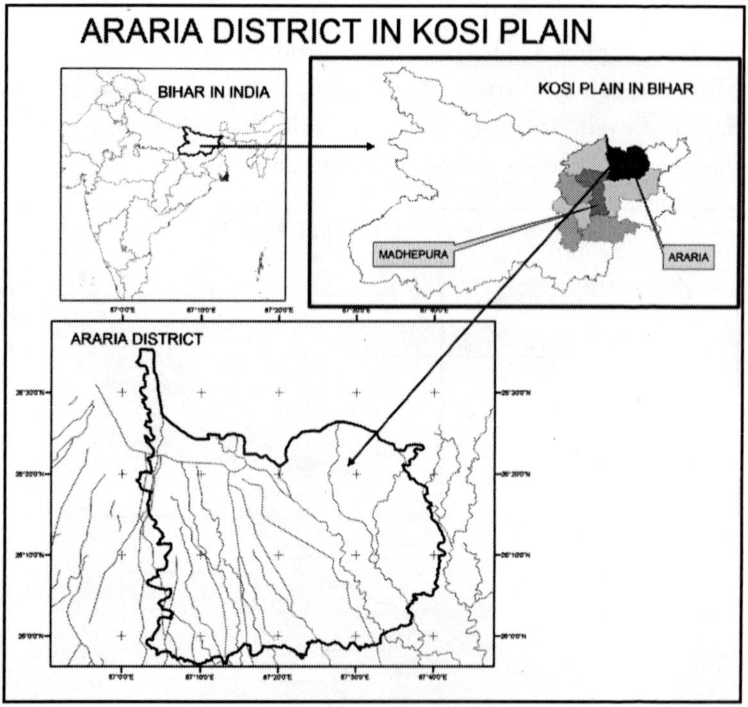

Map 3.6: Map of Araria district

Overall, Kosi is an ancient and mighty river of northeastern Bihar. It has its source in Himalayas falling in Nepal. Several streams and rivers join together to form this great river. It is known for its unpredictable nature, frequent change of course, flood havoc, and difficult navigation. However, the human force and technology has tried to tame this grand river through embankments and wide network of canals. Its plain consists of several districts of northeast Bihar.

Together they have mainly alluvium soil; relatively level plain; gentle slope; and a mix of numerous *dhar*, marshy land, *diyara*, and *tal*; and pleasant climate. So, Kosi and its plain seem to provide favourable geographical and physical conditions for the beginning and growth of human life, a complex society and culture, and ultimately civilization.

NOTES AND REFERENCES

1. Northeastern Bihar consists of several districts including Madhepura. The other districts are Supaul, Araria, Kishanganj, Saharsa, Khagaria, Purnea, and Katihar.
2. That is why; it is also called 'Sapt Kosi.'
3. Chatra is a place in Nepal, where 'Sapt Kosi' debauches in the plains.
4. Ram Chandra Prasad, *Bihar* (New Delhi: National Book Trust, 1992), pp. 7-8.
5. Tribeniganj is located in Supaul district. It is one of its C. D. Blocks.
6. They join this powerful river from the right side.
7. In the process, it passes through the Nepal *Tarai* region and northeastern Bihar.
8. R. R. Diwakar, *Bihar through the Ages* (Calcutta: Orient Longmans, 1958), p. 30.
9. Mohammed Eharar Alam, 'Socio-Economic Profile of Muslims in the Kosi-Mahananda Doab: A Geographical Analysis', unpublished Ph.D. thesis, Department of Geography, Jamia Milia Islamia University, New Delhi, 2002, p. 36.
10. This district borders Kosi plain from west.
11. It has been shown in the Revenue Survey Map of 1870-74.
12. It falls in Bhagalpur district.
13. Diwakar, *Bihar through the Ages,* p. 31.
14. P. C. Roy Choudhary, *District Gazetters of Purnia* (Patna: Superintendant, Secretariat Press, 1965).
15. One of the best recent examples of its widespread devastation is the flood of 2008. It completely inundated the several districts of northeastern Bihar including Madhepura district. Latter was immensely affected by the flood. Eleven out of total thirteen C. D. Blocks were

badly affected. As far as numbers of affected *Panchayats* are concerned, at least 140 out of 170 were inundated. Majority of the village numbering 370 out of 449 was ravaged by the flood. Murliganj, Kumarkhand, and Madhepura C. D. Blocks were among the worst hit areas. Not surprisingly, all the wards falling in Madhepura *Nagar Parishad* and Murliganj *Nagar Panchayat* were submerged under Kosi flood. This flood caused untellable destruction of man and material. Probably, the people of the region may take number of years and in fact decades to come out of the shock and loss.

16. Kosi brings large quantity of sand and *kankar* and leaves them raising the bed and changing its course consequently.
17. The great liability of Kosi is due to the still persistent steep Himalayan gradients that provides it with high velocity during the period of heavy precipitation, and a sudden change from a deep V-shaped valley to a broad and shallow depression in the plain.
18. Diwakar, *Bihar through the Ages,* p. 30.
19. Arthur Geddes, *Nepal: A Cultural and Physical Geography* (Lexington: 1960).
20. They use *kachcha pul* (country made bridge), country made boats, flowing branches of trees, banana stems, and sometimes even foot etc. The *Kachcha pul* is generally made up of bamboo and branches of other trees by local people in the light of governmental indifference towards such problems.
21. This term is locally used to refer to the bank of a river that has been modified for public's use for different purposes such as bathing and crossing the river (through boats) etc. One can presume it to be a country version of port.
22. Sometimes even government has developed such *ghats.*
23. William Wilson Hunter, *Imperial Gazatteer* (1909), vol. 8, p. 33.
24. In fact, before the building of Kosi embankments and barrage, its floodplain included most of Madhepura district.
25. According to Buchchanan's account, parts of Madhepura were notoriously malarious in last centuries. Cholera usually occurred in localized epidemics from April to June and August to October. It was very severe and widespread in 1900. Even deaf-mutism was prevalent

to some extent. Some of these could be probably related to Kosi flood and its aftermath.

26. It was a type of revenue system which flourished in eighteenth and nineteenth centuries.
27. Hunter, *Imperial Gazatteer*, pp. 34-35.
28. URL: http://www.madhepura.nic.in/ - 24k (Accessed on 20 January 2011).
29. But in last few years, the incumbent Nitish government has shown interest in its cleaning and maintenance. The researcher could see earth remover machines operating in various canals during the course of field work.
30. Hunter, *Imperial Gazetteer*, p. 25.
31. Alam, 'Socio-Economic Profile of Muslims in the Kosi-Mahananda Doab: A Geographical Analysis', 2002, p. 41.
32. Hunter, *Imperial Gazetteer*, p. 25.
33. In 1906, a serious distress was caused by Kosi's flood in the west of Madhepura. The crops were entirely destroyed.
34. Sukhdev Singh Chib, *This Beautiful India – Bihar* (New Delhi: Light and Life Publishers, 1980), pp. 34-35.
35. It means the western division of Purnea district. The Kosi flows through the western edge of the district to join the Ganges.
36. William Wilson Hunter, *A Statistical Accountof Bengal* (1877).
37. Dilip K. Chakrabarti, *Archaeological Geography of the Ganga Plain- The Lower and the Middle Ganga* (Delhi: Permanent Black, 2001), p. 192.
38. The grove of mango and litchi is locally called *kalam* or *bagicha.* The bamboo grove is known as *basbaira* or *basbitti.*
39. It refers to a market place located at the intersection of several roads.
40. *Rabi* is cropping season falling between November and March. In contrast, *Kharif* falls between the months of June and October.
41. It is a kind of crop cultivated in marshy and wet lands. Kosi region produces one of the best qualities of its kind in world.
42. Hunter, *A Statistical Accountof Bengal.*
43. Chakrabarti, *Archaeological Geography of the Ganga Plain- The Lower and the Middle Ganga*, p. 192.

44. URL: http://www.purnia.nic.in/aboutpurnia.htm - 24k (Accessed on 15 September 2010).
45. This population figure is according to 2011 census.
46. P. C. Roy Choudhary, *The Old District Gazetteer of Bhagalpur* (Patna: Superintendant, Secretariat Press,1911).
47. Chib, *This Beautiful India – Bihar*, pp. 47-51.
48. It refers to an area surrounded by river on all sides.
49. *Tal* lands suffer from annual inundation, water loggings, and deposition of soil.
50. The crack varies from 1 cm to more than 5 cm wide. Sometimes, it is more than 50 cm deep
51. URL:http://www.munger.nic.in/ATMA/Munger/Munger%20district (Accessed on 20 November 2010).

4

Ecological Setting

Human being needs to be aware about his immediate environment. An individual is in constant touch with the atmosphere around him. He carries his activities in the midst of nature that consists of mountains, plateaus, rivers, streams, plains, flora, and fauna, etc. Person uses nature and its resources to survive and grow. He cultivates land; collects fruits and vegetables; extracts minerals; uses such natural forces as light, air, water, and fire, etc.

But interestingly, people are hardly conscious of being product of this environment and constant influences of cosmic and geological processes. In this backdrop, it becomes imperative to explore, analyze, and reconstruct the ecology of Madhepura District. As already mentioned, the district is divided into two administrative subdivisions. A separate ecological analysis of each of these areas might provide a clearer picture.

The discussion would also involve micro analysis of the climate of Kosi plain and Madhepura district. The general characteristic of seasons, rainfall, temperature, humidity, and special weather phenomenon such as cyclone and thunderstorm etc., is also explained. Then the type and nature of soil of the area is evaluated. No discussion about the ecological settings could be complete without reconstructing the floral and faunal elements of the area. Moreover, since no ecology remains unchanged forever, the modification and alterations in Madhepura's ecological settings is also investigated.

MADHEPURA SUBDIVISION

Madhepura subdivision forms the northern half of Madhepura district. It consists of seven C. D. Blocks out of the total thirteen. These are Madhepura, Murliganj, Kumarkhand, Singheshwar, Shankarpur, Ghailarh, and Gamharia.

Madhepura subdivision mainly contains younger alluvial soil. We can further divide this *Khadar* soil into *chiknee* (fine alluvial), *domat* or *kraree* (hard when dry and soft when wet),[1] and *baluhaee* (sandy) soils. The altitude of this area varies between 50 to 100 meters above the sea level. Its slope is generally from north to south.[2] But, if it is viewed at micro level, the area is of undulating nature which in itself is very significant to explain and establish levels of interaction of the past societies.

Generally, most of the areas of this subdivision are free from flood for the greater part of the year. But during rainy season, we find inundation affecting some pockets especially in low lying areas, either due to pressure in Kosi's distributaries and canals or acute water-logging (Map 4). There is little *diyara* area too. The southeastern portion of Murliganj C. D. Block is marshy.

The natural water resource in the form of surface and sub soil water seems to be fairly conducive to human settlement and subsistence. The sweet drinking water is available at 15 to 25 feet.[3] The general vegetation of Madhepura subdivision is hardly different from that of the whole district. The central portion of this administrative area is especially rich in scrubs and grasses.

Kosi's active and dead distributaries lattice the subdivision including Bharahi *nadi*[4] and several Kosi *dhar*. The area possesses several water canals such as Murliganj, Beldaur, Sonbarsa Raj, Dhabauli, and Gangapur distributaries built under Kosi project. As far as *minor* (locally used to denote narrow artificial water channels taken out of canal) is concerned, it includes Kewatgawan, Jitapur, and Parwa, etc.

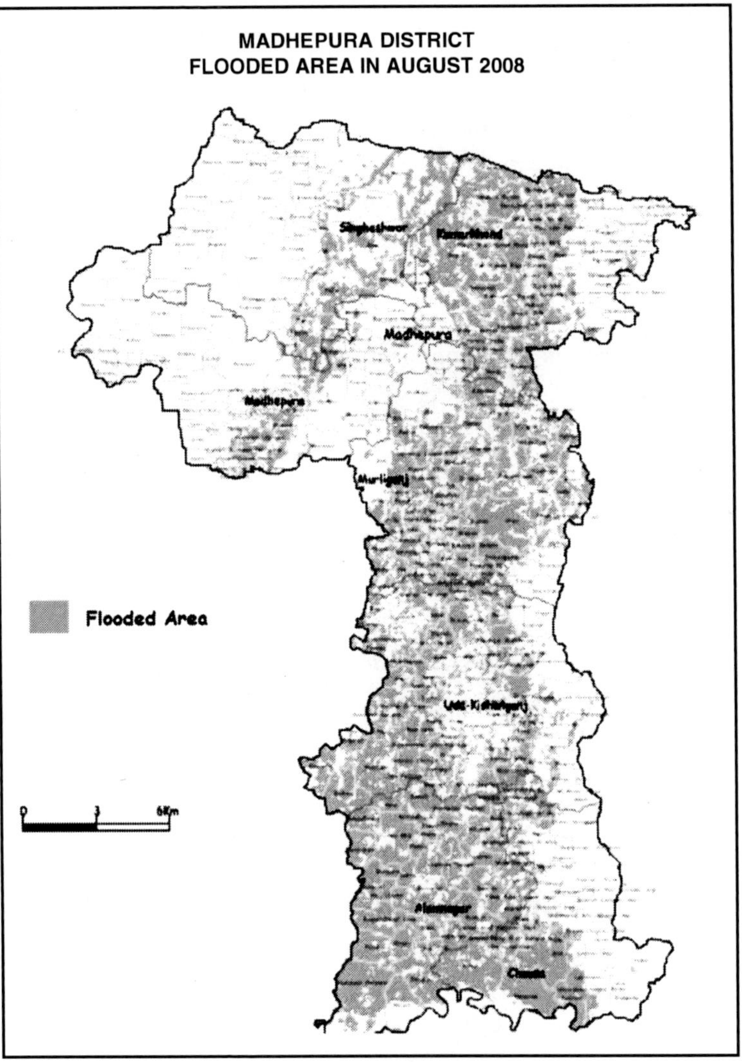

Map 4: Inundation in different areas of Madhepura district during 2008 flood

The landuse pattern in Madhepura subdivision goes along the general trend seen in the Kosi plain. In western part of this division consisting of four C. D. Blocks namely Ghailarh, Gamharia,

Singheshwar, and Madhepura; rice, wheat, and maize are the main crops of cultivation. Whereas, jute along with rice and wheat are predominant crops in central and eastern portion of the area including Shankarpur, Kumarkhand, and Murliganj C. D. Blocks. Green gram (*Mooang*) and *Khesaree* (one type of lentil) are also grown in some pockets alongside the above mentioned crops. Overall, landscape and ecological pattern has a favourable look.

UDAKISHUNGANJ SUBDIVISION

Udakishunganj is the second subdivision of Madhepura district. It consists of six C. D. Blocks such as Alamnagar, Puraini, Chausa, Gwalpara, Bihariganj, and Udakishunganj. Like its northern counterpart, Udakishunganj is also mainly made up of younger alluvium. But certain areas in northwestern part of the subdivision (Gwalpara and Udakishunganj C. D. Blocks) bordering Saharsa district consist of *Tarai*, saline and saline alkali soils.[5] In the central part of the division especially Udakishunganj C. D. Block, we find a mix of *baluhaee*, *matiyaree*, and *domat* soils.[6]

Like Madhepura subdivision, the general altitude of this area above the sea level varies from 50 to 100 meters. The slope of the Udakishunganj subdivision is in line with the general pattern of the rest of the district. The sweet drinking water is usually available at 20 to 30 feet. But in some places, it is accessible only at 30 to 45 feet.[7] In few cases, water has more iron content.[8]

At present, the central portion of the subdivision is not an active flood plain area. But according to local inhabitants, it was so just 40 to 50 years back. The southeastern part of the Udakishunganj subdivision (Alamnagar C. D. Block) is still an active flood zone especially during monsoon season (Map 4). Ghagree, Bagmatee, and Kosi rivers flow through this part. Muddy flats are very common in this administrative area. Besides that some areas also have swamps. The northeastern portion of Bihariganj C. D. Block touching Purnea district is chronically water logged. We find *chap* (area of depression) in Pipra-Karotti and Fanhan area. Western part of Kishanganj C. D. Block is having some waste land too.

Like Madhepura subdivision, Udakishunganj subdivision also possesses several canals such as Beldaur, Khuran, Sukhasan, and Kishanganj distributaries besides having several *minor*. There is one canal in Alamnagar C. D. Block which is linked to Kosi barrage. Kosi's active and dead distributaries crisscross the division including Bharahi *nadi* and Kosi *dhar*. According to local populace, there are several *dhar* in the subdivision. One of them is Arar-Murliganj-Gohumani *dhar*.[9] Another *dhar* is west to Mazora[10] which is a dead channel (locally called *maria dhar*) now. There is one dried Hareli *dhar* 4 kilometers west of Laxmipur village. One also finds an embankment known as Bandh Tutna which has been notorious for flooding the area.

The landuse pattern of this area is not much different from Madhepura subdivision. In its southwestern part (Gwalpara, Udakishunganj, and Alamnagar C. D. Blocks) rice and maize are main crops. But in other parts, people also cultivate wheat. Like the northern half of the district, green gram and *Khesaree* are favorably grown in some pockets alongside the aforesaid crops. The flora of the subdivision is not much different from its northern counterpart. Unlike Madhepura subdivision, the overall landscape pattern in this part of the district seems to be relatively less encouraging for human settlement and subsistence.

CLIMATE

By and large, Madhepura district has pleasant climate. Like any other temperate zone, it has four seasons. The winter season commences in November and lasts till February. It is followed by summer spell in the month of March continuing up to early June. Thereafter, monsoon period arrives and extends up to mid September. The autumn starts in late September and continues up to late November. These fall months have pleasant climate.

As far as temperature is concerned, it remains low during the winter months. In fact, December and January are the coldest months. Generally, summer is hot. The higher temperatures are recorded in the months of May and June and again in September. By and large, Madhepura district has a humid climate. Humidity is higher in the second half of the summer season. The summer afternoons are generally drier. But, the winter afternoons experience lower humidity.

The average annual rainfall of middle Gangetic plain is about 1000 mm. In contrast, the average annual rainfall in Kosi-Mahananda *doab* and Kosi plain[11] is 1630.3 and 1228 mm respectively.[12] The rainfall decreases from west to east.[13] Overall, Kosi belt receives good amount of rain. Madhepura gets majority of rainfall during the monsoon months.[14] The yearly variations are not much. During the fifty years period 1950-2000, the highest and lowest rainfall occurred in 1966 and 1984 respectively.

Madhepura also experiences some special weather phenomena. Storms and cyclones occur in the late and post monsoon period. They generally originate in Bay of Bengal. These weather phenomena affect the area with strong winds and heavy rainfall. The summer of 2010 experienced a marauding cyclone emerging in Bay of Bengal. It inflicted huge destruction on man and material in the whole Kosi region. Madhepura district was also immensely affected. The wind was so strong that a number of trees, houses, and public buildings were blown away and destroyed. The area was lashed with heavy rain.[15]

Another special weather occurrence is thunderstorm. This is common in the district during monsoon months. But, it may also occur in November and pre-monsoon months. Thunderstorm tends to be violent especially incase of the latter. The monsoon season of 2010 experienced more violent thunderstorms leading to the loss of a number of lives in the region.[16]

SOILS

Largely, Madhepura district has unconsolidated sedimentary rock such as alluvial soil. It possesses good clays intermixed with sand. Since it is watered by Kosi, some soil is also sandy. It is to be noted that this is the area through which Kosi has flown for a number of years and therefore deposited some sand in pockets. Soil is ordinarily friable.

Broadly, the soils could be divided into Aquents-Orthents,[17] Orthents-Aquepts-Ochrepts,[18] and Ochrepts[19] sub-order of association.[20] Madhepura district also has *chaur* (low marshy land) as well as some *diyara* lands.[21] *Diyara* land was used for indigo cultivation during nineteenth and early twentieth centuries under colonial rule.[22]

The contour of Madhepura district on the whole is extremely flat with undulations noticeable in old river beds of Kosi. Rain and flood waters accumulate in the area. As a result, the soil is suitable for paddy and jute cultivation.[23] The farmer gives more emphasis on the cultivation of *Rabi* crops as there is a possibility of destruction of *Kharif* crops by flood. But the new techniques, hybrid seeds, fertilizers, etc., have facilitated the cultivation of other crops too. *Rabi* crops are unpopular in clay soil due to unwanted rains in winter and pre-monsoon season especially in April.[24] Although soils are rich in nitrogen and phosphate, they are not available in the suitable form for the plants.[25]

FLORA[26]

The flora of Kosi plain in general and Madhepura district in particular is stimulating. Like other things, Kosi adds dimensions to the floral pattern of the area as well. As discussed earlier, the present and past beds of Kosi and its distributaries intersect the region. In earlier days, their banks were covered with dense vegetation. In fact, the sides of Kosi's old channels are still covered with tall grasses intermixed with plants. The low banks of these old channels and the borders of the marshes and swampy lands are also cultivated with paddy and jute.[27] Since these banks are covered with sand, they are suitable for the growth of low grassland flora with typically moisture loving perennial species like *Vetiveria zizanioides, Pharamites karka, Arunde doney, Eleusine aegyptica, E. indica,* and various polygonums.

The sluggish streams and lakes are covered with water weeds such as reedy grasses (*pattiyo wali ghas*),[28] bulrushes (*narkat*),[29] and tamarisks (*Tamariscus - jhau*).[30] Near villages, small shrubberies are found rich in mango (*Mangifera indica- Aam*), sissoo (*Dalbergia sissoo - Sissu or Sheesham*), blackberry (*Engenia jambolana - Jamun*), various species of ficus, tamarind *(Tamarindus indica - Imali),* and few other spontaneous and useful species.

One can find numerous man made ditches along the roads and railway lines in the area. They receive a supply of spill water and silt that retains their beds in a sandy condition. Therefore, the water they collect percolates very fast. They may develop *spirogyra* and other algae in the rainy season. The old ditches show many aquatics particularly perennate by means of root stock and tubers like *Aponogeton* spp., *Asteracantha longifilia*[31] and *Impomer raplans. Lemmas,* and *Wolffia* are also found that serves food for the ducks and other birds which migrate to the area from distant places.[32]

The sand covered uplands that do not accumulate rainwater grow in them a high grassland flora consisting of *Cynodom dactylor,*[33] *Dichanthium, Annululatum, D. caricosum,* and other grasses. These areas are heavily grazed. Tall grasses such as *Themeda strigesa, T. quadrivalvis,* and *Apluda nutica* can grow in protected areas. Even few annual climbers also grow.

In other places only the dwarf and hardy species such as *Chrysopogon acicolatus,*[34] *Paspalidium flavidum, Impeila,* and *Cylindrica* can grow. The lands which have recently been covered with sand due to shift in the course of the Kosi River are covered with very deep layers of sand and fairly elevated. On such land only the very hardy types of grasses such as *Polliniduim agnustifolium,*[35] *Sacokarym spontaneum,* and *Chasysopogon aciculatus* can grow.

The area contains small remnants of the deciduous monsoon forests because of heavy rainfall and favourable temperature throughout the year. A large number of lianos and climbers[36] grow up in the trees. Epiphytes are numerous.

The rest of the region is under cultivation. The crops like capsicum (*shimla mirch* or *pahari mirch*), maize (*Zea mays - makai*), turmeric (*Curcuma longa - haldi*), kidney bean (*Phaseolus vulgaris - mooang*), black gram (*urad*), sweet potato (*Ipomoea batatas - shakkarkandi,*), etc., are gown in the area where soil is sandy, but covered with the layer of silt and never get inundated. Paddy (*Oryza sativa - dhan*) and Jute (*ptuwa*)[37] are grown in the similar condition except that it should be in the lowlands. Here land gets inundated periodically and thus receives the enriching silt. A crop of paddy is followed by rich winter crop of wheat (*gehun*),[38] barely, and gram, etc. The other crops cultivated are red gram (*arhar*), oats, mustard, and sugarcane.

There are two types of land such as *sali* and *dosali.*[39] The area is rich in pasture lands. A *chaur* land provides abundant grazing space. In fact, scarcity of fodder is seldom experienced even in periods of drought or famine.[40] At the turn of nineteenth century, Buchchanan remarked that agriculture is the main occupation of the people. Paddy, jute, maize (*Zea mays - makai*), wheat, *marua,*[41] and sugarcane (*Saccharum officinarum - ikh or ketari*) are the main crops of the region. One interesting crop cultivated in the region especially by the poor people is *Koni.*[42] Incase the rice field has been harvested and not immediately ploughed, one finds *Ammonia pygmea.*[43]

People grow several trees in villages[44] such as mango, jackfruit (*Artocarpus heterophyllus - kathal*), guava (*amrud*),[45] blackberry, custard-apple (*Annona reticulate - sharifa*), drumstick (*sohijana*), pipal *(Ficus religiosa - pipal)*, neem (*Azadirachta indica - neem*), banana (*kela*),[46] pineapple (*Ananas comosus - ananas*), and palm (*Palma-tar* or *khajoor*),[47] etc.

The commonly grown vegetables and lentils are tomato (*tamatar*),[48] red chilies (*lal mirch*), nigella (*kallongi*),[49] fenugreek (*Trigonella foenum-graecum- methi*), and mustard (*Mustum - sarson*). In towns one finds such trees as *Cyropha, Umbraculifera, Cocos, Nucifera, Area calechus, Bottle plams, Michelia champacca, Polyathia longifolia,* etc. These are used for timber, medicine, flower, and other purposes.

Madhepura shows some interesting plants such as *Drosera burmanni, Sundew, Utricularia, Stellats, V. flexuosa,* and *Bladderworts.*[50] *Piper longum* (*pupar*) and *Piper betal* grow spontaneously. *Dioscorea* spp. (*khamalu*) is common and serves as food for the poor. Among the fruits, *Anona reticulata* (*anta*) and coconut grow.[51] We find the remnants of *Shrikhand Chandan*[52] (a variety of Sandal wood) in Nayanagar village of Udakishunganj C. D. Block (central southern part of Madhepura district).[53]

M. Ahmad opined about the flora of the region in the following way:

> "The region abounds in marshes and swamps, not seen anywhere. They bear many farming species. The damp hot climate favours growth of plants like cane palm, coconut and pine apples. It is predominantly jute and rice growing region and…show a typical monsoon forest."

The study area still consists of small shrubs and trees especially in bad land ravines such as *sissoo, siras (Albizzia lebbek), banyan (Ficus glomerata), pakar (Ficus infectorisa), pipal, tamarind, neem, babul (Acacia arabica), kaitha (Feronia elephantum), chilbil (Ulmus integrifolicus),* and *lisora (Cordial myxa),* etc.

FAUNA[54]

As far as the faunal species of Kosi plain and Madhepura district are concerned, it seems to be quite different from those of the earlier days. Earlier, plausibly the wide varieties of herbivores and carnivores flourished due to the presence of dense forest in the Kosi region. The animals like elephants, lions, tigers, rhinoceros, black bucks, and wild ass, etc., might have roamed in this area as evident in other parts of Gangetic plain. At the turn of nineteenth century, tiger was found occasionally in the high grass jungle of Kosi.[55] Not surprisingly, the cattle fair of significance was held at Singheshwar during nineteenth century.[56]

But today, we find mainly wolf, fox, jackal, hyena, ox, buffalo, cow, dog, goat, and sheep. Several species of wild cats including palm civet or toddy cat (*Paradoxurus niglo*) are also found. Wild hog is common doing considerable damage to the crops. They are even used by 'lower caste' people for food.[57] Among the birds, house sparrow; green parrot; pigeon (blue as well as white);[58] crow; hen; cock;[59] duck;[60] dove; black raven; white heron; eagle; and vultures are quite common. There are migratory birds like wild goose and teals, etc. Figure 2 shows some elements of present fauna.

Figure 2: A flock of sheep and goat being herded in Madhepura (on the way from Singheshwar to Raibhir)

MODIFICATION IN LANDSCAPE

In fact, the landscape of Madhepura district has undergone drastic modification. People have carried intensive colonization of the area.

They have heavily deforested the region. The natural vegetation cover has been obliterated to a great extent. This is also because of the vagaries of Kosi besides the immense human pressure and manipulation. Kosi area was once rich in *Mahua* tree (*Bassia latifolia*), red cotton (*Bombax malbaricum- Simmar*), *Dhak* (*Butea menosperma*) trees jungle, *Sal* (*Shorea robusta*), Indian Ebony (*Abnus*), and Teminalia.[61] Not surprisingly, the remains of tropical deciduous woodland could still be seen in the heavily degraded and isolated patches in the area.

It seems that the ecological balance has reached a delicate stage. The balance between the progressive tendencies of vegetation and retrogressive tendencies of man is very much evident. Probably, the vegetation has reached an apparent equilibrium in relation to the variations in rainfall and temperature. It may get disturbed at any moment. At present, soil is supporting the existing population of man and animals. It seems to be at the stage of dry grassland and thorn scrubs level. But if the populace of the area go for further exploitation, the amount and nature of vegetation is liable to change with enormous consequence.

In the above discussion, an attempt has been made to reconstruct the past and present ecological pattern of Madhepura district. The physical feature, climate, soil, flora, and fauna of the district have been systematically investigated. It seems that once upon a time, the area enjoyed dense forest coverage teeming with variety of flora and fauna. In addition, if the present condition is a reliable indicator, then Madhepura was also having an ideal climate with intermixture of cold, hot, and rainy seasons punctuated by spring and autumn in between. Nonetheless, the present landscape is not pristine and appeared to be heavily modified by men and nature.

Thus Kosi plain in general and Madhepura district in particular look like a preferable location for the early people by natural selection. But probably, there were at least two hindering factors such as the dense forest coverage and the highly unpredictable nature of Kosi. Usually, human beings by nature would not like to settle down in extremely dense forest areas due to threat of wild animals and difficulty of movement in a harsh terrain. Moreover, the recurrent flood of Kosi and its frequent shift of course would not have been much to the taste of the first settlers especially given the limitation of technology in those days.

NOTES AND REFERENCES

1. *Domat* consists of sand, soil, and moisture. It is generally fertile.
2. In fact, to be more precise, it is from northeast to southwest.
3. This is based on the information given by informants during field trips.
4. It means river.
5. Saline alkali soil consists of alkali, a water soluble chemical that reacts with acids to form salts which is harmful to agriculture.
6. This is found in Kunharpur village. *Matiyaree* and *kraree* soils are seen in Murli Chandwa and Taldiha villages.
7. It is so in Madhelee village in Alamnagar C. D. Block.
8. The local inhabitants believe that it may be due to 1934 earthquake.
9. It is also known as Balua *dhar.*
10. It is 2 kilometer from Laxmipur village.
11. Here, it refers to the part of Kosi plain falling in Madhepura district and some nearby C. D. Blocks of Supaul and Saharsa districts such as Chattapur, Basantpur, Tribeniganj, Sonbarsa, Sour bazaar, and Raghopur.
12. Mohammed Eharar Alam, 'Socio-Economic Profile of Muslims in the Kosi-Mahananda Doab: A Geographical Analysis', unpublished Ph.D. thesis, Department of Geography, Jamia Milia Islamia University, New Delhi, 2002, pp. 27-41.
13. One of the district of Kosi plain, Purnea receives very heavy rainfall and is considered to be Cherapunji of Bihar.
14. According to Directorate of Statistics and Evaluation, Bihar; Madhepura district received 1044.90 mm (84.14 %) and 1212.90 mm (86.69 %) of rainfall during monsoon season in 1997-98 and 1998-99

consecutively. In comparison, it stands about 82 % on average during 1950-2000 incase of whole Kosi-Mahananda *doab*.

15. In fact one of the police buildings caved in.
16. People were generally surprised at such a high number of occurrences. It was widely covered and reported in the media.
17. Aquents are poorly drained soils generally formed in human transported material or on excavated (cut) landscapes. This is a soil with an aquic or peraquic moisture regime. It lacks distinct soil horizons in the subsoil. Orthents is an entisols that lack horizon development due to either steep slopes or parent materials that contain no permanent weatherable minerals such as ironstone. Typically, Orthents are exceedingly shallow soils. They are often referred to as "skeletal soils" or as lithosols.
18. Aquept is a suborder of the soil order inceptisol that develops in areas where restricted natural drainage results in water saturation. It is characterized by a dark surface horizon over mottled or gray subsoil.
19. It is a suborder of the soil order inceptisol with horizon below the surface. Ochrept lacks clay and humus.
20. P. C. Roy Choudhary, *District Gazetters of Purnia* (Patna: Superintendant, Secretariat Press, 1965).
21. It especially holds true about the Udakishunganj and Alamnagar C. D. Blocks of Madhepura district.
22. William Wilson Hunter, *Imperial Gazetteer* (1909), vol. 8, p. 30.
23. It was found in an experiment that although jute and paddy could be grown, none of the *Rabi* crops could thrive well.
24. It makes the threshing of crops very difficult.
25. Choudhary, *District Gazetters of Purnia* 1965.
26. The list of common flora found in research area with their English, scientific, and local names have been given in the form of several tables in Appendix-I.
27. It is because their soil are wet and rich in organic matters
28. These are tall slender water plants with jointed stalks that grow in marshes and other wet areas. Their genus is *Phragmites and Arundo.*
29. This is again a waterside plant with leaves like grass that grows in wet conditions. It belongs to *Scirpus* genus.

30. Tamarisk is a tree or bush with leaves resembling scales. Its flowers are white to pink. Its genus is *Tamarix.*
31. In English, it is called Hygrophila and Marsh Barbel. Its Hindi and Sanskrit names are *Talimkhana* and *Kokilaksha* respectively. This is under shrub and an annual herb. It grows to a height of about 60 centimeters. Generally, the plant is found on wet places. It flowers during September-March. In Ayurveda, it is used for treatment of rheumatism; urinary tract infection; inflammation; jaundice; hepatic obstruction; and pain etc. Interestingly, it is believed to enhance sexual desire.
32. *Wolffia* and *Lemna* are small angiospermic plants.
33. Its Hindi name is *dub* or *dooba.*
34. In Hindi, it is called *Gandar* and *Khas-khas.*
35. It is believed to be a high value medicinal plant.
36. It is a kind of plant that attaches itself to other plants or objects (posts and walls, etc.) as it grows.
37. Jute belongs to genus *Corchorus.*
38. Wheat belongs to genus *Triticum.*
39. *Sali* refer to a land which could be cultivated only once a year. But *dosali* could be used for growing two crops a year.
40. Hunter, *Imperial Gazatteer*, p. 31.
41. It looks like mustard seed but smaller in size and dark brown in colour. Generally, people make its powder and bake bread out of it. But these days, it is not in popular use. Still, it is a sacred food on the occasion of a local festival known as *Jitya.* The latter is performed for the well-being of son by a mother.
42. It looks like mustard seed but smaller in size and creamish in colour. *Koni* is cooked like rice. Although now a days it is not in vogue, it still serves as poor men's rice.
43. It is a typical rice field flora. Generally, only few of these are grazed upon by the cattle. The rest of them serve to conserve the water supply of the soil for next season's crop. It also adds to the humus content of the soil on decay.
44. They grow trees either in group or isolation.
45. Its genus is *Psidium.* Guava is native to tropical America.
46. Its genus is *Musa.*

47. Generally palm trees are few.
48. It is native to South America and belongs to genus *Lycopersicon.*
49. It is native to Mediterranean and Western Asia region. Nigella belongs to genus *Nigella.*
50. They are insectivorous plants. As far as *Drosera burrmannii* is concerned, it has been named in honor of Burman. It produces large amounts of seed. *Drosera* burrmannii has been considered a powerful rubefacient in *Hindu* medicine. *Utricularia* is a carnivorous bladderworts.
51. Choudhary, *District Gazetters of Purnia* 1965.
52. It is considered to be one of the best varieties of sandalwood having very high value and demand.
53. It was found during the field work conducted in July-August 2010. The villagers believed that this tree does not grow outside their village. It grows only in their village because of the blessings of the local goddesses (*Bhagwati*).
54. The list of common flora and fauna found in research area with their English, scientific, and local names have been given in the form of several tables in Appendix-I.
55. Hunter, *Imperial Gazatteer* p. 27.
56. Hunter, *Imperial Gazatteer* p. 31.
57. It is used for food by Dom and Chamar castes in the area.
58. Pigeons are commonly domesticated in the area and used for food.
59. Like pigeons, even hen and cock are domesticated by people.
60. Domestication of ducks is common especially among Muslim inhabitants of the area.
61. Hunter, *Imperial Gazatteer*, pp. 26-27.

5

The History

Kosi region in general and Madhepura district in particular have great saga. The inception of human life and culture could be traced back to at least the early historical period.[1] But the neighbouring area of southern Gangetic plain experienced human activities much earlier during prehistoric period.[2] Madhepura district and the surrounding area also experienced the formation of *Janapada* and *Mahajanapada.*

Thereafter, Magadha seemed to have brought it under its sway. Nanda, Maurya, Gupta, post-Gupta, and Kushana appear to have ruled the area or at least exercised some authority. Pala, Sena, and some Rajput rulers also brought the district under their influence. After that Madhepura tasted the rule of Delhi Sultanate as well as Mughal in successions, which was followed by British rule. The district also played a very important role during the freedom movement.

The Munger and Bhagalpur districts lying south of Madhepura[3] have been home to prehistoric and proto-historic people. The area is abounding in prehistoric settlements in places such as Paisra, Bhimbandh, Jamalpur, and the surrounding areas of Antichak. Lower Paleolithic tools have been found in Bhimbandh.[4] In fact, the hilly tract of Munger district was occupied by Acheulian man.[5] The cultural remains of the Middle Paleolithic come from Bhimbandh and Jamalpur.[6] The collection consists of scrapers, denticulate tools, and flakes. Surface material on Neolithic artifacts of mixed assemblages has been found at Oriup in Bhagalpur district.

Findings of Neolithic tools have also been reported in Jamalpur. The traces of proto-historic settlement have also been discovered in the region at such places like Oriup, Lalpur, Champa, Kumrail, and Gawa Chalk.[7] Evidences of Black and Red ware, NBPW (early, middle, and late) and its associated pottery, Kushana, Gupta, post-Gupta, and Pala period have been discovered in the area. The region is very rich in late historical settlements.

The Kosi region has been at the hub of early historic civilization. Many territorial states (i.e., Videha and Magadha) flourished in this area during early historical period. Vaishali was the strongest republic in North Bihar during that time. Anguttarap lay beyond. It consisted of a small *Janapada* known as Apana which probably included the part of the Madhepura district.[8] Probably the people of this area were outside the influence of Lichchhavis. Several sites related to this period in this district were eroded and destroyed by river Kosi- Bitarpur, Budhiagarhi, Budhnaghat, Buddhadi, Pithahi, and Mathai.[9] According to local legends, Buddha and Mahavira passed through Madhepura during their missionary activities and delivered important sermons.

Kosi belt continued to be independent till the beginning of the 6th century B.C.E. For sometime even the great Magadha remained part of Anga. But soon, the latter's prosperity seemed to decline. Bimbasara, the king of Magadha seemed to have annexed Anga. Nonetheless, Anguttarap maintained its independence. The western portion of Supaul district as a part of Mithila continued to enjoy its independence. This was the characteristics of whole north Bihar until the conquest of Ajatsatru.

He defeated Lichchhavis and other independent republics of Bihar and annexed the whole territory to the kingdom of Magadha. The Magadhan Empire grew rapidly and the whole of Bihar came under its sway under Nanda and Maurya. In early twentieth century, a hoard of 58 punch marked coins of Mauryan period was discovered from Gorhoghat. R. K. Choudhary found the same type of coins from Patuaha in 1958. He also came across some Black Polished Ware near Mahishee and surroundings. Mauryan Pillars are found in Sikleegadh[10] and Udakishunganj.[11]

As a province of Magadha, Madhepura district witnessed along with the other parts of the empire, vicissitudes of fortune and a change of ruling dynasties. The Haryak, Sisunagas, the Nandas, the Mauryas, the Sungas, the Kanavas, and the Guptas ruled in chronological succession over it. Madhepura seemed to have also felt the burnt of Kalinga, Satavahana, Greek (Menander), and Kushana invasions. The Bhant communities living in villages of Basantpur and Raibhir under Shankarpur C. D. Block claimed to be the descendants of the Kushana dynasty. The end of Kushana rule towards the first half of the second century C.E synchronizes with the rise of the Bharasiva Nagas, who set up their rule in Uttar Pradesh and east and west Bihar.

The Gupta rule also extended over the Kosi area. The whole Bihar was consolidated as Tirabhukti (a province) with its capital at Vaishali.[12] A copper statue of Buddha delicately executed, discovered at Sultanganj, testifies to the importance of the place and its vicinity as producing marvelous specimens of handwork in bronze and other metals. Later Guptas of Magadha ruled over the Kosi region with the break up of the Gupta Empire. An inscription of Adityasena has been found on the Mandara Hill (Munger).

After the decline of Guptas, the vacuum was utilized by several chiefs. The Varmans of Kamrup extended their authority up to the confines of Kosi. The territory of Purnavarman included the present district of Saharsa.

Madhepura's sovereignty also passed to Harshavardhana. Hieun-Tsang visited the Kosi region (Champa) during Harsha's time. Gopala, the Pala king of Bengal, conquered Magadha and south Bihar in the third decade of the eighth century. Dharmapala, the son of Gopala founded Vikramshila Vihar on a hillock besides the bank of the Ganges in this part.[13] It has been identified with present Antichak village in Bhagalpur district. Pala provided stable administration to the area.

As Kalachuris pressed in present Jharkhand region (erstwhile south Bihar), Pala shifted to Bihar and probably Saharsa served as it's headquarter during the reign of Vigraphapala III. Saharsa was also strategically situated to become Jayaskandhavar, the temporary capital city when they were surrounded by enemies on all sides.[14]

In the eleventh century, the southern Gangetic plain was invaded by Jatavarman, the founder of the Jadava dynasty of east Bengal[15] and the Gangeya king of Dehala. After Palas, Karnata in Mithila, and Sena in Bengal became their legal successor. Both of them claimed authority over Kosi region including Madhepura district and so very often entered into armed conflicts. One of the earliest Karnatas, Nanyadeva established his rule over an area extending from Champaran to Purnea. He was an ally of Vijyasena in the beginning but fell afterwards over the division of territory. The Deopana inscription of Vijyasena indicates that Nanyadeva was defeated and imprisoned in Supaul district. Later on, his son Gangadeva liberated him.

The Sanokar inscription of Vallalasena pointed towards the extension of his rule up to Bhagalpur district. The two sons of Nanyadeva such as Malladeva and Gangadeva drove the Sena further east.[16] Gangadeva was succeeded by Narasim-Hadeva whose reign saw the separation of Mithila and Nepal.

Muhamad Bakhtiyar Khilji marched his Turkish troops to Bihar and Bengal and brought them under his sway. Thus Kosi belt was brought under the Sultanate rulers of Delhi and were ruled by the Turco-Afghans, Saiyyads, Lodis, and later by the Mughals in chronological succession.

The last king of Karnatas was Harshimadeva who lost to Ghiyasuddin Tuglaq in a protracted struggle. But slowly Tuglaq's authority weakened in Mithila region. Haji Ilyas of Bengal invaded

Tirhut and defeated its ruler. He divided Tirhut into two parts. The District of Saharsa came under the control of Oinwara rulers.[17] Their rule was followed by a chaos.

The Gandhavariya Rajputs got the upper hand in the region.[18] They trace their descent from the Tirhut's chiefs. Madhepura remained under the dominance of Bhar rulers during Rajput rule. Present Raibhir village under Singheshwar C. D. Block was a stronghold of Bhar. However, the whole area was dotted with a number of Hindu and Muslim chiefs. They even gathered courage to defy the central Mughal authority. In fact, Karranis and Afghans in collusion with local Rajput rulers and chiefs had made Saharsa and Madhepura district as the center of the revolt.

The Saharsa district formed the parts of Sarkar Tirhut, Sarkar Munger, and Sarkar Purnea during the Mughal rule. As a matter of fact, most of the *Parganas* of Saharsa district was assessed by Raja Todarmal during the time of Akbar.[19] It clearly shows the importance of the Kosi area during those days. Even the town of Bhagalpur is occasionally mentioned in *Akbarnama* and *Ain-i-Akbari.* It is mentioned as the chief town of *Pargana* Bhagalpur. Akbar's troops are known to have passed through the town during 1573 and 1575 while invading Bengal. A mosque from the time of Akbar is still present in Sarsendi village under Udakishunganj. Sikander Sah visited the district, which is evident from the coins discovered from Sahugarh village

When the East India Company assumed the *diwani* rights of Bengal in 1765, Bhagalpur district formed the eastern part of the Muhammadan Sarkar of Munger. A stretch of 1813 sq. km. north of Ganges was added to Bhagalpur in 1864. Saharsa and Madhepura also passed with the rest of Bengal under the rule of East India Company in 1764.

The area was the center of the revolt during 1857. The revolutionaries operated unchecked by the administrations of Purnea and Bhagalpur. Since then Madhepura district remained the center of several agitations during the freedom movement. The Home Rule Movement and Satyagraha *Andolan* received widespread support from its people. The prominent freedom fighters were Sarvashri Mahtab Lal Yadava, Shivanandan Mandal, Nand Kishore Choudhary, Rajendra Mishra, Ram Bahadur Sinha, Yadunandan Jha, and Rajendra Lal Das.

The jail of Madhepura and Supaul were full of freedom fighters. The people of the district got agitated when Rajendra Prasad was man handled by police at Bihpur jail (Bhagalpur). Picketing took place throughout the district. Even *Kisan* (farmer) movement was going on during 1930-1942. The August revolution of 1942 proved to be watershed in the history of Madhepura in relation to the freedom movement. On the thirteenth of August, the people of the district under the leadership of Sarvashri Bhupendra Narayan Mandal and Deto Singh hoisted the national flag in Madhepura court compound.[20] Most of the police station was overtaken by revolutionaries.

A number of people were killed in police firing on the twenty ninth of August in Saharsa. Jay Prakash Narayan visited Madhepura after escaping from Hazaribagh prison, while on the way to Nepal. Sri Shiyaram Singh of Bhagalpur formed the Siyaram Dal which had several branches in Madhepura district. He met Jay Prakash Narayan in Nepal in 1942 at a conference of Bihari workers under the leadership of Shivanandan Mandal. The district played an important role in the subsequent events during the freedom struggle.

Thus, the history of Kosi region and Madhepura seemed to be interesting and fascinating through the ages. The district has a history of at least two and half millennium starting in the early historic period and continuing up to the present. It experienced mixed fortunes during this long period. It would not be an exaggeration to say that Madhepura was a part of great cultures and civilizations for centuries and played a very important role in the history of Bihar and South Asia.

NOTES AND REFERENCES

1. The historical period refers to that phase of past for which we have written records and could be utilized for historical reconstructions. The literary as well as archaeological sources are used for the reconstruction of its history. Generally speaking, historical period could be further divided into ancient, medieval, and modern phases. But in Indian history and archaeology, especially in the context of northern India and middle Gangetic plain, the period between c. 500 B.C.E to 1000 C.E represents the historical period. Historical period could be divided into several cultural sequences such as early historical period (500 B.C.E-300 C.E) and late historical period (300 C.E - 1000 C.E). The early historical period could further be divided into two halves, first half (500-200 B.C.E) consisting of *Mahajanapada* phase and Mauryan phase. The second half of early historical period (200 B.C.E - 300 C.E) consists of Sunga-Kushana phases. Like its predecessor, late Historical period too could be divided into two halves, first half (300 C.E - 600 C.E) consisting of Gupta period and second half (600-1000 C.E.) representing Pala period.
2. Prehistory refers to the time before written records appeared. It generally includes the Stone Age, the Bronze Age, and the Iron Age. The nature and events of prehistory can be partially reconstructed through archaeology.
3. They form the part of southern middle Gangetic plain.
4. A. Gosh, *An Encyclopedia of Indian Archaeology* (Delhi: Munshiram Manoharlal Publishers Pvt. Ltd, 1989), p. 22.
5. *Indian Archaeology- A Review*, 1960-61 and 1965-66, pp. 5-6 and pp. 7-8.
6. They lay in Munger district.
7. *Indian Archaeology- A Review.*
8. It definitely consisted of a part of Saharsa district. Since Madhepura is adjacent of this district and even once formed its part for sometime, it can be presumed that some parts of Madhepura may have constituted the Apana *Janapada.*
9. These sites are known to have been associated with Buddhism.
10. It is located in Purnea district and almost at a distance of 22 km from the eastern border of Madhepura district.

11. Since the area was a border region even in those days, the Mauryan ruler apparently took special care to guard its frontier.
12. Henceforth, the province was called as *Bhukti* and District as *Vishaya.* In Bihar, there were two *Bhukti* such as Tirabhukti and Pundravardhanbhukti. Former consisted most part of Bihar. Pundravardhanbhukti included parts of Madhepura, Purnea, and north Bengal.
13. R. K. Mookerji, *Ancient Indian Education* (London: Macmillan and Co., 1947), p. 587.
14. They also came into contact with Nepal through this region only.
15. It is known from the Belava copper plate of Bhojvarman.
16. It is indicated by the setting up of Gangapur Rajni (named after Gangadeva) in Pargana Nishankpur Kurha and Maldiha (named after Malladeva) on the border of Saharsa and Purnea. Probably village Malhad in Supaul district is also named after Malladeva.
17. Its most famous king was Shivasimha whose court was adorned by the poets like Vidyapati.
18. They are also alternately called as Ganbharia.
19. Todarmal had fixed the revenue settlement of Subha Bihar in 1582.
20. The flag was hoisted in treasury building.

6

Historical Places in Madhepura Subdivision

An intensive archaeological cum historical exploration was conducted in Madhepura district. This exercise helped in indentifying a large number of sites belonging to historical (ancient), medieval, and modern periods.[1] There were some previously reported sites. They were also visited as far as possible. A description of all these sites in terms of their name, location, area, form, size, condition, cultural remains, geographical conditions (soil, water, flora, and fauna, etc.) has been provided. The general beliefs and legends associated with these sites wherever applicable have been given. There is also an attempt to establish them in a time frame.

All these places have been arranged and described in the administrative and alphabetical frameworks.[2] As far as the administrative arrangement is concerned, the sites have been divided into two subdivisions of Madhepura districts namely Madhepura and Udakishunganj. The present chapter deals with the sites related to the former. Where as, the historical places falling under the ambit of Udakishunganj subdivision form the part of the next chapter.

DESCRIPTION OF THE EXPLORED SETTLEMENTS IN MADHEPURA SUBDIVISION

1. Basantpur: E H, 25°58'30" N 86°54'30" E, Shankarpur C. D. Block

Basantpur is one of the villages falling under Shankarpur C. D. Block. The Bhant community of this village claimed to be the descendents of Kushana dynasty. Unfortunately, there is not much information about them. If their contention is considered to be true then Bhant's history could be traced to early historical period.

2. Belo Goth or Belogoth (Lukeshawaree Sthan): L Med and Mod, 25°52'30" N 86°53'15" E, Murliganj C. D. Block

This site is located east to Belo Goth village. A part of it is famous with the name Lukeshawaree Sthan. The settlement is spread over an area of almost 20000 square meters. The dimension of primary settlement area is 50 × 40 meters. In contrast, the measurement of secondary occupation area is around 500 × 350 meters. Overall, the site consists of a mound, modern structures, and farmlands over it.[3] The mound is sloping downward on all sides with a maximum height of 3.5 meters from the surrounding surface level. (Figure 3). Gradually, the site is eroding. It is being encroached by human habitations and arable lands. (Figure 3.1).

Figure 3: Villagers standing on the mound

As far as the cultural remains are concerned, baked bricks and potsherds are found. Former is seen in abundance. The measurement of one full-size brick stands to be 32 × 22 × 4 centimeters. (Figure 3.2). There was one well in the west-south corner of the site. It was made up of brick and now almost extinct. The remnant of a wall was also seen near to the site. One of the informants had found a big pitcher (big size *ghara*), a small size Goddess statue, and seven stone boulders. Villagers reported that one tool (mason's *sahul* type) was also found.

The site and surrounding area possesses *domat* soil. This type of soil is generally useful in making bricks. It is noteworthy that numerous bricks were found in and around site during exploration. There are *chiknee* and *baluhaee* soils east and west of the site respectively. Two canals are passing by this medieval settlement. One

Figure 3.1: Arable lands with cultural remains over the site

of them is Durgapur or Belo *Nahar* running almost half kilometer west to the site. Whereas Beldor *Nahar* is passing almost 5 kilometers east of the site. Generally, water is found at 10 feet with some variations in iron content. But drinking water is available at 25 feet. The general flora and fauna in and around the site did not differ from the general trend seen in the district.

Figure 3.2: A baked brick with 15 centimeters scale

Local populace believed that this place is of Lukeshawaree *Mata*[4] and thus considered sacred. People from near as well as distant places come here for fulfilling their wishes (especially related to wounds) by worshipping the Goddess. Traditionally, they offer *gur* and *batasha*[5] besides other sweet to Lukeshawaree *Mata*. Local villagers believed that one *kalshaee*[6] full of coins moves in the night. But when quipped, villagers replied that they have only heard about it and never actually saw it.[7]

It seemed that the popularity of the place increased dramatically in the last few decades.[8] Tuesday is a special day when a fair is also held here. According to one estimate more than 10000 people throng the place on this day. It is especially visited by women folk. According to informants, there was a British *Kachharee*[9] and some Britishers resided here. According to them, that's why it is also called *gadh*. The site seemed to be occupied from at least late medieval period to modern period.

3. Bindraban or Brindaban (Ram Jankee Thakurbaree): L Med and Mod, 25°51'52" N 86°56' E, Murliganj C. D. Block

The medieval site locally known as "Ram Jankee Thakurbaree" is located 65 meters east of Bindraban village.[10] The dimension of primary occupation area is 45 x 38 meters. The site consists of a building, pond, two wells, and some idols[11] besides few plants and trees. The building is in a dilapidated condition.[12] According to local populace, twenty one statues made up of eight different types of minerals (*dhatu*) and of an estimated value of 2.5 million rupees were stolen a few years ago.[13] There is one pond just east of the site. One could see arable land in and around the settlement. The overall condition of the site is not good.

It consists of black soil. The vegetation goes along the general trend of the district. There is one canal nearby called "Baluha *dhar*." Sweet drinking water is available at 20 feet in the two wells located on the site. According to informants, there were fourteen generations of *Mahant*.[14] But, they could name only seven generations of Mahants such as Baba Bhagwan Das, Ganga Das, Parmeshawar Das, Amar Das, Anup Das, Surendar Das, and Rajeshawar Das.[15] It seems to be a late medieval site.

4. Gohumani-I (*Deeh*): L Med and Mod, 25°57'40" N 86°50'30" E, Singheshwar C. D. Block

There is a mound locally known as "*Deeh*"[16] located southwest of Gohumani village.[17] Presently, its cultural remains could be seen in 1350 square meters. But according to inhabitants, once upon a time it was spread over 403562 square meters. Currently, it lay almost one meter above the ground.

Undoubtedly, the site is in highly disturbed state. The settlement appears to shrink drastically. The dramatic expansion of agriculture appeared to have destroyed much of the site. In fact, the settlement is on the verge of complete extinction if not protected immediately. The soil in and around the site is of *domat* type. Generally, the sweet drinking water in the area is available at 15 to 25 feet. The cultural remains attest to its existence since late medieval period and continuance up to modern period.

5. Gohumani-II (Lala Than): Mod, 25°57'40" N 86°50'30" E, Singheshwar C. D. Block

It is a modern site with the local name "Lala Than" situated 1.5 km west of Gohumani village. The site is exactly located in Lala Pattee *Bastee*[18] of the village. It is spread in almost 500 square meters. General public associate the place with a legendary figure Lala Maharaj. According to them, there were some structures upon the site earlier. But now it is destroyed and in the process of being replaced by a new structure.

According to GPS (Global Positioning System) record, the elevation of the area is 41.45 meters.[19] The area is endowed with *domat* soil. Sweet drinking water could be found at 15 to 25 feet. There is a canal passing west to the site. The people associate Lala Maharaj with another local legendary hero Khedan Baba. Both of them are considered close friends. Khedan Baba is highly revered among the district populace in general and Yadava caste in particular.[20] The site belongs to late modern period.

6. Gudar Chakla: L Med and Mod, 25°50'45" N 86°59'17" E, Murliganj C. D. Block

This site is situated at Amari school near Gudar Chakla and Dumaria villages.[21] It is spread in 10000 square meters. As far as primary occupation area is concerned, its maximum length and breadth are 90 and 76 meters respectively. Presently, the settlement consists of a modern building, pond, and well. The site is in dilapidated condition. The old temple and well have broken down. So, the idols were shifted to a new building.[22] The pond is also in a bad condition.

There are two types of soil in the site area such as *baluhaee* and *domat*. The site has usual plants and trees commonly seen in Madhepura. There is a canal passing 60 meters north of the site. A lake is located almost 1½ km east of the place. The well situated on the site has depth of 20 feet. Sweet drinking water is also found almost at the same level in the locality. Overall, the geographical conditions are quite promising for the human settlement.

There are several legends associated with the site. According to one of them, a virgin cow used to be milked by a sage called Gudar Das. Once it was seen by the local inhabitants who were surprised. Later on, they constructed a house out of respect for the sage over there.

According to the second legend, once upon a time, Maharaja Darbhanga sent his forces here. They asked for some fishes from the aforesaid sage. Gudar Das gave them a jackfruit which got converted into fish. When the king's military personnel ate that, they suffered from dysentry. Then they demanded taxes from Gudar Das. He gave them two horses which became tigers. When the king heard about all this, he came to see these miracles himself. Later on the Maharaja asked for forgiveness and granted 151 acres of land to the miraculous sage. However, according to another version, the king gave 7 *beegha* of land which miraculously got converted into 700 *beegha* in the copper plate record.[23]

According to informants, there were fourteen generations of sages. But the name of only eight of them- Gudar Das, Tulsee das, Gopal Das, Bojran Das, Bhikam Das, Lal Das, Ramadheen Das, Mangneeram Das, Balram Das, and Ram Narayan Das- could be put forward.[24] It is a late medieval settlement which continued to be occupied to this day.

7. Itahari-I (Itahari *Deeh*): L Med and Mod, 25°58' N 86°50'15" E, Murliganj C. D. Block

This site locally called "Itahari *Deeh*" is placed almost 500 meters west to Itahari village.[25] It is spread in 111000 square meters. But the dimension of primary occupation area is estimated to be 500 x 300 meters. The settlement was quite large once upon a time. But now, a very disturbed and small mound (5 × 5 meters) could be found. (Figure 3.3). Some cultural remains such as bricks and potsherds were visible in its section. Few plants like *chius* and grasses have grown over it.

The site is in a highly disturbed state. Villagers were virtually farming on the site and surrounding areas.[26] (Figure 3.4). So, they removed most of the cultural remains in the process.[27] Yet some of them were scattered here and there. Informants reported that villagers

Figure 3.3: A small mound left on the Itahari-I site

Figure 3.4: Agricultural farmland on Itahari-I site

had seen three wells in site area which were extinct now. But it could not be verified during the course of field work.

Domat soil was observed in and around the site. As far as vegetation is concerned, it was not different from the general vegetation trend in Madhepura district. A canal called "Itahari *Nahar*" is running east of the site. The area becomes flooded during monsoon season. Overall, the site and surrounding bears a favourable look for human settlement and has remained under occupation from late medieval period to modern period. According to GPS, the elevation of site area is 40 meters above sea level.[28]

8. Itahari-II (Deeh): Ghailarh C. D. Block[29]

There is a site with the name "*Deeh*" near middle school in Ithari village falling in Ratanpura Panchayat of Ghailarh C. D. Block. But unfortunately, no further information could be retrieved about it.

9. Jorgawan-I (Batola Deeh): Mod, 25°54'42" N 86°58' E, Murliganj C. D. Block

It lays 400 meters southwest of Jorgawan village and almost 3 kilometers from Murliganj C. D. Block headquarter.[30] Locally, the site is known as "Batola *Deeh.*" It is spread in 5087 square meters. The settlement seemed to be a habitation site. It is an early modern site.

10. Jorgawan-II (Samedh): L Med and Mod, 25°54'42" N 86°58' E, Murliganj C. D. Block

There a site locally known as "Samedh" 500 meters west to Jorgawan village.[31] There are two roads running in north (500 meters away) and south (80 meters away) of the site. A river flows almost 1 kilometer away from the settlement. As far as cultural records are concerned, one could observe potsherds scattered on almost 17000 square meters. It seemed that the past human activities were more concentrated in a relatively smaller area such as 1000 square meters. This part of the site was almost 75 centimeters above the surrounding area. Presently, the site also consisted of a brick house, brick well, and *machan.*[32] The settlement was in a highly disturbed state. Most of the area is under cultivation.

It is a flat area which consisted of common vegetation and fauna. The soil is black and sandy. It seemed that the past human settlement had moved from west to east and from low lying area to relatively higher ground. This trend is visible even now. It has been probably due to flood problems in the area. The presence of three ponds almost in a linear line between Batola *Deeh* and Samedh is noteworthy.[33]

There are interesting legends associated with the site. Villagers said that a *Mahant* used to live on the site. There was a well with charismatic water. The sick people used to get healthy after drinking this water. People also believed that there lived a *Jin*[34] in that well who gave dreams to spinster girls. He used to put vermillion on the girls forehead in sleep and then endowed them with a lot of wealth. But the girls used to die after six months. The site seemed to be occupied from late medieval to modern period.

11. Kaurihar and Fulkaha/Phulkaha villages (Itahdeeh): L Med and Mod, Gamharia C. D. Block[35]

There is a site locally called "Itahdeeh" near Kaurihar and Fulkaha villages.[36] It was spread in 1000 square meters area. But this past settlement is almost extinct. The informants saw some cultural remains such as bricks and cowries. Even today, sometimes villagers find the cultural remains in the form of some structural foundation here and there. The bricks are Belodeeh type. The natural vegetation is in line with the flora of the district. Interestingly, *Sakhuwa*[37] is found in the area. The settlement seemed to belong to late medieval period and habitation continuing up to modern period.

12. Khusroopattee (Nawratna Hatta): L Med and Mod, 25°52'35" N 86°57'48" E, Murliganj C. D. Block

This site is locally known as "Nawratna Hatta". It is located on the bank of Kosi *dhar* and 500 meters west to the village Khusroopattee.[38] It was very difficult to reach the exact site due to being surrounded by river and marshy land. The dimension of primary occupation area is estimated to be around 150 x 120 meters. The settlement was covered with long grasses of almost 1 meter height called *kharee*[39] and some trees besides having electric poles. No other remains could be seen. But informants said that once upon a time there was a fort as well as two ponds lying east and south of the site.[40] There are arable lands in the vicinity of the settlement. The site appeared to be almost destroyed.

The soil is sandy. In fact, it is a *diyara* area. The sweet drinking water is available at 15 to 26 feet. The general vegetation seemed to be of quite a normal type.[41] As far as fauna is concerned, according to informants, almost 40 years ago they could easily spot ass and mule in the surrounding. There is a perennial river which flowed in north-south direction in relation to site. It seemed that human settlement had moved from west to east and south.

According to legends, there was a lesser king known as Lal Thakur who ruled the area under the overall sovereignty of Raja Darbhanga Maharaj.[42] He built a fort which was surrounded by brick wall. Overall, the settlement belongs to the late medieval period and continued to be occupied in modern period as well.

13. Kolhaipatti (Baba Chilka Ram): Mod, 25°50'45" N 86°58'45" E, Murliganj C. D. Block

The site of Baba Chilka Ram is situated in *Pashchim Tola*[43] of Kolhaipatti lying 500 meters west of the Raghunathpur village.[44] Presently, the site consists of a modern building of two rooms (temple), a well, and 76 meters long open field behind it. There is a well in front of the temple which is 15 feet in depth. The total area of the site is around 3391 square meters.

The soil type is *chiknee*. There exits a marshy low land behind the site. As far as the site relationship with the surrounding area is concerned, there is arable land in the vicinity. Normally, it gets flooded due to a nearby seasonal river, Beanga *Nadi*. The vegetation is of regular type.

According to local populace, previously, there was an *Akhara*[45] on the present site. It was established by a person known as Chalabala. He was cremated on the site upon his death. Later on, the villagers constructed a temple after having a dream related to him. They believe that non-lactating mothers and animals could be made to milk here. Moreover, people also visit this place to get other wishes fulfilled. The site is being protected by villagers and a caretaker. It is a modern period site.

14. Pakilpar (Baba Jatadharee Shivalaya Sthan): Mod, Murliganj C. D. Block[46]

There is a site with the name "Baba Jatadharee Shivalaya Sthan" located near Pakilpar village.[47] The site is situated almost 5 kilometer from Murliganj C. D. Block headquarter. But, there is no proper road connecting both of them. A *kachcha* (non-metallic) road was used to reach the site. As the name suggests, it consists of a Shiva temple, a rectangular platform, and two trees (Pipal and Banyan). The size of primary occupation area is 900 square meters. There is also a well on the site with 45 feet depth.

A river with the name Pakilpar *dhar* flows 350 meters away from site. The direction of its flow in relation to the site locus is north to south. The area becomes active flood plain during rainy season. The soil in and around the site is *chiknee*. There are arable lands nearby.

Villagers believe that originally there were four trees in place of the present temple. They also talk about a *Baba* and several associated legends. People believe that one's wishes (*manokamna*) can be fulfilled here. It seems to be almost 150-200 years old and so qualifies to be a modern site.

15. Parwaha (Daitya Pokhar): L Med and Mod, Gamharia C. D. Block[48]

There is a site with the local name "Daitya Pokhar" (monster's pond) in Itwah near Parwaha village.[49] According to legends, a monster dug up seven ponds in one night. It was dawn by the time he reached Itwah and so got converted into stone. The local inhabitants commemorate the event by holding a fair every *Kartik-Poornima*[50] month. According to villagers, they had seen seven ponds (1 in Kamaljukee, 2 in Tehree, and 4 in Itwah) earlier, but almost extinct by now. Informants also said that there are two stones in Itwah which looked like monsters. But, these could not be verified during field visits. On the basis of local populace's information, it seemed to be a late medieval to early modern period site.

16. Piprahi (Mahwariya Gadhee): Mod, 25°51'40" N 86°52'42" E, Gamharia C. D. Block

This site locally known as "Mahwariya Gadhee" lies near to village Piprahi.[51] But the cultural remains are almost extinct by now. General public believes that it belonged to a king. There is not much information about it. It qualifies as an early modern site on the basis of information provided by inhabitants.

17. Rajni (Mangnee Baba Ka Sthan): Mod, 25°49' N 86°58'30" E, Murliganj C. D. Block

There is one site with the name "Mangnee Baba Ka Sthan" almost 1.5 kilometers east of Rajni village.[52] It is spread over 850 square meters. The site consists of some structures in the form of temple[53] and a well. It could be seen in Figure 3.5. No other past cultural remains could be found on the site. Presently, it is protected by a *kachcha* fence (bamboo fence). There are arable lands around the site.

The soil is of *domat* type. It is a *chap* and marshy area. Some flood water enters during rainy season. Generally, water is available at 15 feet. But one could get sweet drinking water around 25 feet.

It is believed that there was one *Baba* known as Mangnee Ram who lived here. One king, Diyara Singh belonging to Rajni *Dyorhi*[54] asked for *Malgujaree* or tax. When he and his forces (*Sipahee*) compelled him to yield, *Baba* converted one *bachchee* (female calf) into a tiger. Thereafter, the king asked for forgiveness and granted him some land. Local inhabitants also believe that a diarrhea patient could be cured by visiting this place.[55] The site seemed to be at least 200 years old and thus belongs to the modern period.

Figure 3.5: First Author standing on the Rajni site and pointing towards a modern structure on it

18. Raibhir-I: E H, 25°59' N to 25°60' N and 86°52' E to 86°53'30" E, Shankarpur C. D. Block

Like Basantpur, Raibhir village seemed to host an ancient community. The village is located adjacent to Basantpur already mentioned above. The Bhant community residing in Raibhir also consider themselves to be the descendents of Kushana dynasty. Their claim could not be verified from other sources.

Anyhow, Raibhir is endowed with ideal ecological condition for the beginning and survival of human settlement for a long period of time. The village is made up of younger alluvium with presence of *baluhaee* soil. The area is rich in water resources. Presently, Sonbarsa Raj distributary and couple of *minor* are latticing the village and neighbouring areas. If the legends are taken to have some semblance of truth then the history of some people living in the area could be traced back to early historical period.

19. Raibhir-II: L Med, 25°59' N to 25°60' N and 86°52' E to 86°53'30" E, Shankarpur C. D. Block

There is another site in Raibhir village. It is situated 300 meters away from present human habitations. The settlement is approachable only through a narrow *kachcha* road. In fact, the area was waterlogged when visited. The mound is almost 400 square meters in area and 35 feet high from the surrounding ground level. It is in arch shape and covered with green grasses.

As far as the cultural remains are concerned, potsherds and baked bricks are visible. According to informants, earlier it was a very large mound but disturbed and contracted over a period of time due to Kosi's vagary and intensive human activities. The site is surrounded by farmlands which are slowly encroaching. Presently, it is in a highly disturbed state and on the verge of extinction.

The surroundings of the settlement tend to represent favourable environment for human settlement and subsistence. This past settlement and surroundings are endowed with rich greenery. The soil is *baluhaee.* Generally, people believed that a Raja Basant used to live and rule from here. It seemed to be a habitation site belonging to the late medieval period.

20. Rampur (Thakurbaree): Mod, 25°53'30" N 86°57'30" E, Murliganj C. D. Block

This site with the local name "Thakurbaree" is situated 230 meters east to Rampur village and 12 meters across a metallic road.[56] It is spread over 950 square meters. As far as the dimension of primary occupation area is concerned, the length and breadth is 30 x 28 meters. The site consists of a modern building constructed over the funeral remains of a Thakur Maharaj six years ago and a mud *pindi* or *piri.*[57] There are arable lands near the site. A pond and a canal are located 90 meters and 45 meters away from the site respectively.

The site area and surroundings bear usual type of vegetation. The area mainly consists of *chiknee* soil. The vegetation is of the usual type. It is almost 200 years old and an early modern period settlement.

21. Rohwa (Hasangadh): L Med[58]

This site locally known as "Hasangadh" is located near the village Rohwa. It is a *Thakurbaree* also called as "*Jagah*."[59] The primary occupation area of the site is 850 square meters. The elevation of the site area is 41.14 meters.[60] According to informanst, presently, there are 101738 square meters of land under the ownership of *Jagah*. Half of this land is lying in the north where as another half on the south of the immediate settlement area.

The site consisted of a small temple and three buildings (two *pacca* and one *kachcha*).[61] The temple consisted of some stone and metal idols (Figure 3.6 and Figure 3.7). There is also a well on the site. It is full of normal vegetation found in the area. The nature of the soil is *baluhaee* also called *dorasa*. The water was reported to be sweet in the site expanse. It is an active flood plain area. There is a narrow canal (*chchahree*) running 300 meters east of the site. A dead canal (*maria dhar*) also seen west of the site.

According to the informants, the people throng the place to get their wishes fulfilled through worships and offerings. The incumbent *Mahant* Jagarnath Das told that almost eleven Mahants survived here.[62] He himself got this position in late 2009. It seemed that the site has been inhabited since the late medieval period.

22. Rupauli (Itahdeeh): L Med and Mod, Singheshwar C. D. Block[63]

There is a site called "Itahdeeh" lying 2 kilometers southwest of Rupauli village and 4 kilometers from Singheshwar C. D. Block headquarter.[64] The site spreads in 850 square meters. The elevation of the site is 41.14 meters.[65] As far as the cultural remains are

Figure 3.6: Inside of Hasangadh Jagah temple

Figure 3.7: One of the idols in the Hasangadh Jagah temple

concerned, potsherds and bricks could be found. But, the site is in an extremely disturbed state. The villagers were farming over it.

The natural vegetation is not different from the general pattern seen in the district. The land in the area is relatively less fertile. The nature of soil is *baluhaee* as sandy sediments (*bharna mittee*) has been deposited by Kosi's flood. Generally, sweet drinking water is available at 25 feet. But, according to villagers, at some places proper drinking water is available only at 60 feet depth. Overall, the area bore a relatively less positive look for human settlement and subsistence. The site seemed to be inhabited during the late medieval and early modern period.

23. Sahugarh: E Med and L Med, Madhepura C. D. Block[66]

This site stood in Sahugarh village of Madhepura C. D. Block.[67] It has been reported previously. According to the earlier report, some past cultural remains such as an old house or castle of Sikander Sah's time,[68] the ruler of Bengal, had been found in *Sahugarh* village. That has been substantiated by the discovery of coins bearing the date of his reign.[69] The villagers informed that one could see the remains of a metallic boat in the local river (passing by this village) during summer season when the river water receded. But, this could not be independently verified due to water logging during the course of fieldwork.

The vegetation is of normal type. The type of soil in and around the site is *baluhaee.* The area is also prone to flood water especially during rainy season. On the whole, the area has appealing look for human settlement and subsistence activities. It seemed to be an early to late medieval period site.

24. Sarsendi: L Med and Mod, Gwalpara C. D. Block [70]

Sarsendi village and surrounding areas consisted of several mounds, a mosque, and tank. The mosque was on an elevated ground with a possibility of earlier ruins lying concealed therein. One of the mounds is believed to be a *gadh* (fort) of Raja Bairisal.[71] Bairisal is considered to be the head of Gandhavariya/Ganbharia Rajput. According to local legend, he was very rich and so hoards of gold and silver coins may be lying underneath these ruins. It was reported that some cultivators even found silver coins.

As aforesaid, there were a tank and another mound to the east and southwest of the *gadh* mound. The local people believed that it was the prison of the king. It is generally held that Ganbharia Rajputs came from some other place and gradually settled down here. According to another legend, during the reign of Bairisal, two *faqirs*[72] refused the summons of the king's men and in the scuffle killed these state personnel with their miraculous *khurpis.*[73] Bairisal fearing the consequences of interference from Delhi Sultans got his sister Dai Thakurani married to one of these *faqirs.*

It is also said that all the seven members of the king's sister's family were later killed. The presence of seven graves belonging to them in an enclosure with remnants of earthen horses and elephants (seen on outside wall) is also claimed. A mosque of the time of Akbar is also present in this village. These ruins seemed to be at least 500 years old. So they belong to late medieval period and continued to be inhabited to at least early modern period.

25. Singheshwar (Singheshwar Sthan or Singheshwarsthan): L Med and Mod, 25°58' N 86°47' E, Singheshwar C. D. Block

The site famous as "Singheshwar Sthan" is situated at a distance of 8 kilometers from Madhepura district headquarters.[74] Singheshwar Sthan is renowned for its historical and religious importance. The site is almost spread in 8000 square meters. It consisted of a well built temple (Figure 3.8), one *pokhar* (pond), and few shops. The dense habitation is found around the site. The temple consisted of a *Shiva-Linga*[75] (Figure 3.9) which lay below the modern surrounding surface level. The temple precinct contained few sculptural fragments.

One of them is possibly a *Bhairava* image of c. eleventh to twelfth centuries CE.[76]

There are several myths regarding to the emergence of Singheshwar Sthan. Its references are found in *Barah Puran.* It mentions that once upon a time the area was deeply forested. One day, the cattle herders regularly roaming in the area saw a virgin cow sprinkling milk at a particular place. So, they became curious and dug that place out to finally find a *Shivalaya.* Thereafter, people began to worship it and in the mean time, a temple was constructed over this *Shivalaya.*

Figure 3.8: The partial view of Singheshwar Sthan temple

Figure 3.9: The Shiva-Linga established within the Singheshwar Sthan temple

Surprisingly, *Barah Puran* put forward another version too. According to this version, the three Gods Brahma, Vishnu, and Indra visited Kailaspuri in order to discuss some worldly matters. They did not find Lord Shiva there and finally realized that he was residing in a lonely place in the guise of a deer inside a deep forest. These three Gods caught that deer with his horn at three places which finally broke down and Lord Shiva disappeared. Each of them had one part of horn and Vishnu installed his share in Singheshwar Sthan for the welfare of the mankind. Interestingly, Shiva was worshipped here through *Vaishnava* cult.

According to another myth, Raja Dasharath performed a *mahayagyna* (major worship) presided over by Shringi *Rishi* who worshipped Lord Shiva on that occasion. It is believed that the seven

Havana Kunds[77] created on that sacred occasion got converted into ravaged tank later. Singheshwar Sthan is also considered to be the meditation place of Shringi *Rishi*. However, with the passage of time, the residential place of this great *Rishi* became famous as Singheshwar Sthan.

Another myth said that the three Goddesses such as Maha Kali, Maha Laxmi, and Maha Saraswati were assimilated into the form of Goddess Durga. She being the lion rider is called Singheshwari. On the other hand; Brahma, Vishnu, and Mahakal Shankar were assimilated into the form of an eternal god called Singheshwar. People believed that the three part of the present *Shiva-Linga* represent this *Trimoorti* (Figure 3.9).

There is yet another myth which propounded that Pandit Mandan Mishra was residing at Singheshwar Sthan and engaged in a scholarly debate with *Adi* Shankaracharya. Thereafter, Mandan Mishra adopted *sanatan* cult. Interestingly, some interpreted Buddha's statue of Awalokishawar on one of the walls of the temple as the acceptance of Lord Shiva's eternal omnipresence.[78]

The site might belong to early medieval period. Presently, although it is being looked after by a temple committee with district higher authorities on the board, the site seemed to be under immense threat of extinction due to excessive human intervention in and around it. There is urgent need of policies and action on the part of government and committee for its protection.

26. Sirinagar: E H, L Med, and Mod, Ghailarh C. D. Block[79]

This site falls within Sirinagar village. It lays northwest to the present human habitations.[80] This site has been previously reported by others.[81] The site is spread in large area. The cultural remains are scattered in almost 1 square kilometer. At least two mounds, Mound-I and Mound-II[82] (Figure 3.10 and Figure 3.11) could be located which is separated by a distance of almost half a kilometer.

Figure 3.10: First author standing on Mound-I and indicating towards the present vegetation on it

Figure 3.11: Informant and other villagers standing on Mound-II

Mound-I which is bigger of the two spreads over 80000 square meters. It is almost 5 meters high from the surrounding ground level. The mound is sloping upward. The potsherds and bricks are seen all over the site. The general elevation of the area is 40.53 meters.[83]

Figure 3.12: First author standing on Mound-II besides the standing stone pillar or column

Mound-II is relatively smaller and extends over an area of approximately 200 square meters. It is in arch shape and contains some pillars, Shiva-Linga, broken sculptures, and some unidentified remains with engravings and inscriptions besides a modern temple (Figures 3.12-3.18).[84] Most of these cultural remains are made up of black sandstone. All these seemed to represent elements of a religious structure. The modern temple contains several black sandstone images; probably carried away from Mound-II area by villagers.

The archaeological remains of forts, tanks, and temple have been stated in earlier reports. The name of one of the tank has been

Figure 3.13: An unidentified cultural remain on Mound-II

Figure 3.14: A cultural remain on Mound-II having inscription

Figure 3.15: Cultural remains on Mound-II

mentioned as "Gupa." According to it, the temple contained stone pillars with some inscriptions. But it could not be deciphered. Probably, the inscription recorded the visit of a Hindu Magaradhvaja Jogi whom Cunningham called a simple mendicant. He said that the inscriptions recording his visit are found at four places in India, one

Figure 3.16: Fragments of cultural remains on Mound-II

Figure 3.17: Temple besides the Mound-II

Figure 3.18: The stone sculpture in the temple

of which is Gorakhpur district of Uttar Pradesh.[85] The site is in a highly disturbed state. It needs the attention of the department concerned and authorities for its protection and preservation.

According to a legend, a ruler Raja Srideva lived here with two brothers. One of them was known as Bijal-deva who built his own fort at Bijapur. It is said that Srideva was the Bhar chief who lived 300-400 years ago. According to one of the informants, there was a lowland area in Sirinagar which was called *Hatsar* where elephants used to be washed.

There is one folk-song of "Loree-Ken" eulogizing a powerful and able-bodied man known as Loree-Manihar. According to this song, he belonged to some Ugra-Pawar lineage. One finds the mention of Delhi (*Dilli*) and one village Goa-Gojan in this song. Loree-Manihar migrated from some obscure place and came to Hardee-Bazar which was famous in 14 *kos* (almost 42 square kilometers). He fought with the king Harewa-Barewa whose capital was in Sirinagar. He is believed to have belonged to Dusad Kul (Shudra ancestry). Loree-Manihar finally won in the battle.

The site and surrounding areas are endowed with lush greenery consisting of common type of flora seen in the Madhepura district. Overall, the area has a very favourable look from the human settlement point of view.

Probably this site belongs to later part of the late historical period. According to D. R. Patil, it could be dated to the late 8th century. Garrick and Cunningham take the dates to *Shaka* era. But it continued to be occupied during Medieval and Modern periods as well. This seemed to be one of the most interesting sites in Madhepura district. It has great potential. Any attempt at further systematic exploration and excavation may yield wonderful results.

Overall, the exploration activities in Madhepura subdivision produced dozens of sites with great archaeological and historical importance. Sites belonging to several periods were found in varying numbers. The general cultural remains includes potsherds, bricks, stone idols and statues, wells, remnants of walls, coins, jata,[86] and silla-lauree etc.[87] Not surprisingly, almost all of them are in a disturbed state. In fact, some of them are almost extinct or on the verge of extinction. Most of these site areas bear a favourable geographical look from the perspective of human settlement and subsistence.

NOTES AND REFERENCES

1. The definition of the historical period has already been provided in the previous chapter. As far as medieval period is concerned, the phase from eleventh century up to mid eighteenth century has been included. The settlement belonging to this phase have been further divided into early medieval (1000-1526) and late medieval period (1526-1757). Modern period has been considered from 1757 onwards. All these divisions can not be absolute. Many times, they have been adopted for the sake of convenience.
2. This has been done so mainly for the sake of convenience. The arrangement could have been done in other ways as well like culturally and geographically. Anyway, these sites have been arranged alphabetically within these administrative zones.
3. The devotees have built some sort of *Dharmshaala* (resting houses for votary) in some portion of the site.
4. This word is locally used for mother and even female Goddesses.
5. *Gur* means jiggery. *Batasha* refers to one type of sweet made up by boiling sugar with water.
6. It refers to a special shaped vessel which has a narrow neck.
7. It is interesting to note that such kind of legend is very common in the district. Similar kind of stories could be heard in several other places and contexts.
8. According to informants, almost 50 years ago, only few people used to visit this place.
9. It means a British period court.
10. But some portion of the village also overlooks the site from eastern side.
11. As far as idols are concerned, they mainly consist of *Shaaleegram* statues.
12. Some portion of the building is destroyed. Yet some part has been repaired.
13. Four of them weighed at least 4 kilograms each.

14. Traditionally, temple and religious order and institution have been granted land along with various rights and privileges in the area. They enjoy enormous influence among the local public. Their heads are generally called *Mahant.*
15. They have been arranged in chronological order from older to recent.
16. This word is locally used to denote a residential plot or a house.
17. The population of Gohumani village is 5447.
18. *Bastee* and mohalla are words commonly used to refer to a colony or a residential area in South Asia.
19. There is possibility of error for almost 3.65 meters on upper or lower sides (+ or -).
20. He is popular especially among Yadava community. Their main profession is domestication of animals. Whenever, their cattle stops milking, they pray to Khedan Baba with some offerings for cure.
21. The population of Gudar Chakla village is around 644.
22. These idols are of Ram, Jankee, Laxman, Gopaljee, Shaaleegram, Bajrang Bali, and Krishna.
23. *Beegha* is a local unit of land measurement. One *Beegha* is equivalent to almost 3391 square meters.
24. They have been arranged in chronological order from older to recent.
25. The population of Itahari village is 2892.
26. The large area of site has been converted into farmland by villagers.
27. Villagers reported that they used to find bricks of Belo Goth type (Figure 5.2). These bricks were carried away by them.
28. It is with the possible error margin of 3.65 meters above or below the given measurement.
29. The site or village is not mentioned on the Topo-sheet used for determining their latitude and longitude. It is because of the fact that the geographical area in which the site falls seemed to be beyond the ambit of the concerned Topo-sheet. Moreover, the cultural identity of this site could not be established due lack of sufficient data.
30. The population of Jorgawan village is 6387.
31. The population of the Jorgawan village is 6387.
32. *Machan* is a local word used for referring seat made up of bamboo sticks and rope.

33. There are two ponds such Bba Jee *Pokhar* and Jagdish *Pokhar* towards east and west of the site respectively. Latter is almost 100 meters west from the main site.
34. It refers to disturbed soul of a man who dies as a bachelor.
35. The site or the village is not mentioned on the Topo-sheet used for present research work.
36. The population of Kaurihar village is 1732.
37. It is a very durable and costly wood. *Sakhuwa* was generally grown in Madhepura district earlier. But now, it is rarely found.
38. The population of the village is 1536.
39. It is local name for a type of long grass.
40. I was told by the informants that one pond to the east has already been submerged into the river. But another one almost in 23750 square meters lie 220 feet south to site. But as the area was densely covered with grasses and almost inaccessible, it could not be verified independently.
41. The general plants and trees in the area are *jilebee*, catechu, sissoo, and bamboo.
42. It seemed that the king of Darbhanga was having a large area under his control including Kosi region during late medieval and British periods.
43. It means an area lying in the western part of the village. Generally, this is how a portion within a village is referred to in the area.
44. The settlement is placed towards the western end of Kolhaipatti. The population of Raghunathpur village is 13331.
45. It refers to a wrestling place.
46. The site or village is not mentioned on the Topo-sheet used for determining their latitude and longitude.
47. The population of Pakilpar village is 3344.
48. The site or village is not mentioned on the Topo-sheet used in present research to determine latitude and longitude.
49. Parwaha's population is 3792.
50. It is according to traditional Hindu calendar.
51. Piprahi's population is 4931.
52. The population of Rajni is 11402.
53. There are one half built *pakka* and two *kachcha* temples.

54. It is used to denote the family and house of traditional chiefs, landlords, and kings in the area.
55. It was reported that one girl from Rajni village presently living in Murliganj got cured from diarrhea after drinking the site's well water.
56. The population of Rampur is 7366.
57. It is an arch shaped round mud object worshipped by people locally.
58. It falls in Patarghat C. D. Block of Saharsa district but also forms the part of Madhepura district in some respect. The site or village is not mentioned on the Topo-sheet used for present work to determine latitude and longitude.
59. Literally, *Jagah* means a place. Traditionally, it is a revered place in the area with a temple. Generally some deities are worshiped here. It is also alternately called *Thakurbaree and Math. Jagah* is headed by *Mahant.* It holds large lands generally granted by a king or rich men in the society. Sometimes, they represent a particular faith like *Kabirpanthi.* Moreover, very often, they are a part of larger network of *Jagah* belonging to same faith. These *Jagah* wields huge influence upon local populace. Besides being a religious center, they also offer medicinal advice, and especially in earlier days enjoyed extra-terrestrial rights. Hasangadh is a part of the network of *Jagah* headed by of Bindraban *Jagah* (already mentioned as site number 5).
60. It is according to GPS with the possible error margin of 3.65 meters above or below the given measurement.
61. *Pacca* means concrete building. In contrast here *kachcha* meant non-concrete traditional house.
62. Generally one Mahant's reign is for 20-30 years.
63. The site or village is not mentioned on the Topo-sheet used for present research to determine latitude and longitude.
64. The population of Rupauli village is 11290.
65. It was recorded with the help of GPS. There is possibility of 5.79 meters variations.
66. The site or village is not mentioned on the Topo-sheet used in present research work to determine latitude and longitude.
67. The population of this village is 15359.
68. He was the son of Iliyas Sah.

69. D. R. Patil, *Antiquarian Remains in Bihar* (Patna: Kashi Prasad Jayaswal Research Institute1963), p. 507.
70. The site or village is not mentioned on the Topo-sheet used for present research to determine latitude and longitude.
71. Patil, *Antiquarian Remains in Bihar*, p. 513.
72. It refers to beggars.
73. It is a small tool generally used for minor digging.
74. The population of Singheshwar Sthan village is 4237.
75. It is a symbol for Lord Shiva.
76. Dilip K. Chakrabarti, *Archaeological Geography of the Ganga Plain- The Lower and the Middle Ganga* (Delhi: Permanent Black 2001), p. 192.
77. It means fire-altars.
78. It is located on the southern wall of the eastern side of the temple.
79. The site or village is not mentioned on the Topo-sheet used for determining latitude and longitude.
80. The population of Sirinagar village is 9218.
81. It is mentioned in the *District Gazetteer.*
82. It has been named like this just for the sake of convenience.
83. This was recorded on GPS with possibility of 3.04 meters variations on either side.
84. These inscriptions are almost unreadable.
85. Patil, *Antiquarian Remains in Bihar*, pp. 551-52.
86. It generally consisted of two round and polished grinding stones. A pulley is fixed in the middle of one of these stones (lower one). In case of second one (the upper one) a hole is made so that it could be fixed to the pulley of the first stone. Then the upper stone is revolved over the lower with the help of a handle attached to it. Traditionally, the local inhabitants use it for grinding pulses and grains.
87. It consists of two grinding stones. One of them is bigger in size and used as a base stone in the grinding process. The second one is generally round in shape and smaller in size. This is used in rubbing and grinding the material on the base stone. Even today, it is widely used for grinding by local populace in the area.

7

Historical Places in Udakishunganj Subdivision

As mentioned earlier, all the explored and previously reported past settlements in Madhepura district have been divided into two administrative subdivisions. The description of sites belonging to Udakishunganj subdivision has been provided here. Like their counterparts in Madhepura subdivision, these sites have also been described in terms of their local name, location, area, cultural assemblage, legend and myth, geographical condition, suitability from human survival perspective, and cultural period. Again the sites have been arranged alphabetically.

DESCRIPTION OF THE EXPLORED SETTLEMENTS

1. Alamnagar: L H and E Med, 25°34' N 86°53'30" E, Alamnagar C. D. Block

This site is located in Alamnagar.[1] It has been reported earlier. According to previous investigation, there were some past cultural remains in the forms of ramparts and tanks whose traces were visible till the beginning of twentieth century.[2] It is claimed to be a principal village of the *Chandel* chiefs. Now, the site is almost extinct. But, if earlier reports are presumed to be true then this site must have been quite large.[3]

As far as general ecological condition is concerned, it does not seem to be different from the general trends seen in the Udakishunganj subdivision. The area bore a favourable look from the perspective of human settlements. This site may belong to late historical and early medieval periods.

2. Biri Ranpal-I (Bhatwa Jameendaree): Mod, Udakishunganj C. D. Block[4]

There is a site locally called "Bhatwa Jameendaree" in Biri Ranpal village.[5] It has been named as Biri Ranpal-I as there are two sites in this village. The total area of this site is around 10000 square meters. As far as the dimension of primary occupation area is concerned, its maximum length and width are 100 and 50 meters respectively. According to informants, once upon a time there were some buildings and a big well on the site. Potsherds and bricks were also found. But at present, the site is in a disturbed condition. People are farming sugarcane and other crops upon it.[6]

So far as the vegetation is concerned, it is of an usual type. There is *domat* soil in and around the site. Drinking water is normally available at 25 feet. There is a drainage almost 225 meters east of the site. According to villagers, it was a *kamat*[7] of Bhatwa Jameendar. Its main place was Bihpur. Here, they controlled around 700 acres of land. It is an early modern period site.

3. Biri Ranpal-II (Jagah-Kabeermath): Mod, Udakishunganj C. D. Block

As mentioned above, Biri Ranpal village consists of another site which is locally known as "*Jagah*" and named as Biri Ranpal-II in the present work. It is located west of the village. The area of the site is 10000 square meters. The dimension of the primary occupation area is 100 x 50 meters. The elevation is 25.90 meters.[8] A building stands on part of the site (Figure 4).[9] It consists of a newly built boundary, two wells, and similar number of tube-wells. The settlement is the seat of *Kabeermath*.[10] The total land under this *Math* is around 20 acres.

It is considered to be the oldest *Math* of *Kabeer-Panthee*[11] in the area. The *Math* is headed by a revered sage. According to

Figure 4: A partial view of the Biri Ranpal-II site. The incumbent head of the *Math* is being interviewed by the first author

informants, its followers do not accept idol-worship. They venerate Chaitanya and a *Guru* Maharaj.[12] It is believed that the wishes of people could be fulfilled here. Moreover, populace also visits the *Math* for medical advice and treatment. The incumbent head of the *Math* informed that Gopal Baba, Bateshwar Baba, Mangal Baba, and Ganga Baba preceded him.[13]

The vegetation of site and surroundings represents the general flora of the area except some useful Ayurvedic plants which are found in and around it. The type of soil is *domat* type. There is *chap* area at the back of the site. Drainage is located almost 250 meters east of the settlement. Generally, the area is prone to flood. But, they do not encroach upon the site's primary occupation area. Overall, the topography bore a positive look from a human settlement point of view. It is an early modern site.

4. Khuran village (Dakneesthan): Med, Alamnagar C. D. Block[14]

This site is locally called as "Dakneesthan" and situated in Khuran village almost 5 kilometers from Alamnagar C. D. Block headquarter.[15]

It is spread over 135000 square meters of land. The elevation of the area is 38.40 meters.[16] The cultural thickness is around 0.60 meters. It consists of a building, a temple, a boundary wall, and some densely vegetal area. Some potsherds and bricks are scattered all over the site. The trace of a brick wall was also found.[17]

The temple complex is stretched in 3050 square meters. The temple consists of a composite idol with three distinct parts.[18] (Figure 4.1). It is of white colour and called "Chandmistaka."[19] The idol is covered with two metal sheets. The first metal cover is of 9 kilograms and second and the topmost one of 19 kilograms.[20] The second one is made up of a combination of gold, silver, brass, bronze, and copper etc. According to an informant (priest of the temple), 68 years ago, the idol was shifted 15 meters away from its original location. Thereafter, a temple was constructed over it. Recently, there was an unsuccessful attempt to steal the idol.[21]

It is considered to be a *Deeh* of Raja Bhor. People believed that their wishes could be fulfilled by praying to the goddesses established within the temple precinct. According to legend, nobody can stay in the site area during night. The geographical scenario is quite interesting. A usual kind of vegetation is noticed in and around the site. The soil is of *domat* type. According to villagers, the drinking water is generally sweet and available at 30-35 feet. The site belongs to medieval period.

5. Kushathan (Jaso Yadav ka Tila): Mod, 25°45'5" N 86°59'30" E, Bihariganj C. D. Block

There is a site locally called as "Jaso Yadav ka Tila." It is situated 1 kilometer west to Kushathan village and 1 ½ kilometers from Bihariganj C. D. Block headquarters.[22] The nearest metallic road is almost 1 kilometer from it. The settlement is in the form of a mound almost 0.90 meters above the surrounding area.

It is spread in almost 4000 square meters. But according to informants, the site was spread in almost 8000-10000 square meters

Figure 4.1: Partial view of the interior of Dakneesthan temple

50 years ago. As far as the dimension of the primary occupation area is concerned, it is 46 × 30 meters. The site seemed to be quite disturbed and with no observable surface cultural remains. In context of site relationship with surroundings, arable land can be seen around the site. The site is contracting fast. According to villagers, the local people believe that the ancestors of Jaso Yadav lived 50 years ago on the site and then moved away from there.

The geographical condition is interesting. The type of soil is *chiknee*. It is a *chap* and active flood plain area. A canal is passing 500 meters west to the site. The site seemed to be occupied from early modern to late modern period.

6. Madhukar Chak-I (Dargah / Gachee / Bageecha): L Med and Mod, 25°35'30" N 87°1' E, Bihariganj C. D. Block

This age-old mound is locally known with several names such as "Dargah", "Gachee", and "Bageecha" (Figure 4.2). Since, there are two past settlements in Madhukar Chak village, this site has been named as Madhukar Chak-I. It is located 1 kilometer south of

Madhukar Chak village.[23] The site is spread in almost 40000 square meters of area. It is almost half a meter above the surrounding ground level. The dimension of primary occupation area is 150 × 100 meters.

Its cultural affinity is disclosed by presence of potsherds, bricks, and *jata*. The informants told that a *silla-lauree* of the size 90 × 45 centimeters was found from the site.[24] There exists a well over the site (Figure 4.3 and Figure 4.4). One *kachcha* path crosses the site almost in the middle. In the immediate vicinity of the settlement arable land could be seen.

Figure 4.2: The first author pointing towards the Madhukar Chak-I site

As far as surrounding micro-level natural condition is concerned, there are lot of trees and grasses in and around the site. The nature of soil is black and *domat*. The area south of the site is *chap* and marshy. The site area remains surrounded by water during rainy season. Although, the water is available at 15 feet, sweet drinking water could be found only at 25-30 feet. Generally, the area bore a

Figure 4.3: The well on the site being pointed out

Figure 4.4: The closer view of the brick well on the site

positive look and must have been attractive to past human beings. It is a late medieval site that appeared to remain under occupation up to early modern period.[25]

7. Madhukar Chak-II, (Thumb): Mod, 25°35'30" N 87°1' E, Bihariganj C. D. Block

Figure 4.5: The mound representing the Thumb site covered with grasses

There is a site locally called "Thumb"[26] (Figure 4.5) located ½ kilometers south of Madhukar Chak village. It is named as Madhukar Chak-II as the village consists of two sites. The area of the site is 350 square meters. But the dimension of the mound is 6 × 5 × 5 meters which is in arch shape. The site is contracting very fast.[27]

The cultural remains are collected in form of bricks and potsherds.[28] The site is surrounded by flat land. There is a pond in the vicinity of the mound lying almost 6 meters away. Normal vegetation is visible in the area. The soil is of *domat* type with brown colour. The site belonged to the modern period.

8. Mohammadpur Balia (Ido Ka Khet): L Med, Puraini C. D. Block[29]

There is a site with the local name "Ido Ka khet" lying nearer to Madhelee[30] and Mohammadpur Balia villages.[31] It is situated almost 800 meters besides a canal. In fact, the site got discovered during the construction of this canal. It spreads in 340 square meters. In regard to cultural remains, informants reported that earlier some amount of potsherds, *silla-lauree*, gold ornaments, hearth, and *jata* were found. But the site is almost extinct by now. Local populace believed that Mohammadpur Balia village belonged to the Mughal period. It can be dated to at least the late medieval period.

9. Muraut: E Med and L Med, 25°29'15" N 86°52'45" E, Alamnagar C. D. Block

A site is located in Muraut village which is 12 kilometers south of Alamnagar C. D. Block headquarters.[32] The village is located on the bank of Kosi's distributary.[33] The site is spread in almost 68000 square meters. It consisted of rich past cultural remains such as potsherds, terracotta figurines, bricks, and wells etc. According to informants, some silver and copper coins, and *kalshaee* also found from the site. The brick had a trapezoid shape. (Figure 4.6).

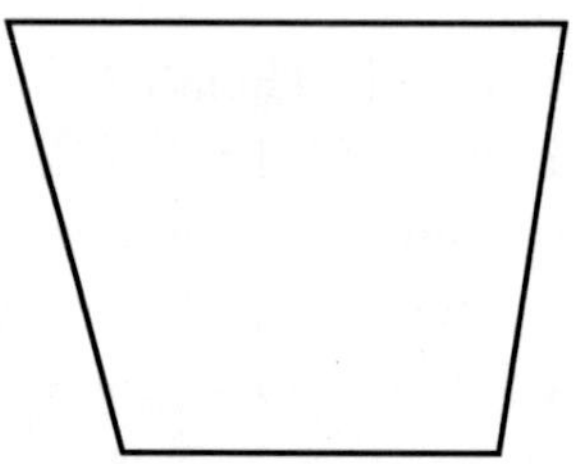

Figure 4.6: The rough shape of the brick found in Muraut site

As far as the geographical situation is concerned, it is a *diyara* area. But, the vegetation is almost similar to that of district's flora. The area is an active flood zone with *baluhaee* soil. According to villagers, sweet drinking water is generally available at 55-60 feet. The only hindering factor to any human settlement is the acute water logging and flood probability. But, it is surprising to note that many of the present habitations lay on the bank of river.[34] It is an early and late medieval site.

10. Nayanagar (Bhagwatee Sthan): L H and E Med, Udakishunganj C. D. Block[35]

This ancient site locally known as "Bhagwatee Sthan" is located in Nayanagar village.[36] It is situated 8 and 35 kilometers from Udakishunganj C. D. Block headquarters and Madhepura district headquarters respectively. But the communication system to the village and site area is very poor as well as hazardous. The site is lying almost 91 meters east of modern human habitation (*bastee*) in the village. Although the total land under the trust looking after the temple and its affairs is 88784 to 90801 square meters, the primary occupation area is 10090 square meters.

The site consists of a temple (Figure 4.7), pond, well (Figure 4.8), arable land (5087 square meters), black sandstone idols, stone plates, some temporary sheds, and petty shops. There are a number of idols ranging from small to big, intact to broken, and meaningful to abstract. Goddess Durga seems to be sitting on a lotus flower in a peaceful gesture. There are statues of Lord Chowmukh Mahadeo (Figure 4.9), eleven Ubhay Lingas, and Sun God etc. The main idol 'Bhagwatee Pratima' (Figure 4.10) is 0.75 meters lower than present surface level. Villagers believe that this idol is connected with "*yantra*" a rectangular black stone plate few meters away (Figure 4.11), by a stone pillar. They consider it to be a seat of *Siddhi/Tapasya*[37] by saints. According to informants (Figure 4.12), there is a *Surang* (underground tunnel) besides the Bhagwatee idol.

The big pond existing before the temple is used for bathing the sacrificial animals before offering to the Goddess. An old brick well is found in the pond. But now a new well has been built over it.[38] Informants said that potsherds and bricks[39] have been found in and around the site. They also reported about the discovery of a big stone plate during a casual excavation. But now, the site is almost on the verge of extinction. According to villagers, its land has been encroached by a school and certain people. Some portion of the temple land is also under cultivation.

Figure 4.7: The partial view of the temple constructed over the site

The temple associated with the site is famous for *manokamna siddhi* (fulfilling of wishes) in the entire Kosi belt. The devotees throng the area to offer floral and other tributes including animal sacrifice to Goddess Bhagwatee. The so called Bairagana *Mela* (fair) is held here on every Monday, Wednesday, and Friday.[40] According to villagers, a *Bhagta*[41] from Anandpura (nearby village) used to sing a *Bhagat* (religious song) in which he used to mention "Raja Rajdev ki jay" (glory to king Rajdev). According to them he belonged to some *Debher* family. Probably, he was the devotee of this place.

Figure 4.8: The brick well in the pond

Figure 4.9: Chowmukh Mahadeo

Figure 4.10: The Bhagwatee Pratima

As far as micro-level natural environment is concerned, the vegetation is of usual type except the presence of sandalwood trees.[42] Sandalwood is mainly used in worship and ritual associated with Goddess Durga and not sold for commercial purposes. The area is endowed with *domat* soil. Drinking water is available at 25-35 feet.

It is generally sweet but with more iron content. A distributary of Kosi locally called "Dahra ghat" flows (from Arar) west to Nayanagar village and almost 500 meters east of the site. Although, it is not an active flood plain, but water-logging in *chap* area is a matter of concern. The site belonged to late historical and early medieval periods.

Figure 4.11: "*Yantra*", the stone plate

Figure 4.12: First author interviewing the Nayanagar villagers

11. Udakishunganj: E H, 25°40' N 86°56' E, Udakishunganj C. D. Block

This site has been reported previously. It is located near Udakishunganj.[43] The site is spread in 340 square meters. Once upon a time, it probably formed a part of the Mauryan Empire. It is attested by the discovery of a Mauryan pillar. Interestingly, another Asokan pillar is situated just 36 kilometers away in Sikleegadh near Banmankhi C. D. Block headquarters falling in nearby Purnea district (Figure 4.13).[44] Overall, it seems to belong to first half of the early historical period.

Figure 4.13: The Asokan pillar in Sikleegadh

Almost a dozen sites of significant archaeological and historical importance have been found in Udakishunganj subdivision. The broad cultural sequence in relation to past human settlements emerging in this administrative area is again the historical, medieval, and modern periods. Again, like their northern counterparts, the sites in this subdivision are also in a disturbed state. In many cases, these past settlements are located in chap, waterlogged, and flood prone areas and near to some watery bodies such as ponds, canals, drainage, and distributaries etc. The general cultural remains in Udakishunganj subdivision seems to be more varied than its northern counterpart. This administrative area also possesses less number of religious sites in comparison to Madhepura subdivision. Overall, Madhepura district remained under occupation from historical period up to present.

NOTES AND REFERENCES

1. It is Alamnagar C. D. Block headquarters as well as a small town with a population is 24105.
2. D. R. Patil, *Antiquarian Remains in Bihar* (Patna: Kashi Prasad Jayaswal Research Institute1963), p.2.
3. It should been at least equivalent to a village.
4. The site or village is not mentioned on the Topo-sheet used for determining the latitude and longitude in present work.
5. The population of Biri Ranpal village is 3636.
6. At the moment, the site area comes under the ownership of Arun Yadav, son of Sukhdev Yadav, a resident of Biri Ranpal village.
7. If somebody has a good amount of land far away from his home, he tends to build a house and make other necessary arrangements there in order to farm and look after those lands. Usually, it is referred with the name *kamat* in Kosi region.
8. It is according to recording done with the help of GPS. There are possibilities of 3.04 meters variations on either side.
9. According to informant, the building is 60 years old.
10. It refers to a place where followers of Kabeer live and practice their faith.
11. It refers to the follower of Kabeer.
12. Latter is relatively obscure.
13. This genealogy is from earliest to recent.

14. The site or village is not mentioned on the Topo-sheet used for present work to determine latitude and longitude.
15. The population of the Khuran village is 3477.
16. This is according to the recording done with the help of GPS. There is a possibility of 3.35 meters variations.
17. The dimension of one brick is 37 x 20 x 6 centimeters.
18. But local populace sees them as separate idols. Two of them are called Jaya and Vijya. The central one's head is cut. The idol is depicted with three blood flows. The main flow is shown in Jogni's mouth. People believe that two *dhara* (flows) represents Jaya and Vijya's mouth.
19. It is believed to be also found in Rajappa (a place in Jharkhand state).
20. The latter one cost Rs. 165000.
21. He seemed to be a lunatic man. The person accepted the charges levelled against him.
22. The population of Kushathan village is 5880.
23. Madhukar Chak's population is 7318.
24. But the family who allegedly possessed it refused to acknowledge so.
25. According to villagers, no body has seen any human habitation on the site at least since four generation.
26. The word is also used to refer to a kind of mound in the locality.
27. Its height is also going down.
28. The size of one brick measured as 6 x 3 x 1½ inches.
29. The site or village is not mentioned on the Topo-sheet used in present research to determine latitude and longitude.
30. The site is located northeast to Madhelee village.
31. The population of Mohammadpur Balia village is 926.
32. The population of this village is 4273.
33. It was almost inaccessible by road. One had to use a country made boat to reach the village as well as site.
34. In fact, one of the villagers was seen constructing his new house literally on the edge of the river. When quipped, he cried about the lack of options. This probably shows human's resilience and power to negotiate with the environment.
35. The site or village is not mentioned on the Topo-sheet used in present work for determining latitude and longitude. It is because of the fact

that the geographical area in which the site falls seemed to be beyond the ambit of the concerned Topo-sheet.

36. The population of Nayanagar village is 12647.
37. It means meditation.
38. It is Belodeeh type brick.
39. The bricks are in round shape as well as Belodeeh type.
40. The main temple on the site has been constructed with contribution and cooperation from the common people and a trust (consisting of five members) has been formed to look after its affairs and management. But the villagers of Nayanagar in general cooperate in its matters. Usually, the government has not taken any deep interest in either the protection or development of the site area. Only recently, it seemed to show some concern to develop it as a tourist place. According to informants, the District Magistrate of Madhepura had visited the place and took stock of the situation.
41. It refers to a person who is religious and presumed to possess some super natural power to heal the people. He is revered and approached especially when somebody is presumed to suffer from *jadu-tona* (influence of some evil forces).
42. Interestingly, a high quality, costly, and scented Sreekhand Chandan (a variety of sandalwood) is unique to this place which is said to be only found in 1 kilometer radius around the site area. According to villagers, its planting is not successful even in very nearby areas.
43. Udakishunganj's population is 8690.
44. It was surveyed in field season of July-August 2007. But interestingly, local people with the active involvement of some authorities have declared it to be the "Prahlad Stambh."

8

Historical Places in Kosi Plain

As already mentioned, Kosi plain is a large geographical area encompassing several modern districts of northeastern Bihar besides Madhepura. The other important districts are Saharsa, Purnea, Bhagalpur, and Munger.[1] All these districts have common historical experiences and cultural bondage. Somewhat, their fate has been intricately attached with each other. So, it is desirable to explore past human activities in these quarters as well in order to better understand and appreciate the historical developments holistically in the region.

Number of historical sites has been reported from Saharsa district from time to time. Some of them are Viratpur, Bangaon, Pirnagar, Mahisi, Jhitkiya, Kandaha Sun temple, Sihaul, and Dhabauli. Bangaon has remains of large stupa, monastic building, and a *Gorhi Dihar* or "Fishermen mound." Some punch marked coins have also been reported from here.[2] Sihaul has an eighteenth century fort of Maharaja Amar Singh of Sonbarsa Raj family.[3] Dhabauli also yields a fort of Bhar chiefs.[4]

Pirnagar has an enclosed area of 20 acres. Locally, it is known as "Chaurasi Bigha." It has a fortified Pala period settlement. Like Bangaon, punch marked coins have also been reported from here. A modern temple in Mahisi has Buddha images and Shiva-Lingas of tenth century. It also shows a destroyed structural mound.

Jhitkiya near Maheskhut comprises about ten acres of land which is covered by a jungle and a Muslim *dargah*.[5] This is a structural mound and shows a Pala period temple. The complex can be dated to the tenth century. Kandaha Sun temple could be dated to eleventh and twelfth centuries.[6] Viratpur has witnessed the first scientific excavation in the Kosi region. It has produced early historic potteries and iron objects, Kushana period ceramics and terracotta objects, and sculptures of Pala and Sena Schools of art.

We find many areas of historical importance such as Sikleegadh, Mahendarpur, Jalalgadh, Purnea town, Khagra, and Dhamdaha, etc., in the adjoining Purnea district too. Jalalgadh fort stands as an island in the old channel of Kosi. It has been built by rulers of Khagra family who are the contemporaries of Jahangir.[7] In fact, Khagra has been the seat of an important Muslim ruler since the time of Humayun. The remnants of some of the buildings constructed by this family are found here.[8] Present Purnea town and its surrounding area also show forts, mosques, and other buildings of the Mughal period. Dhamdaha has two late medieval temples.[9]

Sikleegadh shows remnants of an Ashokan pillar, a fortified early historic city,[10] and Shiva-Linga of Pala period.[11] Mahendarpur has produced a base of an image and a thin scatter of brickbats over about thirty acres. This marks the site of a Pala period temple.[12] Gangasagar and Jivaj are the two tanks near Jalalgadh. It has produced a temple mound and a small ancient lintel. This seems to be a Pala period temple site. The Bhutnat temple in Purnea town has a large Vishnu image of c. twelfth century.[13]

As far as Bhagalpur district is concerned, it has been the hub of a number of exploring missions. Antichak, 13 km north of Kahalgaon railway-station is remarkable from the historical point of view. It has succeeded in attracting the attention of archaeologists and historians. The researches have produced significant remnants such as brick made structures with chambers and antechambers with *pradakshina-pathas*; a *chaitya*, inscribed votive stupas; a large monastery with cells; stone images of God and Goddesses, bronze images of Buddhist deities; terracotta, stone, iron, copper, silver, and bronze objects; a palette bearing the figure of a bust; and a hoard of stone querns and pestle, etc.

It has four shrines facing the four cardinal directions. One important architectural feature is the arched ceilings in the balconies of the central shrine and cells of the monastic establishment. The flanking walls of the terraces are decorated with terracotta plaques having animals, sacred symbols, and Buddhist and Brahmanical details. A bronze image of 'Vajrapani' is amazing.[14]

Oriup village about 2 km southwest of Antichak stupa is another interesting site in Bhagalpur district. The excavation activities[15] have revealed four cultural sequence such as i) black and red ware (both plain and painted) and black slipped and red wares[16] ii) N. B. P. ware and associated fabric[17] iii) typical Pala pottery[18] and iv) medieval green glazed pottery and red ware. Important findings are elongated lipped bowl bearing white paintings, fire place, fishing tools, terracotta objects, copper objects, iron objects, ivory, beads of glass and terracotta, etc.[19]

Exploration and excavation has also been carried at Champa which is situated 5 km west of Bhagalpur town and 1 km north of Nathnagar-Bhagalpur road.[20] It is the site of ancient city of Champa. The site seems to be occupied from the historical to medieval periods.[21] The important outcomes are terracotta objects, copper coins, cast copper coins, punch marked coins, iron objects, bone points, ghost wall, ring wells, post-holes, rammed brick floor, brick walls, traces of wooden post, precious stones, ivory objects, female and Goddesses figurines, stone moulds, and drain.[22]

On the whole, a broad cultural sequence in Bhagalpur could be constructed on the basis of aforesaid archaeological artifacts, remnants, and ceramic traditions- Early Stone Age, Middle Stone Age, Late Stone Age, Mesolithic culture, Chalcolithic culture, Black and Red Ware, Northern Black Polished ware and other associated ceramics, Grey and Red ware, Pala Period, and Medieval and Late Medieval cultures, etc. The noteworthy findings from the district are Stone Age tools; microliths of Chalcolithic assemblage; terracotta pieces; sculptures of Brahmanical Gods and Goddesses and Buddha; and temples etc.[23]

Besides Bhagalpur, the neighbouring district of Munger is also notable from the historical perspective. The emerging broad cultural sequence is quite interesting- Early Stone Age, Middle Stone Age, Late Stone Age, Neolithic Age, Northern Black Polished ware and other associated ceramics, Red ware, and Pala Period. The important findings from the district are Stone Age tools, Acheulian tools, stone and terracotta objects, sculptures, and sign of human habitation on forested hill tops, etc.[24]

Two places in Munger district have seen large excavation activities- Karnachaura and Paisra.[25] The major cultural sequences exposed are Pala period, medieval period, and late medieval period. But, some peculiar appearance of N. B. P ware and associated black-slipped ware is interesting.

Incase of Paisra village and surrounding areas, the culture sequences revealed are Acheulian and Mesolithic cultures.[26] The notable findings are Acheulian artifacts, massive stone alignment, working floor with post-holes, and Mesolithic objects, etc.[27]

In Bhagalpur and Munger districts, most of the prehistoric settlements (i.e., Paisra, Bhimbandh, Rehna, Reha, Rajjan, Man river bed, and Teprani stream, etc.) are located in southwestern region. In contrast, the north and east portions are abound with greater number of historic and early medieval settlements. Moreover, most of the sites in these districts lie in *tal* area than *diyara.*

Most of the settlement (Paisra, Bhimbandh, Rehna, Reha, Rajjan, Sitakund, and Khakharadih, etc.) in Munger district are situated near to the river flood plain (Ganges, Man River, and Teprani stream). Larger number of the prehistoric settlements falls in densely forested area in this district. Moreover, the occurrence of prehistoric settlement (Bhimbandh locality) in the forested hill-tops is an interesting feature due to its rarity in the country. In case of Bhagalpur again the entire major sites (i.e., Champa, Karnagarh, Oriup, and Antichak, etc.) are presently situated close to the river flood plains (Ganges and Chandan).

Generally speaking, there seems to be several similarities in the historical experiences of Madhepura, Saharsa, and Purnea districts. But, the southern districts of Bhagalpur and Munger shows lot of difference from them. Madhepura, Saharsa, and Purnea districts seem to be rich in late historical and medieval settlements. But, they are completely devoid of prehistoric and proto-historic settlements. Madhepura shows relatively continuous settlement from early historic phase to medieval period. While a huge gap in terms of cultural sequence (between early historic and early medieval period) is noticed in Saharsa and Purnea districts. Overall, the emerging broad cultural sequences in larger Kosi-Gangetic plain are Paleolithic, Mesolithic, Neolithic, Chalcolithic, Black and Red Ware, Early Historical, Late Historical, Early Medieval, Late Medieval, and Modern Period's culture.

Now, one needs to assess the past societies and cultures from different dimensions in the light of all these data. This shall help in understanding the manner in which the people of historical and other periods were arranged over the landscape of the district. This may also enlighten about the broad settlement and subsistence pattern and variations at micro as well as macro levels. These exercises will also aid in knowing the relationship between men and environment.

NOTES AND REFERENCES

1. The last two lay south of Kosi and Ganges. There are other district as well like Supaul, Darvanga, and Khagaria.
2. D. R. Patil, *Antiquarian Remains in Bihar* (Patna: Kashi Prasad Jayaswal Research Institute1963), p. 14.

3. Patil, *Antiquarian Remains in Bihar*, p. 537.
4. Patil, *Antiquarian Remains in Bihar*, p. 114.
5. It refers to a site where a Muslim holy man has been buried. *Dargah* represents tomb of a Muslim saint where a shrine is built. Generally, Kosi region is dotted with *dargah*.
6. Dilip K. Chakrabarti, *Archaeological Geography of the Ganga Plain- The Lower and the Middle Ganga* (Delhi: Permanent Black, 2001), pp. 195-96.
7. Patil, *Antiquarian Remains in Bihar*, p. 181.
8. Patil, *Antiquarian Remains in Bihar*, p. 203.
9. Patil, *Antiquarian Remains in Bihar*, p. 115.
10. Chakrabarti, *Archaeological Geography of the Ganga Plain- The Lower and the Middle Ganga*, p. 194.
11. B. K. Sinha, *Archaeology of North Bihar* (Delhi, 1999), p. 126.
12. Chakrabarti, *Archaeological Geography of the Ganga Plain- The Lower and the Middle Ganga*, p. 194.
13. Chakrabarti, *Archaeological Geography of the Ganga Plain- The Lower and the Middle Ganga*, p. 194.
14. *Indian Archaeology - A Review* (New Delhi: Department of Archaeology, Government of India).
15. B. P. Sinha and Dr. R. C. P. Singh of Department of Ancient Indian History and Archaeology, Patna University explored and excavated the aforesaid site.
16. These are comparable with other chalcolithic sites of western India and Bihar.
17. Latter includes black slipped ware, grey and red ware, and iron objects. These were found 15 cm above the upper layer of the site.
18. It includes plain red ware with chocolate slip and plain grey ware with black slip.
19. *Indian Archaeology - A Review*
20. Prof. B. P. Sinha, B. Narayan, S. K. Kaviraj, A. K. Singh, Sarvashri B. Kumar, J. P. Singh, B. Sahai, P. K. Bose, and Dr. R. C. P. Singh of Department of Ancient Indian History and Archaeology, Patna University explored and excavated this site in different years.

21. The cultural sequences exposed are Black and Red ware, N.B.P. ware (early, middle, and late phase), Black slipped and Grey ware, Kushana Period, Gupta Period, post-Gupta Period, Pala Period, and Medieval Period.
22. *Indian Archaeology - A Review*
23. *Indian Archaeology - A Review*
24. *Indian Archaeology - A Review*
25. Karnachaura has been excavated by Shri Ajit Kumar Prasad, Sharvashri Kedar Nath Singh, Satyakam Prasad, L. P. Singh, N. C. Ghosh, J. Akhtar, U. S. Pandit, and Dr. Sita Ram Roy (Department of Archaeology and Museum, Government of Bihar). Paisra is explored and excavated by Vidula Jayaswal, P. C. Pant, and Postgraduate student of department of Ancient Indian History, Culture and Archaeology, Banaras Hindu University.
26. They have been found at a depth of 3.5 meters and 2.40-2.55 meters respectively.
27. *Indian Archaeology - A Review.*

9

Settlement Distribution

The settlement study is still a bud in Indian archaeology.[1] As far as Madhepura district is concerned, it lacks in general archaeological and historical investigations let alone the work on settlement archaeology. The present exercise is an attempt in that direction. It tries to examine the pattern of distribution of explored settlements over the landscape of this district. First of all, the frequency of settlements in different cultures and areas has been analyzed. It is followed by a discussion on location of the sites.[2] Thereafter, the settlements belonging to each culture have been analyzed in terms of size, thickness of cultural deposition, cultural possession, and frequency of the artifacts discovered.

CULTURE WISE DISTRIBUTION OF SETTLEMENTS

The exploratory work in Madhepura district has produced dozens of settlements scattered over its landscape. These sites belonged to diverse cultural spectrum involving historical to modern periods (Table 3 and Map 5). Interestingly, the maximum number of explored settlements belongs to modern period (47%). Their numbers are 25 out of total 53 settlements. It is closely followed by medieval sites numbering 22 (42%).

The medieval settlements have been further divided into early medieval and late medieval sites. Their numbers are 3 and 19 respectively. This amply reflects the overwhelming dominance of late medieval settlements among the medieval sites. Curiously, the least number of settlements have their place in historical phase (11%). These historical sites have been further divided into early historical and late historical settlements (Map 5.1). Former's strength (04) is more than that of the latter (02). This cultural division of sites reveals following picture.

Table 3: The culture wise distribution of settlements in Madhepura district

Sl. No.	Culture	Number of Sites		Percentage
1.	Historical	6	Early Historical-4	11.32
			Late Historical-2	
2.	Medieval	22	Early Medieval-3	41.50
			Late Medieval-19	
3.	Modern	25		47.16

The aforesaid cultural sequence and the distribution of sites within that give an insight about inception of human life in Madhepura district. First of all, it is to be noted that no prehistoric site has been found during exploration activity in the study area. The earliest explored settlement belongs to early historical period. It means that human life began sometime in the first half of early historical period in Madhepura district. So, Kosi plain seems to be a preferred destination of the people from late historical period onwards.

Moreover, northern part of Madhepura district (Madhepura subdivision) seems to be more preferred than its southern counterpart (Udakishunganj subdivision) by early historical people as their settlements are more in this portion (03 vs. 01).

In the succeeding phase- medieval period- there is a surprising increase in the number of human settlements. The cultural remains of this period have been found from 22 sites (Map 5.2). It is worth mentioning that majority of these sites (15) is located in the northern portion of the district. Only 7 medieval settlements are situated in

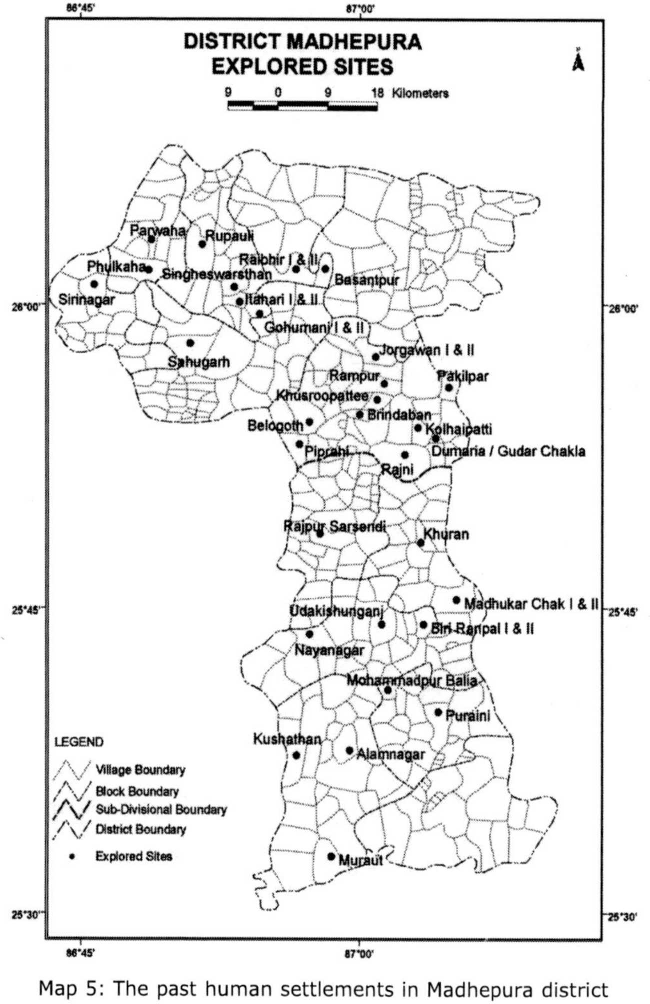

Map 5: The past human settlements in Madhepura district

the southern part. Furthermore, the number of early medieval settlements is moderately more in southern portion than the northern portion of Madhepura (2 vs. 1). All these throw light upon the pattern of distribution of settlements as well as migration of people.

It seems that there is a movement of human settlements from south to north in the district. Interestingly, only one early medieval

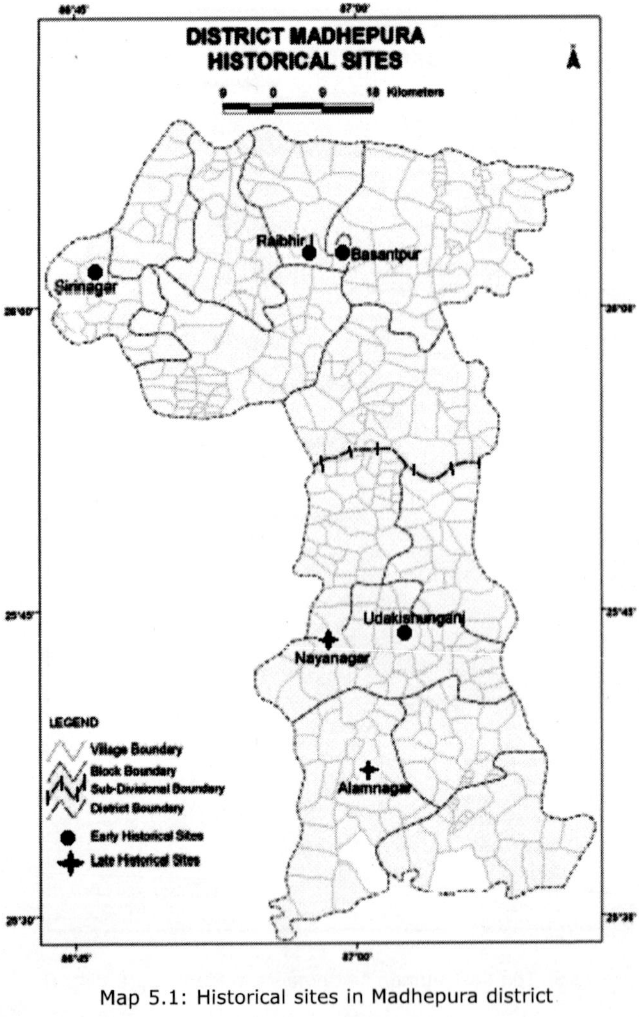

Map 5.1: Historical sites in Madhepura district

site is found in northern portion of Madhepura. This may signify the extension of human habitation to this point in early medieval phase. In another way, it also shows the growing human tendency of breaking fresh grounds for new settlements.

The next phase in the cultural gamut is represented by modern period settlements. The cultural remains of this phase have been gleaned from 25 sites (Map 5.3). This again shows an increase in the number of settlements from the preceding phase. Overall, such a trend reflects the gradual upsurge in the number of settlements with the passage of time starting from early historical period and continuing upto modern times. The distributional analysis of these sites indicates the following features.

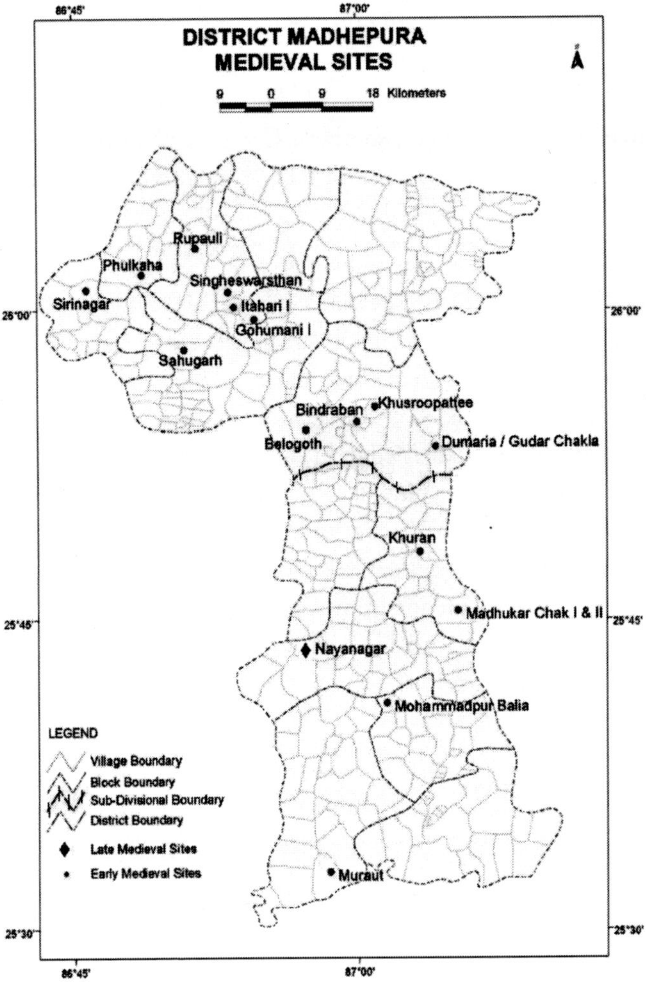

Map 5.2: Medieval period sites in Madhepura district

First of all, like the medieval phase, the concentration of human settlement is in northern section of the district as 19 out of 25 modern sites have been found in this area. The southern portion consists of only 6 human settlements belonging to this period. This reflects the continued preference of past human beings of northern division especially northeastern and southwestern sections.

The emerging pattern of settlement distribution in Madhepura has been compared with its neighbouring districts in Kosi plain or northern Gangetic plain (i.e., Madhepura, Saharsa, and Purnea districts) on one hand and southern Gangetic plain (i.e., Bhagalpur and Munger districts) on the other hand to find out the scenario at macro level.

The cultural sequence emerging in southern Gangetic plain on the basis of reported sites and cultural artifacts are as follows- Early Stone Age, Middle Stone Age, Late Stone Age, Mesolithic, Neolithic, Chalcolithic, Black and Red ware, Northern Black Polished ware and other associated ceramics, Grey and Red ware, Pala Period, Early Medieval and Late Medieval, and Modern cultures etc. Broadly speaking, one finds the human settlements belonging to prehistoric, historical, medieval, and modern phases in southern Gangetic plain (Table 3.1). But in the case of Kosi plain or northern Gangetic plain, the prehistoric settlement is completely absent. This reflects that the southern Gangetic plain had the feel of human life long before the Kosi plain had the same.

Table 3.1: The settlements belonging to different cultural period in northern Gangetic plain/Kosi plain and southern Gangetic plain

Sl. No.	Name of the Area	Prehistoric Settlements	Historical Settlements	Medieval Settlements	Modern Settlements
1.	Northern Gangetic Plain	×	✓	✓	✓
2.	Southern Gangetic Plain	✓	✓	✓	✓

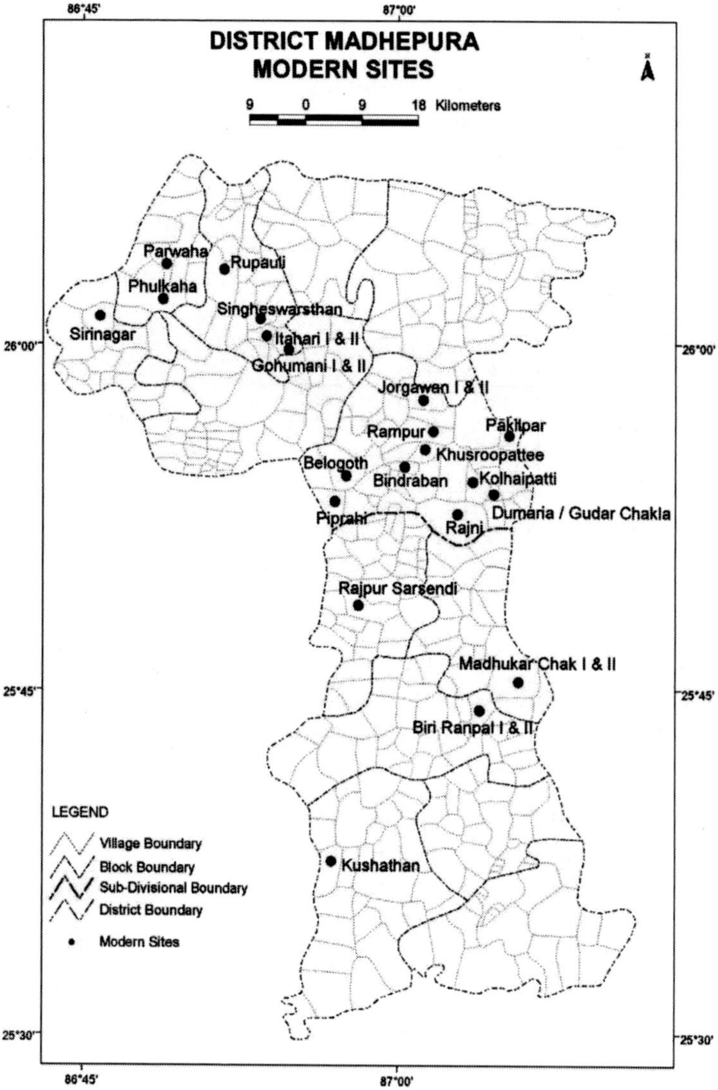

Map 5.3: Modern period sites in Madhepura district

But Kosi plain seemed to be much richer than southern Gangetic plain in late historical, medieval, and modern settlements. All these may point towards a possibility of gradual human movement from south of Ganges to north. Moreover, Madhepura district is having more historical, medieval, and modern settlements than Purnea and Saharsa districts each. Somehow, this reflects that central portion of Kosi plain (i.e., Madhepura district) seems to be better placed than its eastern and western neighbours (Saharsa and Purnea districts) in terms of settlements in cultural sequence.

Table 3.2: The number of settlements in different cultural period in three districts of Kosi plain

Sl. No.	Name of the District	Prehistoric Settlements	Historical Settlements	Medieval Settlements	Modern Settlements
1.	Madhepura	×	6	22	25
2.	Saharsa	×	5	1	1
3.	Purnea	×	3	4	0

LOCATION AND LINES OF EXTENSION OF SETTLEMENTS

The study of site's location, size, cultural thickness, and frequency of artifacts becomes pertinent in any settlement analysis. In this context, it is better to start the discussion with some observations regarding the process of site selection made by people in different cultural periods. All the historical settlements are situated on flat lands. Most of them are located near some or the other water bodies such as depression, natural and man made drainage system, tank, pond, and well etc. In some cases, the settlements are near to *chap* area which is water-logged during most part of the year. These depressions must have received rain water from the adjoining areas.[3] Such water repositories might have catered to the needs of the people for greater part of the year.[4] In addition, it is of note that the sweet drinking water is easily available that too at a very low depth of 15 to 35 feet in these locations.

As far as the size of the settlements during this period is concerned, it seems to be quite large. The best examples are those of Sirinagar and Nayanagar historical sites. Even the depositional thickness is quite impressive in their cases. They seem to be developed and to have thriving settlements.[5] The cultural repertoire of these Historical settlements appeared to be quite rich including potsherds, bricks, stone sculptures, stone plates, stone pillars including a Mauryan pillar, stone inscriptions, forts, ramparts, tanks, ponds, and wells. The frequency of cultural artifacts in terms of potsherds, bricks, and stone objects (especially sculptures and pillars) is appreciable.

Coming to the succeeding medieval period, an interesting picture emerges in regard to settlement's location and its lines of extension. Like historical settlements, most of these medieval sites are located on flat land. But they are situated relatively on a higher ground in comparison to their surroundings. Again the greater number of these sites is located near some form of water bodies such as river, canal, *dhar*, natural and artificial drainages, some water reservoir, pond, tank, and well etc.

Like its preceding counterparts, several of these medieval settlements are situated in *chap*, water-logged, flood prone, and *diyara* areas. But interestingly, according to informants, the water does not reach over the site. That means the past human beings were very careful in selecting the location for their settlements or in site selection. On the one hand, they established themselves in an area where water was easily available for various purposes; while on the other hand, these human beings were also cautious to keep their settlements at a safer distance and height from any threat of water. But surprisingly in some cases (Muraut and Khusroopattee), the site is almost submerged in water. This might be due to the change in the course of Kosi and its distributaries.

Most of medieval settlements are quite large running into thousands of square meters.[6] But yet, there are some sites which are relatively small. One possibility is that these settlements might have contracted with the passage of time.[7] In terms of cultural thickness, some of the sites are still having notable depths running into several feet.[8] But there are sites in whose case, it is difficult to estimate their cultural deposit due to either being highly disturbed or submerged.

The cultural assemblage is also remarkable consisting of baked bricks, potsherds, stone sculptures, idols, sandstone images, pitchers, stone boulders, stone plates, cowries, silver and copper coins, forts, remains of castle, remains of wall and foundation, tunnels, *silla-lauree, kalshaee, jata*, hearth, gold ornaments, and inscriptions etc. As far as the frequency of artifacts is concerned, the occurrence of potsherds and bricks; and stone sculpture, images, and idols are quite impressive. The remains of walls and some structure's foundations are also frequently reported. But the appearance of ornaments and coins are rare.

Like medieval sites, modern settlements are also generally situated on flat land and on relatively higher ground than their surrounding. Again these settlements are located nearer to different forms of water bodies.[9] Most of these sites are also located in *chap* and flood prone areas.[10] Some of them even get submerged or flooded or at least surrounded by water during rainy or monsoon season.[11]

As far as the size of modern sites is concerned a thought provoking picture emerges. Some of them are very big running into several thousand square meters, where as few of them are medium sized spread in couple of thousand square meters. Yet there are several sites which are very small settlements covering an area below 1000 square meters. The thickness of cultural possessions is also intriguing as there is a lot of variation. In some cases, it is around 5 meters (Sirinagar and Belo Goth) whereas in few other cases, it is around 0.5 to 1 meter. But yet, there are some sites where there is no observable thickness. In some cases, no archeological remains of any significance are found.

Like the sites of medieval period, the cultural remains of modern settlements are also notable. Broadly, the cultural assemblage bears similar look.[12] As far as the frequency of cultural artifacts is concerned, like preceding phase, good quantity of bricks and potsherds as well as stone sculptures and idols is seen in modern period settlements too. Moreover, the remnants of walls and other structures are also noticed frequently. In addition, some of the modern sites are still inhabited. On these sites, modern structure in the form of secular and religious buildings could also be seen along with ponds, wells, and tube-wells.

The above discussion amply shows that the origin of life in Madhepura district can be traced to early historical period. Once this process started with limited number of sites, the human settlements registered growth in terms of number, size, depositional thickness, and cultural advancement right from historical to modern phase. Gradually, they spread and colonized the entire district during medieval and modern periods. The number of human settlements kept on increasing in every phase though not so appreciably from medieval to modern period as seen in the case of historical to medieval phase.

The settlements across the periods show rich cultural remains reflecting the potential of the area for human survival and growth. The district enjoyed fertile soil, rich vegetation, favourable climate, and abundant water resources; fulfilling the prerequisites for the emergence and survival of any society and culture.[13] The several other aspects of settlement pattern are the subject matter of next chapter.

NOTES AND REFERENCES

1. But undoubtedly, it is growing and gaining currency day by day.
2. It tries to find out where the sites are located- flat land, high land, low land, in depression, and near water bodies.
3. There is a possibility of such happening at local as well as regional level.
4. Such presumption becomes strong possibility in the light of similar kind of findings in other places. This has been found during field works in Haryana and Rajasthan (India) and Qohaito (Eritrea). Most of the villages located on the way from Delhi to Hanumangarh district (Rajasthan) are endowed with some natural or man made depressions. Villagers informed that these water bodies catered to their needs for most part of the year. Moreover, this is also observed in a historical trip

to Qohaito, one of the historical sites in Eritrea, northeast Africa. There is one man made micro dam locally called "Safira dam" which is believed to have catered to the water needs of people since 2000 years. The rain water from nearby areas collects in the dam. Interestingly, even today people living on the Qohaito plateau use the water of this dam.

5. We expect the same on the basis of earlier report in regard to Alamnagar and Udakishunganj settlements. But now these sites are almost extinct.
6. Some of the examples are in the form of sites such as Nayanagar, Khuran, Khusroopattee, Muraut, Raibhir, Belo Goth, Sirinagar, Gudar Chakla, Gohumani-I, Itahari-I, Jorgawan, Madhukar Chak-I, and Sahugarh.
7. It has already been observed in previous chapters that some of the sites got disturbed due to intensive cultivation or other types of human intervention.
8. This can be observed in cases of Raibhir-II, Madhukar Chak-I, Sirinagar, Khuran, Belo Goth, Gohumani-I, Jorgawan-II, and Itahari-I sites.
9. These water bodies again include river, watercourse, natural depressions, water reservoirs, ponds, lakes, tanks, and wells etc.
10. Almost 10 out of 25 modern sites have been found in such areas.
11. Out of the aforesaid 10 sites, 6 and 4 were submerged and surrounded by water respectively.
12. It involves baked bricks, potsherds, stone idols, pitcher, tools, remains of walls, remains of some foundation and structures, cowries, stone boulders, *silla-lauree*, *jata*, silver coins, metal idols, forts, inscriptions, and pillars etc.
13. The inferences drawn in connection with dispersal of communities on landscape should be treated tentatively and subject to subsequent verification through more research and particularly excavations.

10

Settlement Pattern

The analysis of settlement pattern and location constitutes an important aspect of settlement archaeology. It enhances the understanding of past and their inhabitants. But such studies are challenging in the light of scanty data.[1] The present exercise is an attempt in that direction. It tries to comprehend the pattern of past human settlements in terms of administrative, physiographic, and rainfall zones; hydrology; and land-use pattern etc. In addition, an attempt has been made to determine the size of explored sites and their population. The rank size frequency and demographic analyses has also been made. Moreover, the carrying capacity of Madhepura's past environment has also been probed. The issues such as splitting off tendencies among the past societies have been discussed. The discourses on all these are logical culmination of preceding settlement analyses in terms of location, culture wise dispersal, and cultural deposition and possessions etc.

SUBDIVISION WISE DISTRIBUTION OF SITES

When the past settlements are divided into two sub-divisional administrative areas of Madhepura district, an interesting picture (Table 4 and Map 6) emerges regarding their dispersal over these parts. The data demonstrates that Madhepura subdivision has more number of early historical settlements than Udakishunganj subdivision. But intriguingly, the former did not experience any late historical settlements. Rather Udakishunganj subdivision seemed to be favoured by the people of that period.

Likewise, in early medieval period, slightly more number of sites are found in Udakishunganj subdivision. A close examination of the process of site selection by historical and early medieval people reveals a common approach on their part. Their settlements are almost evenly dispersed over both the segments of the district with slight variations.[2]

Table 4: The frequency of different cultural sites in two sub-divisional administrative areas of Madhepura district

Sl. No.	Period		Madhepura subdivision	Udakishunganj subdivision
1.	Historical	EH	3	1
		LH	X	2
2.	Medieval	EM	1	2
		LM	14	5
3.	Modern		19	6
Total			37	16

By late medieval period, Madhepura subdivision appears to become the favourite of the contemporary people. This is reflected by higher number of late medieval settlements in this part (14) in comparison to the smaller number (5) in Udakishunganj. It may be due to the fact that the inhabitants understood the ecology of these two areas well by this time and found Madhepura subdivision to be more suitable for their survival than its southern counterpart. Another reason can be the possible change in geographical conditions. Yet, another possibility is the probable shift in the course of Kosi leading to relatively favourable situation in Madhepura subdivision. At micro level, the center of gravity of human activities during medieval period seemed to be northwestern and central-eastern part of Madhepura district.

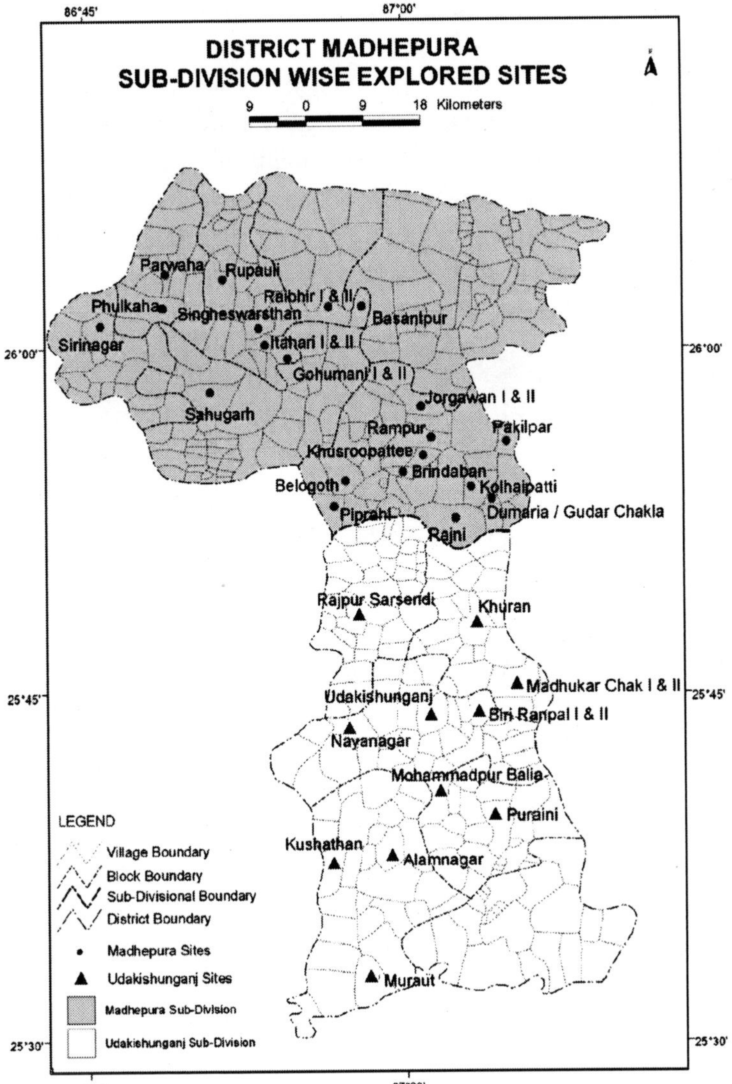

Map 6: Subdivision wise distributions of past human settlements

The human being's tilt towards Madhepura subdivision continued in modern times as well. Udakishunganj subdivision is outnumbered in terms of modern human settlement (06) by its northern counterpart (19). It means from early historical to early medieval periods, the people were still exploring the suitable locale for their settlements. But by the late medieval and especially modern period, they were convinced of the suitability of northern portion of Madhepura district for their settlement and subsistence. As a result from that time onwards the area has become their favourite till now. Like the preceding phases, the center of gravity during modern period again looks to be the northwestern and central-eastern part of the district.

FREQUENCY OF SITES IN DIFFERENT SOILS AND PHYSIOGRAPHIC ZONES

Madhepura district is watered by river Kosi since time immemorial. That's why it has mainly having *Khadar* soil (Map 6.1). Some segment of the district also possesses *Tarai*, saline, saline alkali, peaty, and saline peaty soils (Map 6.1).[3]

The past human settlements are divided into entisols, aridisols, and histosols types of soils and an interesting picture emerges regarding their distribution. Bulk of the sites is located in entisols. Aridisols also possess a reasonable number of sites. But, none of the explored settlements lay in histosols (Map 6.1).

The younger alluvium soil could be further divided into *chiknee*, *domat* or *kraree*, and *baluhaee* soils.[4] It is difficult to separate them in different pockets within the district. In fact, many times they are found coexisted and overlapped each other. The analysis of the frequency of settlements in *chiknee*, *domat*, and *baluhaee* soils produces a stimulating picture (Table 4.1).

The overwhelming majority of past human settlements are located in *domat* and *baluhaee* soils. Only few of the sites are situated in *chiknee* ground. Surprisingly, none of the site has been found in *chiknee* soil up to early medieval period.[5] Earlier inhabitants seem to begin settling on *chiknee* soil from late medieval period onwards.

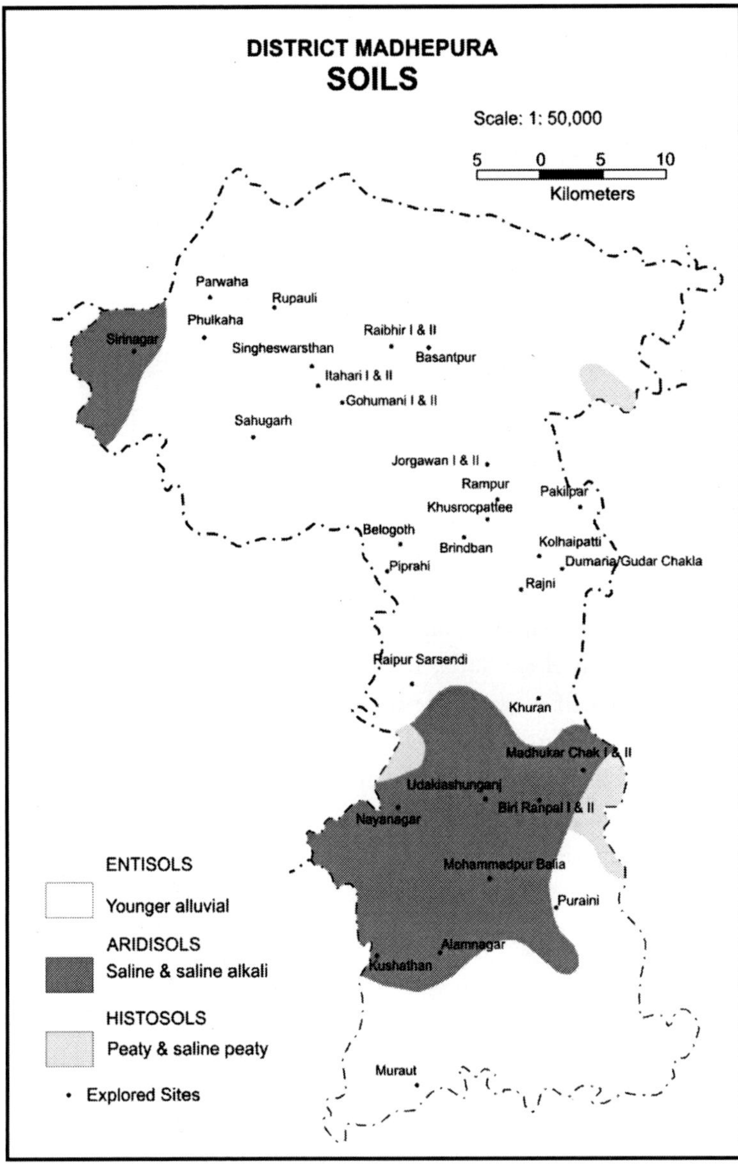

Map 6.1: Distributions of past human settlements in different soils

Moreover, it looks as if *domat* and *baluhaee* were most preferred soils for establishing settlement up to early medieval phase. Although *chiknee* soil too was inhabited by late medieval period, *baluhaee* and *domat* continued to be their first preferences. But, if we compare the presence of sites between *domat* and *baluhaee* soils, both have almost equal share.

Table 4.1: The frequency of different cultural period's site in *chiknee*, *domat*, and *baluhaee* soils

Sl. No.	Period		Chiknee	Domat/ Kraree	Baluhaee
1.	Historical	EH	X	X	2
		LH	X	1	X
2.	Medieval	EM	X	1	2
		LM	1	7	8
3.	Modern		4	11	7
Total			5	20	19

In order to understand the logic behind the location of past settlements in these soils, it's necessary to analyze the latter's characteristics. If we compare their features, *chiknee* and *domat* are relatively more fertile than *baluhaee*. It is due to the fact that the particle of *baluhaee* soil is very big and has less water retention capacity. But the particle of *chiknee* soil is very fine and thus better water retention capacity which makes it more fertile.[6] As far as *domat* is concerned, its particles are of different sizes. Therefore, it has less water retention capacity than *chiknee* but it is more than *baluhaee*.

Earlier settlers seem to be extremely careful in their selection of site. Their preference for *domat* and *baluhaee* soils for establishing settlements is quite understandable. *Domat* is suitable for human settlements as variety of crops can be grown over it. It is also less prone to water logging which has been much to the likings of past human beings as Madhepura district receives heavy rainfall and endowed with several water bodies. The water table in the district is quite high (nearer to surface level). This soil is also more appropriate for the construction of roads and pathways which can serve in all weathers.

Their preferences for *baluhaee* area also appear to be quite reasonable in the light of Madhepura being a flood prone area. *Baluhaee* soil does not retain much moisture. So, it is quite suitable for settlement in order to avoid water logging in a aquatic rich area. This type of soil is also suitable for some types of coarse crops. It is also easily friable which must have been to the taste of past human being as their farming technology and tools might not have been well developed in those times.

The presence of fewer sites in *chiknee* soil is also not surprising. Due to high water retention capacity, this soil can lead to water logging which may not have been liked by contemporary people given the less advanced technology to effectively negotiate with such conditions. A water logged area has more probability of infection and disease.

Besides, it creates difficulty in effective transportation and communication systems. The pathways along *chiknee* soil may not be good for all seasons, especially during monsoon period. It is not also appropriate for the cultivation of variety of crops and plants.[7] The beginning of settlements in *chiknee* soil by late medieval period and their increase in succeeding phase may be due to advancement in technology and human being's negotiation capabilities with the nature.

If we divide the past human settlements into two different levels of elevation such as Physiographic Zone-I (0-50 meters) and Physiographic Zone-II (more than 50 meters), then a thought provoking scenario will emerges (Map 6.2). Curiously, all the explored sites are situated in Physiographic Zone-I. Several possible reasons could be attributed to it. One reason could be the relative unsuitability of the area for human settlement and subsistence.[8] Besides, the complete absence of site in Physiographic Zone-II can be also because of possible destruction of past human settlements by Kosi's havoc.

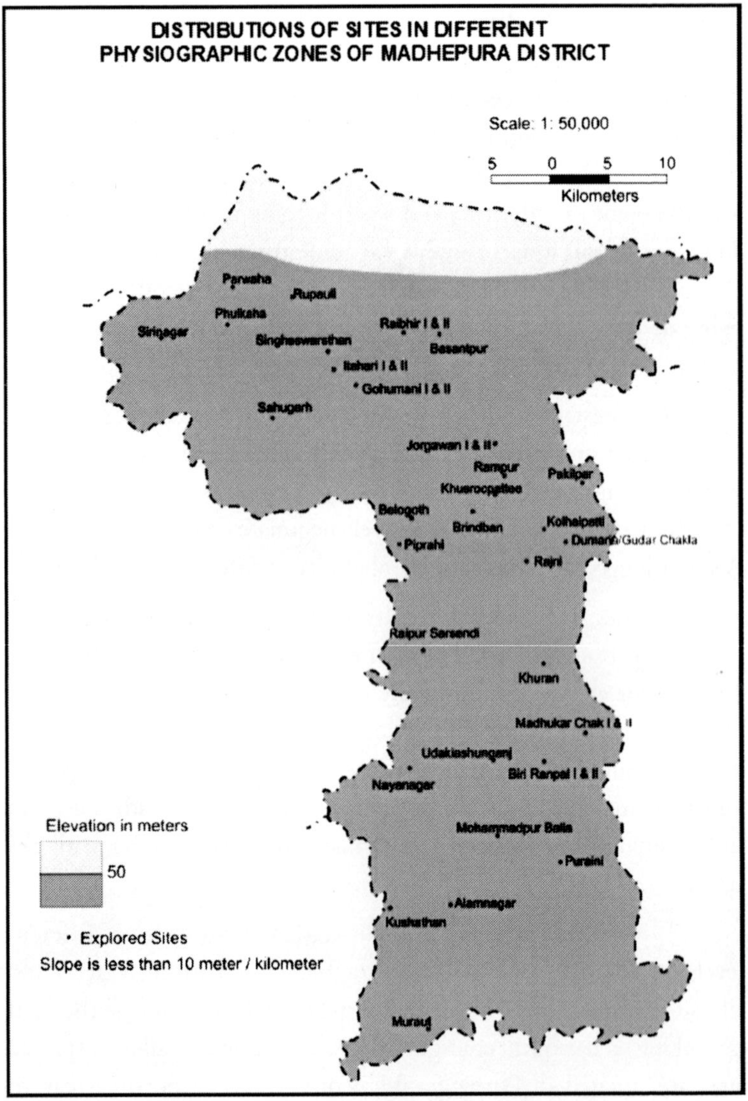

Map 6.2: Distributions of past human settlements in different physiographic zones

SETTLEMENT PATTERNS IN HYDROLOGICAL PERSPECTIVE

By and large Madhepura district is endowed with rich and quality water resources. Usually, the potable water is available between 15-

35 feet. But there are exceptions when it is 55-60 feet deep.[9] Generally, the quality of water is sweet.[10] All the explored sites are located in areas with sweet drinking water. Broadly, the district can be divided into three sub-soil water level zones such as Zone-I (availability of drinking water at 15-25 feet), Zone-II (availability of drinking water at 25-35 feet), and Zone-III (availability of drinking water at 35-60 feet).

Interestingly, majority of the sites (38) across the period are located in Zone-I. Some of them (12) have been found in zone-II. But few settlements (3) are situated in Zone-III. Moreover, up to early medieval period, the past human settlements can be found in Zone-I as well as Zone-II. But from late medieval period onwards, the area with availability of water at 15-25 feet (Zone-I) became the favourite for human settlements. (Table 4.2).

94.33 % of the past settlements are located in areas where water is available with normal iron content. But there are few settlements where the water is with more iron content. One settlement from each of the three periods under analysis is found in such area.[11] This again reflects the prudence of earlier inhabitants in selecting the location for their settlements. They probably understood the consequences of using water with more iron content.[12]

Table 4.2: The frequency of sites in different sub-soil water level zones

Sl. No.	Period		Zone-I (15-25 feet)	Zone-II (25-35 feet)	Zone-III (35-60 feet)
1.	Historical	EH	2	1	X
		LH	X	1	X
2.	Medieval	EM	1	2	1
		LM	15	4	1
3.	Modern		20	4	1
	Total		38	12	3

SETTLEMENT PATTERN IN LANDUSE PERSPECTIVE

Table 4.3: The frequency of historical, medieval, and modern sites in different cropping system

Sl. No.	Period		Cropping Zone-I (Rice, Maize, Jute, Wheat, and Pulses)	Cropping Zone-II (Rice, Maize, Wheat, and Sugarcane)
1.	Historical	EH	3	1
		LH	X	2
2.	Medieval	EM	1	2
		LM	14	5
3.	Modern		19	6
Total			37	16

We can divide Madhepura district into two cropping zones: Cropping Zone-I (area producing rice, maize, jute, wheat, and pulses) and Cropping Zone-II (area producing rice, maize, wheat, and sugarcane). The Table 4.3 and Map 6.3 show the frequency of sites in different cropping zones. The data clearly depicts that historical people were equally settled in both the cropping zones. Gradually, their preference moved towards the Cropping Zone-I, especially in the medieval period.

68 % of medieval settlements located in Cropping Zone-I. In contrast, only 32 % of the settlements which belong to this period are situated in Cropping Zone- II. The preference for Cropping Zone-I continued among modern human being with greater intensity, 76 % of the settlements which belonged to this period are placed in this zone against the 24 % in Cropping Zone- II. Overall 70 % of all the explored sites are located in Cropping Zone- I. This zone seems to be favoured by past human beings in all phases except the historical period.

Madhepura district can also be divided into two zones such as Arable Irrigated Zone and Arable Un-irrigated Zone on the basis of accessibility of irrigation facility for cultivation. Interestingly, majority of the sites fall in the latter. This may be due to the fact that the canal irrigation is relatively a modern practice in the area.

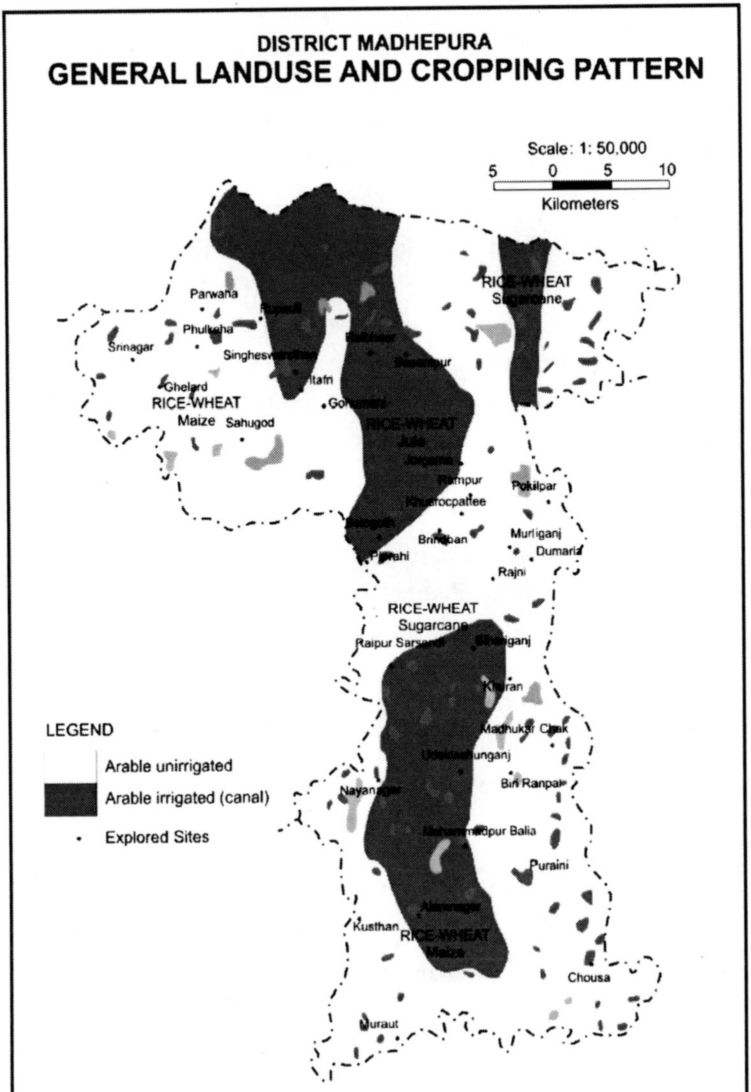

Map 6.3: Distributions of past settlements in different cropping zones

But, it is to be noted that the aforesaid cropping and landuse patterns are based on modern practices in the absence of any archaeological excavation and other relevant researches in Madhepura district. There is a possibility of change in these patterns in modern period especially after independence and green revolution with the introduction of new variety of seeds, fertilizers, modern farming tools and technology, and irrigation facility. But generally speaking, it appears that such changes have had relatively less impact upon the cropping pattern of this district.

During the field work it has been found that still people are following many of the traditional farming techniques and practices. Their cropping system is still largely based on conventional knowledge of crops, information of probable trends of ecology, and techniques of subsistence. But, it is also noticed that some of the crops cultivated earlier have simply vanished or less grown now.[13]

SETTLEMENT PATTERN IN CLIMATIC PERSPECTIVE

On the basis of amount of rainfall, Madhepura district can be divided into three rainfall zones: Rainfall Zone-I (up to 1300 mm), Rainfall Zone-II (1300-1400 mm), and Rainfall Zone-III (>1400 mm). Interestingly, a greater number of sites are located in Rainfall Zone-II. Rainfall Zone-I also has some sites. But Rainfall Zone-III is literally devoid of any settlement. It may be because of the fact that the earlier settlers did not like heavy rainfall area with the possibilities of acute water logging.

RANK SIZE FREQUENCY OF SITES AND DEMOGRAPHIC ANALYSIS

The rank size frequency analysis constitutes an integral part of the settlement archaeology. The ranking depends on the sizes of the sites, the functions performed upon them, their internal differentials, and relationship with the representative sites in the concerned area. But an attempt to such study in Madhepura district is hampered by lack

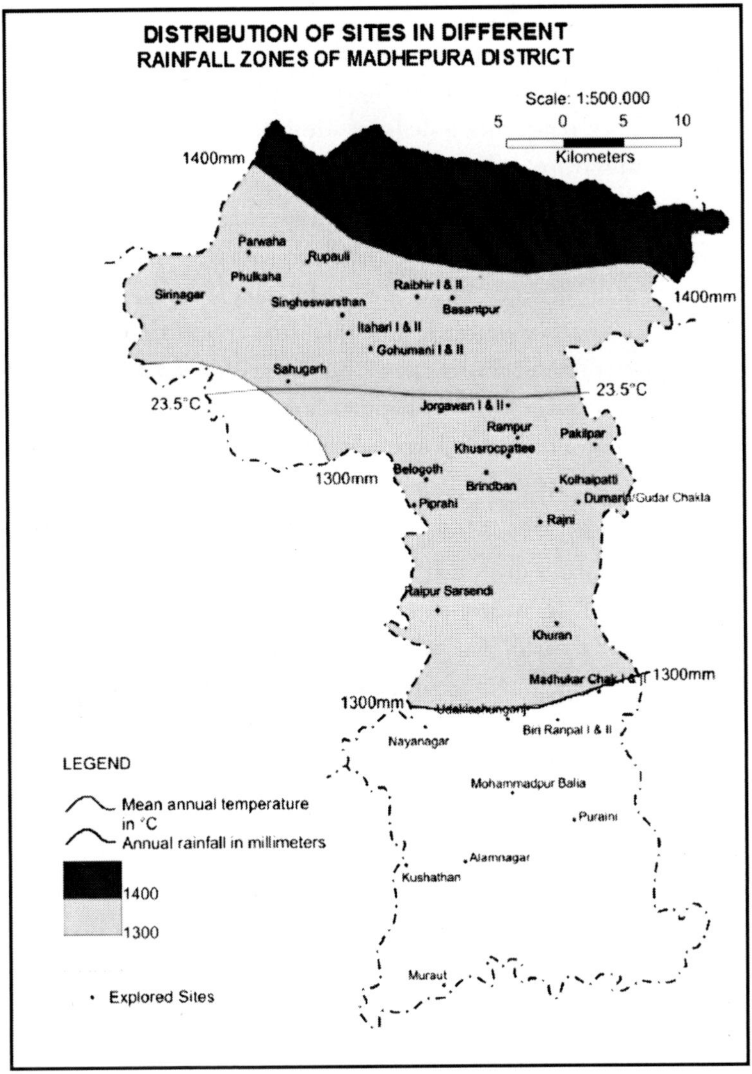

Map 6.4: Distributions of past settlements in different rainfall zones

of excavated settlements, presence of multi-cultural sites, the disturbed nature of single culture settlements, and less number of sites in some cases.

Nevertheless, such an investigation is desired to regain and understand the past settlement's hierarchy and processes.[14] The whole range of explored past settlements has been divided into ten categories. Each category represents a definite size in respect of the area and probable number of inhabitants.[15]

This whole exercise also draws inferences about the demographic trends in different cultural phases. The degree of accuracy again depends upon the careful survey of the size of the sites, niceties in focusing their time span, and conducting horizontal excavations at representative sites.[16] But there is complete absence of horizontal excavation in Madhepura. So, it is difficult to precisely measure the area of circulation of the respective culture especially at multi-cultural sites.

But even incase of single cultural sites, the problem is their small numbers and disturbed state. The degree of sedentariness will also be helpful. In such a situation, there are high probabilities of mistake in analysis of size of site, length of occupations, size and number of families, and occupied accommodation. The population estimates and their bonafides may also get seriously affected. Anyhow, first of all, we will discuss about the available demographic models.

One model has been forwarded by Frankfort. He recorded 20 houses in an area of 1 acre and assumed 6-10 persons per houses. Thus Frankfort estimated 297-497 persons per hectare with 20-34 square meter area for each person.[17] Another model has been advanced by Fairservis. He assigned 6 people per house and 75 square meters per person, so 450 square meters for a house. Fairservis calculated 22 houses in one hectare with 133 persons and 13 people per thousand square meters.[18]

Adam assigned 100[19] and 150 persons[20] to one hectare depending on the way the area of settlement is measured. The former is applicable incase the area is measured in terms of length and breadth. But, the latter is valid when total area is taken into account. On the basis of these calculations, 9 and 12 persons per 1000 square meters are worked out respectively. In his second approach, he took into account non-residential area such as lanes, gardens, public buildings, and well etc. In this case, Adam assigns 3.5 people per family and 200 persons per hectare. In fact, 17 persons are allotted to per thousands square meters.

Makhan Lal has estimated 55 houses per hectare with 4.9 people per house in proto-historic and early historic Ganga-Yamuna Doab. He calculated 175 persons in one hectare.[21] That means 23 persons per thousand square meters and 36 square meter area per person. Overall, his calculation is 12-40 persons per thousand square meters.

In Sonipat area, Dutt estimated 18 persons per thousand square meter and 200 persons per hectare.[22] R. C. Thakran calculated 20 persons per thousand square meters taking into account several possible factors such as lanes, wells, courtyard, storage fuel items, husks, animal den, and living room etc.[23]

However, all the aforesaid models are based on tentative past and present conditions in their respective area. They appear to be convenient working model to ensure minimum possible errors. In fact, all of them should be considered provisional. While keeping all these into mind, 20 persons per thousand square meter is proposed for present study area.

Of the 6 historical sites only three of them (Raibhir-II, Nayanagar, and Sirinagar) have been selected for the purpose of rank size frequency and demographic analysis. This is because of the fact that these three settlements are single culture sites and they are in better physical condition besides having relatively large circulation of cultural remains. Although, rest of other three settlements (Raibhir-I, Alamnagar, and Udakishunganj) are also single culture sites but they are almost extinct by now. The data in Table 4.4 depicts wide variations in the size and population of historical settlements.

Table 4.4: Historical sites: Rank size frequency[24]

Rank Size	Approximate area of sites (in sq. m.)	Number of sites	Population size (20 per 1000 sq. m.)
A	1000	1	20
B	2000	X	40
C	5000	X	100
D	8000	X	160
E	10000	1	200
F	20000	X	400
G	40000	X	800
H	70000	X	1400
I	100000 and above	1	2000

One of the sites falls in category A (1000 sq. m.) where as the second and third comes in categories E and J and they reflect the big size of these settlements. Accordingly, the population spectrum is from 20 to 2000 inhabitants. This reflects the coexistence of small, medium, and big settlements and probably pointing towards their different functions, importance, and rank within the contemporary communities.

Table 4.5 depicts an interesting picture about the rank size frequency and demographic figures of the medieval settlements. But one of the biggest limitation in such analysis is the multi-cultural nature of these sites. It seems that some of the medieval settlements are relatively small ranging from 1000-2000 sq. m. In contrast, few of them are medium sized with a population range of 160 to 400 people. Like historical sites, some of the medieval sites are large to very large encompassing an area of 40000 sq. m. and above and accommodating a large population of 800 and above.

The Table 4.6 shows fascinating picture regarding modern settlements. Modern sites are found in various denominations. There are relatively smaller settlements (10 out of 22) encompassing an area of up to 5000 sq. m. Besides that there are even medium range

Table 4.5: Medieval sites: Rank size frequency[25]

Rank Size	Approximate area of sites (in sq. m.)	Number of sites	Population size (20 per 1000 sq. m.)
A	1000	4	20
B	2000	1	40
C	5000	X	100
D	8000	3	160
E	10000	2	200
F	20000	3	400
G	40000	1	800
H	70000	2	1400
I	100000 and above	4	2000

settlements (08) with an area ranging from 5000 up to 20000 sq. m. The number of larger settlements stands 4 out of 22 modern sites accommodating a population between 800-2000.

Table 4.6: Modern sites: Rank size frequency[26]

Rank Size	Approximate area of sites (in sq. m.)	Number of sites	Population size (20 per 1000 sq. m.)
A	1000	7	20
B	2000	1	40
C	5000	2	100
D	8000	1	160
E	10000	4	200
F	20000	3	400
G	40000	1	800
H	70000	X	1400
I	100000 and above	3	2000

FUNCTIONAL ANALYSIS OF SITES

The past human settlements can also be examined on the basis of their functions. A settlement can have one or several functions. Here, they are analyzed mainly in terms of habitational, religious, and habitational cum religious functions. Table 4.7 demonstrates an interesting picture in regard to these functions of sites.

Table 4.7: The functional analysis of sites[27]

Sl. No.	Period		Habitation site	Religious site	Habitation cum religious site
1.	Historical	EH	4	X	X
		LH	1	X	1
2.	Medieval	EM	2	X	1
		LM	13	1	4
3.	Modern		14	5	5
Total			34	6	11

It looks as if habitation settlements (H-5, Med-15, and Mod-14) dominated the nature of human settlements across the periods. This reflects human occupation with their worldly affairs more than any other things. The number of religious and habitational cum religious sites increased gradually in succeeding phases (H-1, M-6, and M-10). This increase is sharp from historical (1) to medieval phase (6). The almost similar trend is seen in the case of medieval (6) to modern phases (10) as well. This shows that people's thinking and activities became more diverse and complex with the passage of time.

CARRYING CAPACITY AND SPLITTING UP TENDENCY

There is hot scholarly debate upon the definition of carrying capacity of a locale and the variable affecting it. According to some scholars, once the population density of a land reaches to maximum, its carrying capacity can not be increased simply by putting extra input of labour. It can be enhanced either by technological innovations or occupation of pristine land. But there are others who emphasize on the exploiting capacity of a group, the extension of the perimeter of the catchment area, and harmony between them. If this harmony is disturbed (going beyond the economic range of people's exploiting potential), both the carrying capacity of the catchment area and the exploiting potential are likely to deteriorate.

A correlation is sought between the inhabitant's better operative potential and the extending catchment zones to assess the carrying capacity of an area. But, the ineffectiveness of extant technology and non-availability of suitable geographical locales may promote the extension of the catchment area which is against the spirit of the very concept of carrying capacity of a locale.

In fact, the concept of catchment zone[28] may vary from place to place, society to society, and time to time. Sometimes, it includes far-flung areas providing the essential goods and services. While some take the spacing between two settlements as the immediate primary catchment zone. The carrying capacity should be seen in conjunction with operative variables. It can increase with the operative potential of the people. That means there can be change in the levels of carrying capacity and harmony between natural and social variables.

The degree of carrying capacity of an environment depends upon the harmony of aforesaid variables. If the harmonious level is below normal caused by the underdevelopment of the constituent variables, the carrying capacity tends to be affected in all probability.[29] Thus the number of person to be fed in a given space and time with the help of the effective strength of the environment should be conceived as carrying capacity.

The overgrowth of social forces might affect the natural dynamism that may further disturb the harmony. It will increase the probability for diminishing return with improvement in former. Thus the secret of higher carrying capacity lies in optimum balance between the operative variables. The shift in the balance of either side tends to affect the attitude of the residents to stay or march on some suitable locales which brings in the issue of branching off tendency.

In both the cases of minor and major imbalances, there are possibilities of splitting of the human settlements with a view to settle in a new place to maintain the required level of food production. But sometimes, the split may be caused by influx of new population in an area. In semi-arid areas, a setback to the crop owing to fluctuations inherent in rainfall systems may force the people to bud off from their parent settlements especially in absence of provisions for irrigation, storage, and transportation.

Undoubtedly, the people do show remarkable resilient attitude incase of hardships. Sometimes, they try to survive by gathering wild fruits, roots, and rough grains in extreme adversity. They decide to shift to a new area only when there are no options left to them. That is their last choice.

The size of Madhepura's alluvial plain seems to remain almost same throughout the time. But the number of human settlements kept on increasing in every successive period.[30] In addition, the number of sites in both the administrative zones (Madhepura and Udakishunganj) registered increase from historical to medieval phase. This is evidently true in Madhepura subdivision from medieval to modern period as well. Interestingly, this trend continues even today.

Moreover, it is very much apparent from the aforesaid analysis of rank size frequency and demography that the size as well as population of past human settlements increased from one phase to another. This reflects the increase in the carrying capacity of environment with the improving operative potential of the inhabitants. Therefore, the lowest and highest level of population growth pattern is seen in same geographical area. This speaks about the changing level of carrying capacity and the harmony between the natural and social variables.

The less number of sites in northern portion of the district in historical period and then gradual increase in medieval and modern phases subsequently are not because of the absence of extant feature of this zone in ancient phase. But rather other variables of operative potential were not potent enough to utilize the natural resources in the historical period.

Relatively, the number of sites in southern portion did not increase in the same way as its northern counterpart from medieval to modern phase. Moreover, even today though the number of settlements is much greater than previous periods, they are not as big in size and population as the present settlements in northern part of the district. This somehow may reflect the increase in carrying capacity with the passage of time but with diminishing returns.

Besides, the increase in the number of settlements with smaller sizes and populations in Udakishunganj subdivision may also point towards splitting up tendencies. This possibly reflects the disturbances in the harmonious relations between the forces of production. It perhaps happened due to overgrowth of social forces which are very much evident in modern times. This adversely affects the health of natural dynamism which leads to a stage when every improvement in social forces produces diminishing returns. This concern has been discussed in the fourth chapter that the ecological balance may be disturbed anytime with disastrous consequences. The southern part of the district seems to have reached to that point. That's why this area bear less favourable sight than its northern counterpart for human settlement and subsistence.

The wide variations in the size and population of settlements in medieval and modern times also points towards the branching off tendencies.[31] But such tendency should not always be seen in the perspective of saturation of carrying capacity. It may be due to other factors such as arrival of new settlers,[32] change in geographical and climatic conditions,[33] the variations in rainfall,[34] and occurrence of famines[35] and epidemics.

Epidemics do not appear unusual till recent past in the absence of modern medical facilities. One example is the malarial prevalence in the area during preceding centuries as pointed out by Buchanan. The epidemics might forced the inhabitants to desert their settlement altogether. Moreover, the tendency of the young and adolescent to get independent from their elders might also lead to splitting up. This is generally evident in modern times.

As aforesaid, human beings show resilience in adverse conditions to hold back at their parent settlement despite temptation to march on to the new and supposedly better places.

The aforesaid discussion sheds light upon the various facets of settlement pattern of past societies in Madhepura district across different periods. It is lucid that the number of human settlements is decisively more in Madhepura subdivision as compared to Udakishunganj in all the phases except historical one. This was probably because of the fact that this northern portion of the district offered more favourable environment and opportunities for earlier settlers. Not surprisingly, this trend is still continuing. Moreover, cotemporary inhabitants found *domat* and *baluhaee* soils more fertile for their settlements and subsistence than the *chiknee* soil.

Generally the research area is endowed with a good of quality water. It appeared that past human beings preferred to live in an area of low water table (relatively farther from surface level). Besides that they seem to avoid the place where water had more iron content. Moreover, people preferred to establish their settlement in a cropping zone where rice, wheat, jute, pulses, and vegetable etc., could be cultivated. Most of the past settlements appear to be of habitation nature. But, there are some sites which are of habitation cum religious nature. Besides that in few cases the religious element of the sites looks like later development.

There is increasing variety in the sizes as well as population of human settlements in every succeeding periods starting from historical to modern. All these may point towards function, position, and importance of sites in those periods. The ever increasing number of settlements across the phases shows that the carrying capacity of Madhepura's environment increased with the passage of time although with diminishing return after certain period.[36]

Not surprisingly, the branching off tendencies among the settlements is also very much evident. Overall, the human choices seem to be greatly influenced and determined by nature in past. It is because the people in those times lacked the skills and technology to effectively challenge and adapt their nature.

NOTES AND REFERENCES

1. There is lack of information about paleo-ecology, paleo-geography, paleo-geomorphology, paleo-hydrology, and land-use pattern etc., in context of Madhepura district. The effort to gather such relevant data are further impeded by absence of archaeological excavation in the district.
2. There are 3 historical settlements in each case. Incase of medieval settlements, Madhepura and Udakishunganj subdivisions has 1 and 2 settlements respectively.
3. It can be observed in north-western, south-western, and central-western parts (pockets of Gwalpara and Udakishunganj C. D. Blocks) of the district.
4. A discussion upon the nature of Madhepura's soil can be seen in fourth chapter. The *chiknee*, *domat*, and *baluhaee* soils are also called clayey, loamy, and sandy respectively. They have several differences besides the most apparent, colour.
5. Here, it is to be noted that the soil data of some of the sites are not available. It is so incase of 16 sites out of 53.
6. It is noteworthy that *chiknee* soils are of two types such as yellowish and blackish.
7. Besides, the more water logging possibilities compounds the problems.
8. The area may be either densely forested or away from water bodies. It may be marshy or with very low water table. The soil may not have been suitable for cultivation being relatively closer to Tarai region than other parts of Madhepura district. Another possibility is that area may not have been fit of communication. These are only probabilities. The future researches will shed more light.
9. Of course, that is rare.
10. The saline water is not reported from any settlement area.

11. They are Nayanagar (early medieval), Belo Goth (late medieval), and Belo Goth (modern period).
12. Generally the use of such water leads to several types of negative impact upon human health especially hydrocele among men. The past human beings must have come to know about these through observation and trail and error method. A large number of hydrocele cases are reported in the district these days. This is because of the fact that the people are trying to inhabit every nook and corner of the area irrespective of the quality of resources available.
13. However, in the light of these facts the aforesaid analysis should be treated tentative and subjected to fresh enquiries in future researches.
14. The present exercise will take into account as many settlements as possible.
15. Of course, this classification suffers with several limitations. It has been opted for the sake of convenience while dealing with wide range of settlement sizes.
16. All these will allow knowing the actual size and internal structures of the settlements. The contemporary demographic pattern in the vicinity can be taken into consideration to increase the accuracy.
17. H. Frankfort, 'Town-planning in ancient Mesopotamia', *Town Planning Review*, 21, 1950, pp-98-115.
18. W. A. Fairservis, 'Origin, Character, and Decline of an Early Civilization', *American Museum*, Novitates, 2302, American Museum of Natural History, 1967, pp. 1-48.
19. R. M. Adams, *Heartland of Cities* (Chicago, 1981), p. 65.
20. R. M. Adams, *Land Behind Baghdad* (Chicago, 1965), pp. 23-25 and p. 44.
21. Makhan Lal, "Summary of Four Seasons Explorations in Kanpur Districts", *ME*, 1984, p 24.
22. B. Dutt, 'PGW Settlements in Haryana', unpublished Ph.D. thesis, Kurushetra University, Kurushetra, 1980, p. 168.
23. R. C. Thakran, *Dynamics of Settlement Archaeology- Haryana* (New Delhi: Gyan Publishing House, 2000).
24. There is no data about the size of the site in case of two historical settlements (Raibhir-I and Basantpur). They are almost extinct by now.

25. Again, in the case of two medieval sites (Parwaha and Sarsendi), there is no data about their size due to near extinction.
26. Like historical and medieval periods, there are three modern sites (Parwaha, Piprahi, and Sarsendi) for which there is lack of data about the site's size due to near extinction.
27. There is no functional information about some of the sites like Parwaha.
28. It represents the natural environment consisting of soil types, bio-diversity, and ecological forces.
29. If the imbalance is major then it can be amply visible in archaeological data (expansion and contraction etc.) also.
30. The figures are 6 in historical phase, 22 in medieval phase, and 25 in modern period.
31. The sites are found in almost all the categories designed for present analysis.
32. There is possibility of movement of population from southern Gangetic plain to Kosi plain.
33. It is plausible because of frequent change in the course of river Kosi. The nature of soil can also change due to deposit of sand by Kosi's flood as happened in the case of 2008 inundation.
34. It holds true especially in the absence of technology for better irrigation facilities and taming nature.
35. There exited a near famine situation in 2010 monsoon season.
36. This seems to be especially applicable from early modern period onwards.

11

The History of Education

Education is the heart and blood of a culture. It helps in the total growth of a person and society. That's why the developed communities possessed strong educational background. Education is the key for becoming a superpower in the twenty first century. India was a leader in this field during ancient time. In fact, high educational development and attainment has been the hallmark of its cultures and civilizations. India hosted several world renowned educational centers and universities of the time. Not surprisingly, Bihar was in the thick of all this.

It would not be an exaggeration to say that Nalanda and Vikramshila (falling in Kosi region) were the twin academic capitals of India in the late ancient and early medieval periods respectively. They belonged to the elite class of world's oldest universities where students from different parts of the globe came and studied.[1] But things changed with time. Bihar and Kosi area lost their leadership position in education in the succeeding periods. Nevertheless, some revival could be seen during British and post-independence phases.

Nalanda is one of the earliest centers of higher learning in the Indian subcontinent. It flourished between the reign of Sakraditya[2] and twelfth century (1197). The university was patronized by Gupta rulers,[3] Harsha,[4] and later Pala. The site of Nalanda is located about 88 kilometres southeast of Patna. Its ruins occupy an area of 14 hectares.[5] (Figure 5).

Figure 5: Ruins of Nalanda University

There are several theories associated with its nomenclature. According to some scholars, it has been named after the Naga who lived in a tank in the middle of a mangrove. Some believe that Buddha once had his capital here and gave "alms without intermission," hence the name. Xuanzang said that since Sariputra died at the village called 'Nalaka,' so the place got identified as Nalanda.

Sukumar Dutt divides the history of Nalanda University into two phases- the first one of growth, development, and fruition (from the sixth to the ninth centuries);[6] and the second of gradual decline and final dissolution (from the ninth to the thirteen centuries).

Nalanda also has the distinction of being one of the world's first residential universities. In its heyday, the university accommodated over 10,000 students and 2,000 teachers.[7] It was considered an architectural masterpiece and marked by a lofty wall and one gate. Nalanda had eight separate compounds and ten temples, along with many other meditation halls and classrooms. There were lakes and parks. The library was located in a nine storied building where meticulous copies of texts were produced.[8] The subjects taught at Nalanda University covered major fields of learning.[9] Xuanzang left detailed accounts of the university in the seventh century.[10]

Evidence suggests that the Nalanda University was sacked by Bakhtiyar Khilji in 1193.[11] The last head of Nalanda, Shakyashribhadra, fled to Tibet in 1204 at the invitation of the Tibetan translator Tropu Lotsawa. When the Tibetan translator Chag Lotsawa (1197–1264) visited the site in 1235, he found it damaged and looted.[12] Despite all these, remnants of the debilitated Buddhist community continued to struggle on under scarce resources until c. 1400. Chagalaraja was reportedly the last king to have patronized Nalanda.

Vikramshila University was another important centre of higher learning.[13] It was one of the monasteries which grew up during the Pala period in ancient Bihar and Bengal.[14] Vikramshila was established by King Dharmapala (783 to 820) in response to a supposed decline in the quality of scholarship at Nalanda. Atisha Dipankara, the renowned *Pandita* is sometimes listed as its one of the notable abbots.

Figure 5.1: Ruins of Vikramshila University

Figure 5.2: Landscape of Vikramshila ruins including the seating and meditation area

Figure 5.3: Pillars at Vikramshila site

Figure 5.4: The view of Vikramshila's entrance

The ruin of Vikramshila is located about 50 km east of Bhagalpur and about 13 km northeast of Kahalgaon (village Antichak).[15] (Figure 5.1 to 5.4). It prospered for about four centuries. The university is known to have had more than one hundred teachers and about one thousand students. It produced eminent scholars who were often invited by foreign countries to spread learning, culture, and religion. The most distinguished and eminent among all was Atisa.[16] Subjects such as philosophy, grammar, metaphysics, Indian logic, and tantricism etc., were taught here.

According to Sukumar Dutt, Vikramshila appears to have had a more clearly delineated hierarchy than other mahaviharas- abbot *Adhyaksa*, six gate protectors or gate scholars (*Dvarapala* or *Dvarapandita*), great Scholars (Mahapandita),[17] scholars (*Pandita*),[18] professors or teachers (*Upadhyaya* or *Acharya*),[19] and resident monks (*bhiksu*).[20]

It was again destroyed by Bakhtiyar Khilji during fighting with the Sena dynasty along with the other major centers of Buddhism in India around 1200. His marauding armies destroyed this great center of learning. Thus these traditions of learning were lost during succeeding period.

Bihar and Kosi region saw partial revival of education during the later part of British rule. Britishers established a university at Patna along with other centers of high learning, viz. Science College, Patna; Prince of Wales Medical College (now Patna Medical College and Hospital); and Bihar Engineering College (now National Institute of Technology). They also established a system of district schools (locally called Zila schools), located at the district headquarters. In addition, there were semi aided and private schools which were run and administered by local communities. Several of them were known for their high quality education.

This lead was lost in the early post independence period when Bihar failed to get sufficient number of institute of higher education established. However, in 1960s major educational reforms were implemented to streamline the educational structure of state by the then educationist and minister of education late Satender Narain Sinha. But, this phenomenal change was short lived as the successive governments failed to implement it.

During late 1970s and early 1980s, the state government took over management of most privately run schools. This adversely affected the quality of school education since the government was ill equipped to manage them.[21] Though the state accorded them government recognition, the standard began to fall. But, the government did not take over the schools that were run by the Christian missionaries. As a result, these schools became the carrier of quality education for sometime in Bihar.

As in other states, the central government of India runs a number of Kendriya Vidyalaya (Central Schools) and Jawahar Navodaya Vidyalaya for rural students.[22] Both of them have been successful in providing quality education especially to the weaker sections of the society.

The number of private schools, including school-chains, missionary schools as well as madrasas has increased in the post liberalisation phase. Presently, most of the schools in Bihar are affiliated with the Bihar School Examination Board, while some of them to the CBSE and ICSE boards.[23]

Modern Bihar has an inadequate educational infrastructure creating a huge mismatch between demand and supply. This problem is further compounded by massive increase in population. The craving for higher education among the general populace of Bihar has led to migration of the student community from the state.[24]

In spite of the meagre investment on education in Bihar and poor conditions of schools, its students have done well in comparison to other Indian states. National institutes of learning such as IITs, IIMs, and AIIMs have had good representation from this state.[25]

Since 2006-2007, the enrolment ratio at the primary level in Bihar has been increasing and is now better than the average of several large states of India. However, this rate at the upper primary level is one of the lowest. Bihar has a higher out of school rate than the average of India. It is another fact that its percentage has been declining over time.[26] In line with the enrolment numbers, this rate is higher among older children.

Bihar performs poorly in the provision of basic schooling inputs.[27] It has the highest student-teacher as well as the student-classroom ratios among Indian states.[28] The proportion of classrooms in good condition is just 60%.[29]

But, the state has made some progress in recent years in the provision of drinking water in schools, and is now ranked above the average of India on this measure. However, the fact that roughly 10% of the primary schools lack access to drinking water facilities shows a sorry affair. Bihar despite focusing on hiring female teachers for primary school has only 20% of schools with separate toilets for girls.[30]

The state government has taken steps for preventing disease transmission in institutional area by implementing a massive deworming programme in 2011. Some researches have shown that 37.8% of Bihar's teachers could not be found during unannounced visits to schools. This is probably the worst teacher absence rate in India. But the problem is not just confined to teachers but also related with the demand of education. Many parents and children perceive the returns from schooling less than the early employment. Resultantly, people are choosing to under educate themselves. There is also lack of public information regarding the advantages of proper education.

But the situation is definitely changing. The State Education Department has planned to set up 410 model schools and upgrade 750 primary schools to secondary level.[31] This department has also initiated 'Shiksha Darpan Project' which plans to combine education and technology.[32] It is worthy to quote the statement of honourable Chief Minister of Bihar, Nitish Kumar in regard to his government's educational vision in the state.

> "Sound education is the only way which can take out Bihar from its socio economic problems."

Another milestone in the effort for improving the education in Bihar is the plan for establishment, revival, and restoration of the ancient Nalanda University at its original site as Nalanda International University. It is an international joint effort involving countries like Singapore, China, India, and Japan etc. They have planned to raise USD 1000 million to build this university and develop other necessary infrastructure.[33] The Indian Parliament passed a bill approving plans to rebuild the campus as a symbol of India's global ambitions.[34]

As seen above, the Kosi region and Madhepura district have been seat of higher learning in ancient and early medieval time. It is amply reflected by the evidences and ruins of Vikramshila University in present Bhagalpur district. The area has been also home to prolific literary giants and scholars in Sanskrit, Hindi, Maithili, and Bengali during late medieval and modern periods. Mandan Mishra and his wife Bharti of Mahisi (in present Saharsa district) are famous for their scholarly debate with Shankaracharya. But off late, the region has lost its erstwhile glory.

Today, its educational scenario is a pathetic tale of utter neglect and apathy. Even 65 years after India's independence, there are very few institutes and centers of higher learning in the area. Moreover, the quality is big concern in exiting institutes. In fact, one of the reasons is the lopsided and regionally imbalanced educational development in post-independence era in Bihar state.

The capital city, Patna and the neighbouring areas received more favour. Patna has become an educational hub for the state as well as the whole Eastern India. It hosts a reputed university, technical and vocational colleges, and quality schools etc. The city has also developed as an important centre for preparation of competitive exams such as IAS, IITs, IIMs, engineering, medical, management, chartered accountancy, banking, and railway etc. The quality of school education is quite better in Patna than other districts of the state like Madhepura. Resultantly, there is a significant migration of students from the Kosi belt and Madhepura district in search for better and competitive education.

As a matter of fact, the Kosi belt and Madhepura district are lagging behind many of the districts of the state at most levels of education. According to the 2011 census, the literacy rate in the district is 53.78 % (858886). The situation is relatively better in cases of primary and secondary education. There are 834 government schools and dozens of privately run schools imparting education in Madhepura district.[35] But the initiative on behalf of private sector is still poor. Till very recently; Madhepura did not have any national level public school for secondary and higher secondary education.[36] In contrast, Purnea and some other neighbouring districts of Kosi are better placed in different tiers of education.

Especially the former has emerged as the educational hub for almost the whole north-eastern Bihar and border districts of Bengal. According to one estimate, Purnea city and the neighbouring areas are hosting more than 300 schools of different levels. In fact, the city boasts of some well known national level schools. Recently, the foundation stone for an international level school has also been laid. Purnea is also having several institutes of higher and technical learning. Besides the government run and aided institutions; several private Engineering Colleges, Teacher Training colleges, polytechnics, and coaching institutes have mushroomed. At least, three medical colleges are proposed.[37] There is also a plan to set up a private university and a technical College in Parora area on sprawling campuses.[38] The neighbouring districts of Katihar and Kishanganj also boast of medical and engineering colleges run by trust and societies.

Why Madhepura lagged behind is an interesting question to probe. This is more intriguing in light of the prominent leaders representing the district in parliament from time to time. One of the probable reasons is, unlike Purnea, Madhepura district lacks big educational entrepreneurs.[39] Besides, the dearth of general infrastructure and low literacy rate in the district are also to be blamed. Moreover, Kosi's vagaries in the district also seemed to have loomed large on the minds of entrepreneur. The district headquarter is also bounded on two different sides Kosi *dhar*. This impedes the scope of spatial expansion of the town and any big project which may need large space.

Interestingly, the district headquarter hosts the main campus of B. N. Mandal University.[40] Undoubtedly, it has contributed to the development of better educational and academic environment in the district. Besides offering the traditional courses in Arts, Sciences, and Commerce; the university also provides the opportunity for technical and vocational learning.[41] It has dozens of constituent, semi-aided, and self-financed colleges.[42] The government of Bihar has also proposed to open a medical college in Madhepura town under the aegis of this university.[43]

Madhepura town hosts a thriving academic community. Off late, the B. N. Mandal University has hosted several national and other seminars enhancing the educational environment of the district and Kosi belt. But everything is not well with the university. It is suffering from some administrative instability besides other things. In the first four months of 2013, it saw four vice-chancellors. This easily reflects a sorry state of affairs regarding higher education in Bihar. Moreover, when it comes to the number of technical and vocational institutes, Madhepura again lags behind. Besides the government initiatives, there is need for private efforts as well. Recently, one college of education was established in the vicinity of the town successfully.[44]

Moreover, parents as well as children give lot of emphasis in this area on choosing a doctoral, engineering, or administrative profession. The other field of studies such as journalism, fashion designing, animation, research, teaching, and management etc., are broadly neglected. This is because of typical social mindset which does not allow students to think out of box. If Kosi area and Madhepura have to make progress in educational realm then their people will have to come out of this traditional mind set.

Thus we can say that Madhepura and Kosi region has been leading the beacon of education in ancient and early medieval times. This early lead was loosened to some extent in the succeeding periods.[45] It recovered partially in the nineteenth and early twentieth centuries. But, the first five decade of post-independence era was disappointing when compared with the educational development in other states of India. Again the 'sleeping dragon' seemed to wake up in this century. Bihar in general and Madhepura district and surrounding in particular are making progress in educational realm. But lots need to be done.

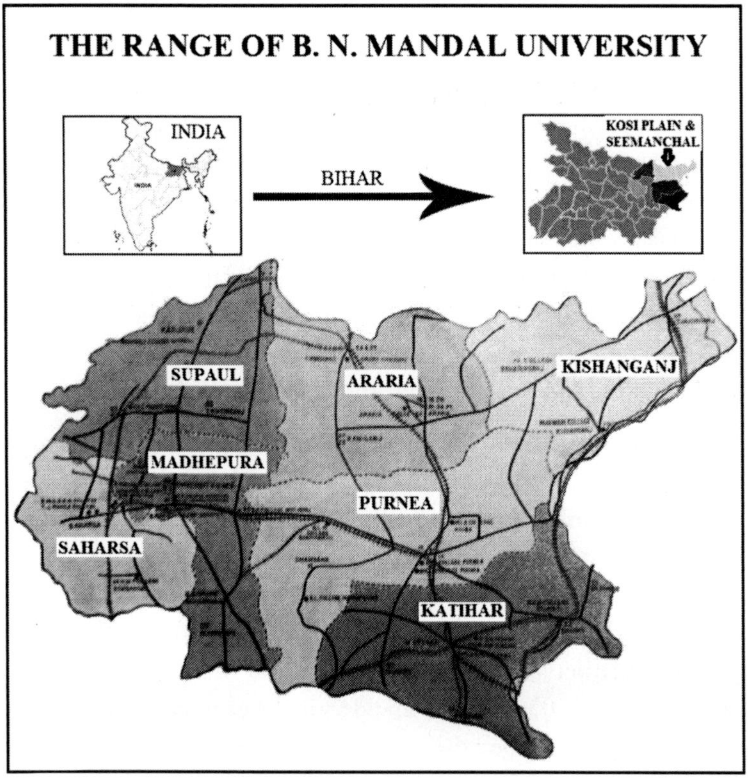

Map 7: It shows the range (Kosi region and neighbouring districts) of B. N. Mandal University

The Bihar government's recent policy initiatives and improvements in primary school enrolment amply show that the former has focused on lowering the cost of schooling in the state through subsidizing or providing textbooks, uniforms, bicycles, and cash transfers for attendance etc. But much remains to be done to boost schooling infrastructure and improve conditions for both students and teachers. Policymakers must universally provide drinking water facilities, and separate toilets for girls in schools. They should also improve the student-teacher ratio and ensure that classrooms are in good condition.

The government needs to indulge in information campaigns regarding the returns of education. It has to understand the determinants of household's decision regarding investment in education.[46] Moreover, the government needs to think beyond the quantity and quality of educational inputs. The performance-related pay for teachers can play an important role in improving the quality of education in the state and district. However, to be able to link student performance to teacher effectiveness, a state-wide data system is a prerequisite. We also require special initiative from the Bihar government and Madhepura district administration to facilitate and open technical and vocational institutes in Kosi region and the district.

All these will help the Kosiite and Madhepurian to access high quality education in their homeland. Moreover, it will also facilitate educational tourism in the area as a better educational infrastructure is bound to attract students from other neighbouring districts. It would be a good idea to emphasize the development of English language skills, given their high returns in the job market today. With proper education and guidance, the youth of Madhepura and Kosi can do wonders. If all the stakeholders make genuine effort towards these goals, there will be a rise and positive change in education system of Bihar, Kosi belt, and Madhepura.[47]

NOTES AND REFERENCES

1. At its peak, Nalanda University attracted scholars and students from as far away as Tibet, China, Greece, Indonesia, Turkey, and Persia.
2. His identity is uncertain. Sakraditya might have been either Kumara Gupta I or Kumara Gupta II of the Gupta Dynasty. The University of Nalanda seems to have been established during his reign. Both Xuanzang (the Tang Dynasty Chinese monk and pilgrim) and Prajnavarman cite him as the founder, as does a seal discovered at the Nalanda site.
3. The entrance of many of the *viharas* in the Nalanda University ruins can be seen with a bow marked floor. The bow was the royal sign of the Gupta.
4. Harsha seemed to have granted 200 villages to the monastery.

5. The complex is built with red bricks.
6. At this time, it was dominated by the liberal cultural traditions inherited from the Gupta age.
7. In the seventh century, Xuanzang records the number of teachers at Nalanda as being around 1510. Of these, approximately 1000 were able to explain 20 collections of sutras and shastras, 500 were able to explain 30 collections, and only 10 teachers were able to explain 50 collections. Xuanzang was among the few who were able to explain 50 collections or more. At this time, only the abbot Silabhadra had studied all the major collections of sutras and sastras at Nalanda.
8. The library of Nalanda is also known as *Dharma Gunj* (mountain of truth) or *Dharmaganja* (treasury of truth), was one of the most renowned repository of knowledge in the world at the time. Its collection comprised hundreds of thousands of volumes, so extensive that it burned for approximately more than 6 months when set aflame by Turkish invaders. The library had three main buildings- *Ratnasagara* (sea of jewels), *Ratnodadhi* (ocean of jewels), and *Ratnaranjaka* (delighter of jewels) - as high as nine stories tall.
9. The courses were drawn from every field of learning, Buddhist and Hindu, sacred and secular, foreign and native. Students studied science, astronomy, medicine, and logic as diligently as they applied themselves to metaphysics, philosophy, Samkhya, Yoga-shastra, the Veda, and the scriptures of Buddhism. They also learned foreign philosophy likewise.
10. He described how the regularly laid-out towers, forest of pavilions, *harmikas* and temples seemed to "soar above the mists in the sky" so that from their cells the monks "might witness the birth of the winds and clouds." The pilgrim states: "An azure pool winds around the monasteries, adorned with the full-blown cups of the blue lotus; the dazzling red flowers of the lovely kanaka hang here and there, and outside groves of mango trees offer the inhabitants their dense and protective shade."
11. The Persian historian Minhaj-i-Siraj, in his chronicle the *Tabaqat-I-Nasiri*, reported that thousands of monks were burned alive and thousands beheaded. Khilji tried his best to uproot Buddhism. The burning of the library continued for several months and "smoke from the burning manuscripts hung for days like a dark pall over the low hills."

12. He found a 90 year old teacher, Rahula Shribhadra, instructing a class of about 70 students.
13. It is known to us mainly through Tibetan sources, especially the writings of Taranatha, the Tibetan monk historian of sixteenth and seventeenth centuries.
14. According to Tibetan sources five great *Mahaviharas* stood out such as Vikramashila, the premier university of the era; Nalanda, past its prime but still illustrious; Somapura; Odantapura; and Jaggadala. They formed a network. There existed a system of co-ordination among them. It was common for great scholars to move easily from position to position among them.
15. It is approachable through 11 km long motorable road diverting from National Highway 80 at Anadipur and about 2 km from Kahalgaon.
16. He is considered as founder of the Sarma traditions of Tibetan Buddhism.
17. There was one each for the eastern, western, first central, second central, northern, and southern gates.
18. They were roughly 108 in number.
19. There were roughly 160 of them including *paGitas.*
20. They were roughly 1,000 in number.
21. Its bureaucrats were trained for law and order duties.
22. Former was started by the late Prime Minister Rajiv Gandhi.
23. The Kendriya Vidyalaya and a few other elite schools including the Christian missionary schools are affiliated to CBSE and ICSSE boards.
24. This has led to thousands of students seeking educational opportunities in other states, such as Delhi and Karnataka especially for higher level education.
25. A survey has shown their better absorption capacity of teaching than students of other states.
26. According to the government record, out-of-school rate in the age group 6-14 was 6.3% in 2007, a big drop from 12.8 per cent in 2006.
27. It holds true both in absolute terms and in relation to other states in India.
28. In 2009-2010, Bihar had 53 students to every one teacher, while the national average was 26. As far as student-classroom ratio is concerned,

it is also very poor, with over 80 students per classroom in all years surveyed, far above the national average.

29. It is below the national average and also 20 percentage points below the best performing state in India.
30. Other studies have found availability of a separate girls' toilet to be an important determinant both of female schooling and teacher attendance.
31. These have been planned with a fund of Rs. 1300 crores. The project will be run under the "Rashtriya Madhyamik Siksha Abhiyan (RMSA)," for which the centre would allocate around Rs. 2000 crores to Bihar.
32. Interestingly, a call centre has also been attached with this project to handle complaints from students, teachers, and general public.
33. On 28 May 2007, *Merinews* reported that the revived university's enrollment will be 1,137 in its first year, and 4,530 by the fifth year. In the second phase, enrollment will reach 5,812. On 12 June 2007, *News Post India* reported Japanese diplomat Noro Motoyasu statement that "Japan will fund the setting up an international university in Nalanda in Bihar." The report goes on to say that "The proposed university will be fully residential, like the ancient seat of learning at Nalanda. In the first phase of the project, seven schools with 46 foreign faculty members and over 400 Indian academics would come up... The university will impart courses in science, philosophy, and spiritualism along with other subjects. A renowned international scholar will be its chancellor." It has been decided that Nalanda would largely be a post-graduate research university, with School of Buddhist studies, philosophy, and comparative religion; School of historical studies; School of International Relations and Peace; School of Business Management and Development; School of Languages and Literature; and, School of Ecology and Environmental Studies. The objective of the school was claimed to be "aimed at advancing the concept of an Asian community...and rediscovering old relationships."
34. It was reported on 13 September 2010 by the *Jakarta Globe*.
35. Some of the reputed schools are B. R. Oxford Residential Public School, Don Bosco Academy, Kiran Public School, Holy Cross, Holy angels, Wisdom Public School, Madhepura Public School, St. Johns Public School, Shiv Nandan Prasad Mandal High School, Keshav Kanya High School, Rash Bihari High School, B. L. High School, Parasmani High

School, M.M. High School, Yadav High School, Project Kanya High school, and Kidzee etc.

36. Madhepura saw the establishment of two reputed school in 2011 and 2012. One of them is situated near to Sukhasan Dhar in the vicinity of the town. The second one named after Subhash Chandra Bose has been established in village Khurda by the family of Papu Yadav, the former Member of Parliament. Both these schools are privately run.
37. These include Bihar government proposed medical college within Sadar Hospital, two medical colleges proposed by minority run society and trust. One of them has been named as Shershah Suri Medical College.
38. The plan for the university was revealed by Dr. Imam of Millia Educational Trust in a personal meeting with one of the authors in the month of August 2012. The proposed technical college has been named as Kosi Institute of Technology and Research to be started in Ganeshpur near Kajha Kothi besides the state highway.
39. Purnea is lucky to have such entrepreneurs like Dr. Imam, Ramesh Mishra, Gautam Sinha, and Vanu etc.
40. There is a popular story related to its establishment. Generally, local populace believes that the seat of university's main campus according to original plan was Saharsa town. But, Lalu Prasad Yadav facilitated its establishment in Madhepura. Interestingly, the university main campus is located in so called Laloonagar area of the town. A new campus is under construction in the vicinity.
41. The courses offered by university include general courses such as B. A, B. Sc, B. Com, M. A, M. Sc, and M. Com. The technical and vocational courses includes B. C. A, B. B. A, Bio-Technology, B. Ed, Engineering, and Medical etc. Surprisingly, for a long time B. Ed was being offered only in very few colleges. But recently, NCTE gave approval to six colleges of this university to start this course from 2012 academic calendar. Interestingly, only one college out of them could start the course in 2012-13 academic calendars. So an opportunity to train hundreds of students was lost for a year. In April 2013 B. N. M. U geared up under the vice-chancellor ship of Anant Kumar to start the B. Ed course for the 2013-14 academic calendar.
42. These colleges include Adarsh College, Ghailarh; Alsam's Millia College, Purnea; ALY College, Tribeniganj; Araria College, Araria; Balrapur

College, Balrampur; BM College, Barari; BNC College, Dhamdaha; BNMV College, Madhepura; BS College, Simraha; BSS College, Supaul; Commerce College, Madhepura; CM Science College, Madhepura; Degree College, Supaul; DS College, Katihar; Evening College, Saharsa; Forbesganj College, Forbesganj; GLM College, Banmankhi; HS College, Udakishunganj; JDSS Mahila College, Forbesganj; KB Women's College, Madhepura; KB Jha College, Katihar; KD College, Raniganj; KND College, Raghopur; KP College, Murliganj; LN College, Bangaon; LNMS College, Birpur; Madhepura College, Madhepura; Marwari College, Kishanganj; MHM College, Sonbarsa; MJM Mahila College, Katihar; MLA College, Kasba; MLDPKY College, Araria; MLT College, Saharsa; ND College, Rambagh; Nehru College, Bahadurganj; Nirmali College, Nirmali; People's College, Araria; Parvati Science College, Madhepura; Purnea College, Purnea; Purnea Mahila College, Purnea; RDS College, Salmari; Ramesh Jha Mahila College, Saharsa; RKS Mahila College, Kishanganj; RL College, Madhavnagar; RM College, Saharsa; RPM College, Madhepura; SAKND College, Madhepura; RY Manhari College, Manihari; SNS Mahila College, Supaul; SNS RKS College, Saharsa; SNSY College, Purnea; SRCD College, Katihar; TP College, Madhepura; UVK College, Karama; and YNP College, Raniganj etc.

43. But, it is still in limbo. The project is marred by lack of seriousness and other problems. Medical Council of India's representatives have visited the site, but refused to give green signal due to lack of sufficient infrastructure.
44. This is M. P. College of Education. It is providing teacher training education.
45. Ahir considers the destruction of the temples, monasteries, and centers of learning at Nalanda and other places of northern India to be responsible for the demise of ancient Indian scientific thought in mathematics, astronomy, alchemy, and anatomy.
46. This could be an important component of academic research and policy.
47. Moreover, the education system and culture can definitely improve if youth takes up the responsibility.

12

Epilogue: The Incredible Madhepura

The present treatise explored and analyzed several aspects of Madhepura district and related areas by now. It begins with a probe into one of the central proposition of this work as how Madhepura is a forgotten land.[1] It has been followed by reconnoitering the location, administrative history, and modern settlement and subsistence pattern of the district. Then it moves on to discuss the geology, topography, physical features, climate, soil, flora, and fauna of Madhepura and Kosi region and modification in them.

Thereafter, an attempt has been made to reconstruct the general history of Madhepura and surroundings from earliest times to present. This is followed by description of the explored past human settlement of archaeological and historical importance in the district. Then the work tries to analyze and understand the distribution of previous communities over the landscape of Madhepura. This analysis is taken further by examining and reconstructing their settlement pattern. Now, it seems appropriate to investigate the second central proposition of this book "Why Madhepura is incredible?"

Madhepura district constitutes a small segment of the great Gangetic plain that has evolved over a very long period of time, from the Tertiary period to the present. Although there are conflicting opinions about the thickness of alluvial deposit of this Indian plain, it seems to be somewhere between 1,000 to 8,000 meters.[2] This sits over older rocks of Gondwana, Cretaceous, Tertiary, and Siwalik formations.

As far as its geological formation is concerned that mainly consists of the Archean rocks, the Gondwana rocks, and the Gangetic alluvium. Latter obscures the extensions of the Chota Nagpur plateau and the Indian Peninsula underneath. This alluvium is the result of thousands of year's deposition by Ganges and her tributaries, including Kosi.

Madhepura falls in the middle Gangetic plain. It forms the continuation of the great alluvial plain of Tirhut, being intersected by several rivers. Madhepura lies exactly in Kosi plain. Kosi and its distributaries flow through it. This mighty river is the "lifeline" as well as "sorrow" for the local people. Kosi is notorious for its frequent flood havoc due to overflow of its channels and shift in the course. The river has been steadily shifting its course from east to west.[3]

This great ancient river practically influences almost every walk of people's life from settlement pattern to culture. The unpredictable nature of Kosi weighs heavily in the psyche of inhabitants of the district. They tend to establish their settlements relatively at safer places if possible.[4] However sometimes, populace is extremely resilient.[5] People's food production,[6] dietary habits,[7] languages,[8] architecture,[9] and in few cases even professions[10] and leisure time activities[11] are heavily influenced by this river.

Generally, Madhepura's soil is productive and possesses two type of alluvium: *Khadar* and *Bhangar*, former being more prominent. Madhepura is largely having a level plain. Its physical feature is characterized by rivers, their dead arms, the old courses, numerous *dhar*, number of tree and plants, and cropped farmlands etc.

The district has a mixed climate consisting of winter, summer, and monsoon seasons. It experiences chilly winter, very hot summer, and rainy monsoon. Madhepura has humid environment. Quite often, it is also lashed by storms, cyclones, and thunderstorms.

Overall, the vegetation of Madhepura district is of a deciduous type, intermixed with evergreen trees. Its present natural vegetation outside the cultivated realm is mainly of savannah and parkland type typified by extensive meadows and grasslands and punctuated by trees. Farm crops, orchards, groves of trees, and clumps of bamboos are in abundance.

Farmers grow two crops a year in *Rabi* and *Kharif* seasons, cereals like paddy, wheat, maize, *marua*, and *koni* are cultivated. The main cash crops are sugarcane and jute. The commonly grown fruits are mango, litchi, jackfruit, guava, blackberry, custard-apple, banana, pineapple, muskmelon, watermelon, pear, mint, palm, coconut, groundnut, pomegranate, papaya, plum, *makhana,* and date, etc.

The local inhabitants produce several varieties of vegetables, such as cauliflower, cabbage, brinjal, lady finger, bitter-gourd, peas, drumstick, sweet potato, pumpkin, potato, onion, tomato, red chilly, capsicum, carrot, radish, turnip, lemon, nigella, turmeric, ginger, garlic, gram, cucumber, and fenugreek, etc.

People also cultivate several types of lentils and oilseeds, like kidney beans, *arhar*, *masoor*, black gram, *kurthee*, mustard, linseed, sunflower, and seasum etc. They adorn their gardens with marigold, rose, jasmine (*chameli*), magnolia (*champa*), *karotan*, *singhara*, and *arhul*, etc.

One can sight other common trees, such as sheesham, siras, banyan, pakar, bo tree (*pipal*), tamarind, azadirachta indica (*neem*), cassia (*tejpatta*), basil (*tulsi*),[12] babul, catechu (*kaitha*), chilbil, stramonium (*dhatoora*),[13] myrtle (*meanhdee*),[14] and castor[15] etc. These are used for several purposes, such as timber, firewood, and medicine etc.

As far as the fauna of Madhepura district is concerned, there seems wide contrast between the present and past scenarios. In earlier days, even up a century and a half back, wide varieties of herbivores and carnivores- elephant, lion, tiger, rhinoceros, black buck, and wild ass - flourished.

Today, mainly wolf, fox, jackal, hyena, ox, buffalo, cow, dog, goat, sheep, horse, hog, hare, rat, ass, sparrows, cuckoo (*koyal*), patridge (*titar*), nightingale, parrot, pigeon, crow, *maina,*[16] *neelkanth, kathphorwa, kohwar rani,* hen, cock, duck, dove, black raven, white heron, eagle, vultures, wild gees, and teels etc., are found. The area abounds in a variety of insects such as flies, butterflies, bees, spiders, mosquitoes, cockroaches, frogs, bedbugs, lizards, scorpions, ants, snakes,[17] tortoises, and fishes.[18]

It seems that the natural phenomenon and people's intervention has drastically altered the natural landscape of Madhepura district. Besides well known Kosi's vagaries, people's intensive farming and deforestation has resulted into the present situation. The natural vegetation has been virtually obliterated[19] and ecological balance has reached a delicate stage. Any further manipulation with nature may cause untold miseries and destruction.

The present research work in Madhepura district helped in identifying dozens of important past human settlements. The broad cultural sequence emerging in the district is historical, medieval, and modern periods. There are sites from Mauryan, Kushana, Gupta, Pala, Sultanate, Mughal, British, and post-British times.

At the micro level, the general cultural pattern in Madhepura subdivision is early historical, early medieval, late medieval, and modern periods. The number of sites belonging to medieval and especially late medieval period is more than that of other periods. There are very few sites from the historical period (2). Moreover, there seems to be a break between early historical period and late medieval period. No site belonging to late historical period is found. Moreover, only one site of early medieval period has been recorded. It could be due to climatic conditions or the violent nature of river Kosi.

Most of the sites are dilapidated. Many are on the verge of extinction. Farming is done by villagers on many site; modern structures have also been built on the site.[20] It seems that the sites occupied in late medieval period in many instances continue to be occupied in early modern and late modern period too.

The cultural remains mainly consist of potsherds, bricks, stone idols, statues, and some wells and remains of walls. In some cases, the presence of coins has also been reported.

The local populace has some awareness of these past settlements. They have their own legends about them. Interestingly, some common or similar types of legends are associated to some of the sites. In many cases, the site is located in *chap* area or near some water bodies (canals and ponds). Usually, the water is sweet except in one or two cases, where it has more of iron content.

In Udakishunganj subdivision, the cultural pattern of the past human settlements is almost similar to of northern counterpart. The number of sites belonging to medieval and modern period is more than that of the historical period. At least one site belongs to early historical period and late historical period each. Seven and five sites are from medieval and modern periods respectively. So, there is no doubt about its continuous habitation by human being from early historical period to the present. Some sites have been occupied across different cultural periods.

The cultural remains found in this subdivision are bricks, traces of walls, potsherds, *jata*, *silla-lauree*, stone idols, stone plates, terracotta figurines, *kalshaee*, silver and copper coins, gold ornaments, *chulla-chakli*, metallic boat, Ashokan pillar, etc. Like Madhepura subdivision, most of the sites in Udakishunganj are also in a bad shape, almost on the verge of extinction.

The number of sites in early historical, late medieval, and modern periods is more in Madhepura than in Udakishunganj. The latter scores over the former in terms of human settlements in late historical and early medieval periods. It reflects that human being had been exploring the area because of suitability for their settlements and subsistence till early medieval period. It seems that they found the northern half to be more favourable and akin to their taste than the southern portion of the district by late medieval period. Thus not surprisingly, Madhepura subdivision became their favourite which continues till now.

But one intriguing matter is the greater number of late historical sites in southern Madhepura instead of the northern one. It could be due to the extinction of some of the sites by Kosi's vagaries. Probably, this enigma could be solved by future researches.

It seems that the northern area of Madhepura district was preferred by people, especially in medieval and modern phases. It could be because the southern half of the district is relatively less suitable for human settlement and subsistence than its northern counterpart. The ecological condition in Udakishunganj subdivision is inhospitable, as the area is marred by saline soil, water with more iron content, muddy flats, greater number of *chap* and *diyara* areas, and proneness to floods.

Overall, majority of the settlements in the district belong to modern and medieval periods. The present exercise resulted into very few historical period settlements. Madhepura district had its first human habitation in the historical phase, and remained under human occupation till now. However, there are relatively less settlements in the late historical and early medieval periods.

Several inferences can be drawn from this. First, although the life which began in historical period, it became favourite only during medieval period. This trend continued in the modern period as well. It may be because the area was densely forested and teeming with variety of fauna, some of which potentially dangerous, and also Kosi's turbulent nature.

The people did not have the sufficient technological knowhow and skills to control and tame nature. Another strong possibility is that many human settlements for the historical phase have been destroyed by natural and human intervention with the passage of time. This is because the sites of this phase have shown rich material milieu, those thriving settlements could not have survived in isolation.

The increase in the number of settlements and their size took place with the passage of time. It may be with some retrograde changes in between. The increasing size of settlements points towards aggradational patterns in the realm of population density at individual settlements and in the context of different geographical locales and at different point of time.

There is also enhancement in area of influence as well as material culture over the period of time. There seem to be gradual evolution in subsistence pattern of the past inhabitants of the district. All these aspects been influenced by the prevailing micro environment and social conditions.

When the past settlements of Madhepura district are compared with those of its neighbouring districts, such as Bhagalpur and Munger, the latter are better placed in terms of continuous human habitation from prehistoric times to medieval period. But Madhepura is in better situation than Purnea and Saharsa districts as far as transition in cultural period from historical to modern phase is concerned. It seems that the human habitation shifted form southern Gangetic region to northern Gangetic area (i.e., Madhepura and neighbouring areas).

This work also explored and analyzed the process of site selection, size of settlements, and their cultural composition. The past humans have been very rational in selecting the sites for their habitation. Most of the sites are located on flat land but at a relatively higher ground from their surroundings in order to be safe from any threat of flood water. This must have been based on the experience and experiments of generations. Secondly, overwhelming majority of the sites is located near water bodies.

The size of site and thickness of cultural deposition show variations across periods. In all the cultures, there are some sites which are quite large. But simultaneously, there are sites which are medium to very small. This may either represent the coexistence of smaller and bigger communities or society performing different functions or the contraction and extinction of sites due to natural and artificial interventions. Former is a strong possibility because of the vagaries of Kosi in the area since time immemorial.

Moreover, the wide variations in cultural possessions may represent the number of years a particular settlement has been inhabited and their material milieu or disturbance and destruction with the passage of time. Impressive cultural remains recorded across culture; include baked bricks, potsherds, stone sculptures, stone idols, remnants of structures. Their quantity is also good enough. But coins, cowries, metal items, and tools are rare.

Since Madhepura district is mainly composed of new alluvium, all the explored sites are located in *Khadar* soil. A very small segment of the district bordering Saharsa is saline and alkali saline. Not surprisingly, none of the settlements is situated in this area. The *Khadar* soil of the district could be divided into *chiknee*, *domat*, and *baluhaee* soils.

The overwhelming majority of the sites are placed in *domat* and *baluhaee*. Moreover, not even a single human settlement has been found in *chiknee* soil up to early medieval period. It seems that nature and its tremendous power weighed heavily upon the choices of human beings. Moreover, they were also helpless given the less advanced level of their technological knowhow.

So, they preferred to settle on *domat* and *baluhaee* soils than *chiknee* as the former two were more suitable for human settlement and subsistence. Perhaps, they could not effectively and efficiently negotiate with the conditions arising out of settlements being in *chiknee* soil- water logging, problems in transport facilities, disease, non-suitability of soil for several types of crops, and deep ploughing, etc.

Generally speaking, the sweet drinking water is available at 15-35 feet in Madhepura district. The overwhelming majority of the sites is found within this water level. Furthermore, the district could be divided into two sub-soil water level zones such as 15-25 feet and 25-35 feet. Majority of the sites are in the 15-25 feet water level zone. Moreover, the water is generally sweet. But at some places, iron content is more. All the explored settlements except one are located in sweet drinking water zone with normal iron content.

The major crops grown in Madhepura are rice, wheat, jute, sugarcane, pulses, and vegetables. The district could be divided into two cropping zones such as Cropping Zone-I (northern half consisting of rice, wheat, jute, mooang, khesaree, and vegetables) and cropping zone-II (southern half consisting of rice, wheat, and sugarcane). Majority of the sites belong to Cropping Zone-I. It seems to have become favourite of human being since medieval period onwards. Since there is a possibility of lot of changes in cropping pattern from historical period up to present so these inferences could only be tentative.

The explored settlements have been divided on the basis of their function in terms of habitation, religious, and habitation cum religious nature. Interestingly, most of the human settlements across the period are of habitation nature. This especially holds true from medieval period onwards. It reflects the increasing involvement of human beings in religious affairs besides their worldly matters and the increasing complexity of their religious belief and practices.

In order to analyze the past human settlements in terms of rank size and demography, the explored past settlements have been divided into ten categories. Moreover, as far as the estimated population in those days is concerned, 20 persons per 1000 sq. m. have been considered. The historical settlements are found in very few categories. Interestingly, the 3 selected historical period sites represent three distinct categorie,s such as small, medium, and large. The medieval and modern sites belong to most of the set denominations.

There is a lot of variety in the size and population of these sites. This may be due to more number of settlements in the case of medieval and modern periods in comparison with historical phase. Moreover, this point towards the increasing complexity with the passage of time.

There is increase in the number of sites from historical to medieval and then to modern phase, though the size of the study area remained same. This may point towards improvement in carrying capacity. Moreover, it may indicate towards enhancement in operative variables determining the carrying capacity. But it is to be noted that although the number of settlements increases across the period, the upsurge from medieval to modern phase was less in comparison to historical to medieval period. It may depict the diminishing return in terms of carrying capacity in spite of improvement in social variables.

Moreover, though the number of sites increased in every succeeding phase, many of these new settlements were smaller in size and population. All these show splitting up or branching off tendencies. Such phenomenon may be caused by declining carrying capacity, influx of new population, change in environment, epidemics, social beliefs and practices, and a new trend in society towards individuality and nuclear family system, etc.

Madhepura is decently endowed with natural resources and beauty. It enjoys one of the best and richest soils in the Indian subcontinent. The district has abundance of good quality water resources. This is a blessing when the different Indian states and people are struggling intermittently over distribution of scarce water resources in their area.[21] The sweet drinking water is available at a very low depth. Although, the district lacks in general mineral resources, nature has gifted it with good quality soil and plenty of sands suitable for pottery making and construction industries respectively.[22]

Madhepura has lush greenery and abundant quality wood for development of timber industry. It has suitable climate with good amount of rainfall. Probably, all these helped it to build a glorious history. The latter start with early historical period and continues to present. The great *Janapada* and *Mahajanapada*, Maurya, Kushana, Gupta, Pala, Rajputs, Delhi Sultanate, Mughal, and British held their sway over the area in succession. Madhepura's people have also played a significant role in the freedom struggle of the country. Besides, the area and its surrounding region has also played and important role in the educational realm as well in past.

All these are amply reflected in the remains and facts of the past. The discovery of number of archaeological and historical sites in the district further proves this point. An interesting picture of human's settlement distribution and pattern emerges over time. There are some very important sites such as Sirinagar, Khuran, Nayanagar, and Madhukar Chak-I. They need to be properly excavated and developed for tourism.

Madhepura occupies a place of prominence across the periods. But, it nearly lost that position in post-independence era due to petty politics. It stands neglected in independent India. The successive central and state governments have handed over pieces of cakes in between which are insufficient. Its land and people deserve better. In recent years, Madhepura and neighbouring districts are developing as centers of education.[23] It is adjacent to the region where two major religions of the world- Buddhism and Jainism originated. All these amply reflect Madhepura's incredibility.

Madhepura is also incredible because it has withstood the vagaries of time, nature, environment, and human activities. It has stood tall and unmoved during all assaults on its existence. Consequent upon all kinds of neglect, it has shown resilience. During different periods, it has moved along with various dynasties and rulers. Madhepura has not only observed them, but benefitted from their cultural, social, economical, and administrative characteristics.

Even during the post-independence period, it has moved ahead despite the onslaught by petty-politics and vested interests. Madhepura is still marching ahead socially, culturally, politically, and economically. Its inhabitants have registered progress in all walks of life and currently endeavouring hard to catch up with the modern fast developing world. Madhepura indeed is Incredible!

NOTES AND REFERENCES

1. In fact, this constitutes part of the central hypothesis of present work "Although Madhepura is a forgotten land, still it is incredible."
2. The thickness in middle Gangetic region may vary between 2,000 to 10,000 feet.
3. In the last two centuries, it has shifted hundreds of kilometers.
4. People tend to construct their houses on higher ground in order to escape and protect themselves from Kosi's flood. For instance, in the aftermath of 2008 massive inundation, several people from the flood affected area moved to higher areas such as neighbouring Purnea district. Moreover, some branches of Kosi which lay un-embanked are still shifting their course. In one case, people of Madrauni village facing the threat of extinction due to shifting of Kosi's course, almost completely relocated in higher locations.
5. There are several villages and hamlets almost situated on the bank of Kosi's *dhar* which may be engulfed any moment. Yet, either due to no option or other reasons, the inhabitants did not relocate.
6. People tend to cultivate different crops for varying altitudes- low lying and highland area.
7. Some of the crops and plants are typical to region.
8. The local dialect spoken in the area is Tenthi which is different from Maithili and Anga (spoken in neighbouring regions) in several ways such as vocabulary and pronunciations.

9. The people build the foundation of their houses high enough to avoid flood water entering into their houses.
10. People living near Kosi or its distributaries are engaged in fishing or transportation activities like playing ferries across the river.
11. People staying near Kosi or its *dhar* are good swimmers. The children learn to play with water at a young stage.
12. This is a sacred plant. It also has medicinal value. Almost every house in the area has having this plant. The ladies worship it and offer flowers and water every morning.
13. It is very common in the area. Stramonium locally called *dhatura* is poisonous. Sometimes, people use it to commit suicide.
14. This is the world famous heena used for dying the hair.
15. Though common, people probably do not know its value. It is wildly grown and generally goes waste.
16. It is yellow-brownish in colour.
17. One finds a variety of snakes such as *nag-nagin* (also called *gohman*), *krait, bahra-krait, dhamna, saguwa, harhara,* and *teleea* etc. *Krait* is about feet and half in size and black in colour. It is considered to be very poisonous. *Dhamna* is very long and believed to suck the milk out of newly mothers. Whereas *saguwa* is small in size and lives on tree leaves. People complain of its bite on head. *Teleea* is very small (roughly 5-20 centimeters) and a thin variety of snake often seen in monsoon season. In fact, snake bite is common especially during rainy season.
18. People breed freshwater fish. Since Madhepura district is rich in water resources such as river, canal, and pond, fishing has become an important activity in the area. Almost every village is having one or more ponds locally called *Pokhar.* Gradually, it has become an important means of livelihood for farmers as well as traditional fishermen.
19. The government has launched awareness and reforestation programs. It has toughened rules and regulations against deforestation. One could see the plantation of several trees especially sissoo and mango along roads and canals.
20. These may be due to lack of awareness about the cultural heritage.
21. The best example is that of Kaveri River water dispute between Karnataka and Tamilnadu and Mullaperiyar Dam (on the Periyar River)

dispute between Tamilnadu and Kerala. In fact, Bihar has the capacity to meet the needs of several water thirsty states of India.

22. The *chiknee* soil is also suitable for plastering the walls of a *Kachcha* house, which is commonly found in the area.
23. The B. N. Mandal University's main campus is located in the district headquarter. Besides, several private educational and training institutes have mushroomed up. The incumbent government is trying to start state engineering and medical colleges. Moreover, the neighbouring district of Purnea has already become the hub of education adding to the strength of Kosi region.

Appendices

APPENDIX-I: LIST OF COMMON FLORA AND FAUNA FOUND IN MADHEPURA DISTRICT AND KOSI PLAIN

FLORA

Table 6: List of commonly produced cereals

S. No	English Name of Cereal	Scientific Name of Cereal	Local Name of Cereal
1.	Barley	*Hordeum vulgare*	*Jau*
2.	Jute	*Corchorus capsularis and Corchorus olitorius*	*Ptuwa*
3.	*Koni*	-	*Koni*
4.	Maize	*Zea mays*	*Makaee*
5.	*Marwa*	-	*Marwa*
6.	Oats	*Avena Sativa*	*Jaee*
7.	Paddy	*Oryza Sativa*	*Dhan*
8.	Sugarcane	*Saccharum officinarum*	*Ketari (also Eekh or Ganna)*
9.	Wheat[1]	-	*Gehoon*

Table 6.1: List of usually grown fruits

S. No	English Name of Fruit	Scientific Name of Fruit	Local Name of Fruit
1.	Banana	*Musa paradisiaca*	*Kela*
2.	Blackberry	*Engenia jambolana*	*Jamun*
3.	Coconut	*Cocos nucifera*	*Nariyal*
4.	Custard-apple	*Annona reticulate*	*Shareefa*
5.	Date	*Phoenix dactylifera*	*Khajoor*
6.	Groundnut	*Apios americana*	*Muangfalee*
7.	Guava	*Psidium guajava*	*Amrood*
8.	Jackfruit	*Artocarpus heterophyllus*	*Kathal*
9.	Lychee	*Litchi chinensis*	*Litchi*
10.	*Makhana*	-	*Makhana*
11.	Mango	*Mangifera indica*	*Aam*
12.	Mint	*Mentha piperita, Mentha spicata,* and *Mentha pulegium*	*Pudeena*
13.	Muskmelon	*Cucumis melo*	*Kharbooja*
14.	Palm	*Palma-tar*	*Khajoor and Tad*
15.	Papaya	*Carica papaya*	*Papeeta*
16.	Pear	*Pyrus communis*	*Nashpatee*
17.	Pineapple	*Ananas comosus*	*Ananas*
18.	Plum	*Prunus domestica, Prunus salicina,* and *Prunus insititia*	*Ber*
19.	Pomegranate	*Punica granatum*	*Anar*
20.	Watermelon	*Citrullus lanatus*	*Tarbooj*

Table 6.2: List of normally grown vegetables

S. No	English Name of Vegetable	Scientific Name of Vegetable	Local Name of Vegetable
1.	Bitter-gourd	*Citrullus colocynthis*	*Krela*
2.	Brinjal	*Solanum melongena*	*Baiangan*
3.	Cabbage	*Brassica oleraceacapitata*	*Baandhagobhee*
4.	Capsicum	*Capsicum annum grossum*	*Shimla mirch or Pahari mirch*
5.	Carrot	*Daucus carota*	*Gajar*
6.	Cauliflower		*Phulgobhee*
7.	Cucumber	*Cucumis sativus*	*Kheera*

contd...

8.	Drumstick	-	*Sohijana*
9.	Fenugreek	*Trigonella foenum graecum*	*Methi*
10.	Garlic	*Allium sativum*	*Lahsun*
11.	Ginger	*Zingiber officinale*	*Adrakh*
12.	Gram	*Cicer arietinum*	*Chana*
13.	Lady finger	-	*Bhiandee*
14.	Lemon	*Citrus limon*	*Neeanboo*
15.	Onion	*Allium cepa*	*Pyaj*
16.	Peas	*Pisum sativum*	*Matar*
17.	Potato	*Solanum tuberosum*	*Aalu*
18.	Pumpkin	*Cucurbita maxima, Cucurbita mixta, Cucurbita moschata,* and *Cucurbita pepo*	*Kaddoo*
19.	Radish	*Raphanus sativus*	*Moolee*
20.	Chilli	*Capsicum annum, Capsicum annum longum,* and *Capsicum frutescens*	*Mirch*
21.	Sweet potato	*Ipomoea batatas*	*Shakkarkandi*
22.	Tomato	*Lycopersicon esculentum*	*Tamatar*
23.	Turmeric	*Curcuma longa*	*Haldi*
24.	Turnip	*Brassica rapa*	*Shalgam*

Table 6.3: List of pulses and oilseeds

S. No	English Name of Pulse and Oilseed	Scientific Name of Pulse and Oilseed	Hindi Name of Pulse and Oilseed
1.	-	-	*Kurthee*
2.	Lentil	*Lens culinaris*	*Masoor*
3.	Bengal gram	*Cacercicer*	*Chana*
4.	Black gram	*Phascolus radiatus*	*Urad*
5.	Horse gram	*Dolichos biflorus*	*Boot*
6.	Lentil green/Green gram/Kidney bean	*Phaseolus vulgaris* and *Vigna radiata*	*Mooang*
7.	Linseed	*Linum usitatissimum*	*Teesee*
8.	Mustard	*Mustum*	*Sarson*
9.	Red gram	*Cazanus indicus*	*Arhar*
10.	Seasum	*Sesamum indicum*	*Til*
11.	Sunflower	*Helianthus annuus*	*Sooryamukhee*

Table 6.4: List of commonly seen flowers

S. No	English Name of Flower	Scientific Name of Flower	Hindi Name of Flower
1.	Hibiscus	*Hibiscus macrophyllus*	*Arhul*
2.	Jasmine	*Jasminum officinale*	*Chamelee*
3.	Magnolia	*Magnolia grandiflora*	*Champa*
4.	Marigold	*Tagetes erecta, Tagetes patula,* and *Tagetes lucida*	*Geanda*
5.	Nigella[1]	-	*Kalauannee*
6.	Rose	-	*Gulab*

Table 6.5: List of commonly grown trees

S. No	English Name of Tree	Scientific Name of Tree	Hindi Name of Tree
1.	-	*Anona reticulata*	*Anta*
2.	Acacia	*Acacia arabica*	*Babool*
3.	Bamboo	-	*Baans*
4.	Banyan	*Ficus glomerata*	*Bargad*
5.	Basil	*Ocimum basilicum*	*Tulsee*
6.	Betel	*Piper betle*	*Pan*
7.	Bulrushes	*Cyperus papyrus*	*Narkat*
8.	Cassia	*Cinnamomum aromaticum*	*Tejpatta*
9.	Castor	*Ricinus communis*	*Aandee*
10.	Catechu	*Acacia catechu*	*Khair and Kattha*
11.	Chilbil	*Ulmus integrifolicus*	*Chilbil*
12.	Kaitha	*Feronia elephantum*	*Kaitha*
13.	Lisora	*Cordial myxa*	*Lisora*
14.	Myrtle	*Myrtus communis*	*Meanhdee*
15.	Neem	*Azadirachta indica*	*Neem*
16.	Pakar	*Ficus infectorisa*	*Pakar*
17.	Pipal	*Ficus religiosa*	*Pipal*
18.	Reedy grasses	-	*Pattiyo walee ghas*
19.	Sandalwood	*Santalum album*	*Shreekhand Chandan*
20.	Siras	*Albizzia lebbek*	*Siras*
21.	Sissoo	*Dalbergia sissoo*	*Sheesham*
22.	Stramonium	*Datura stramonium*	*Dhatoora*
23.	Tamarind	*Tamarindus indica*	*Imalee*
24.	Tamarisks	*Tamariscus*	*Jhau*

FAUNA

Table 6.6: List of familiar animals

S. No.	English Name of Animal	Scientific Name of Animal	Hindi Name of Animal
1.	Black buck	*Antilope cervicapra*	*Kala Hiran*
2.	Buffalo	*Bufalus*	*Bhaians*
3.	Cow	*Bos indicus*	*Gay*
4.	Dog	*Canis familiaris*	*Kutta*
5.	Elephant	*Loxodonta africana, Loxodonta cyclotis, and Elephas maximus*	*Hathee*
6.	Fox	*Vulpes vulpes*	*Lomdee*
7.	Goat	*Capra hircus*	*Bakdee*
8.	Hare	*Lepus americanus, Lepus californicus,* and *Oryctolagus cuniculus*	*Khargosha*
9.	Hog	*Potamochoerus chorcus*	*Suuar*
10.	Horse	*Equus caballus*	*Ghoda*
11.	Hyena	*Crocuta crocuta, Parahyaena brunnea,* and *Hyaena hyaena*	*Lkadbaggha*
12.	Jackal	*Canis aureus*	*Siyar or Geedad*
13.	Lion	*Panthera lio*	*Shaer*
14.	Ox	*Bos taurus*	*Bail*
15.	Palm civet	*Arctictis binturong, Poiana richardsoni, Prionodon pardicolor,* and *Prionodon linsang*	*Gandhbilaw*
16.	Rat	*Rattus norvegicus*	*Chooha*
17.	Rhinoceros	*Rhinoceros unicornis*	*Gainda*
18.	Sheep	*Ovis orientalis* and *Ovis vignei*	*Bhed*
19.	Tiger	*Panthera tigris*	*Bagh*
20.	Wild ass	*Equus hemionus*	*Janglee Gadha*
21.	Wild-cats	*Felis sylvestris*	*Janglee Billee*
22.	Wild hog	*Sus scrofa* and *Sus vittatus*	*Janglee Suuar*
23.	Wolf	*Canis lupus*	*Bhediya*

Table 6.7: List of insects

S. No.	English Name of Insect	Scientific Name of Insect	Hindi Name of Insect
1.	Ant	-	*Cheeantee*
2.	Bedbug	*Cimex lectularius*	*Khatmal*
3.	Bee	*Apis cerana*	*Madhumakkhee*
4.	Butterfly	*Glaucopsyche xerces, Vanessa cardui, Limenitis archippus,* and *Danaus plexippus*	*Titalee*
5.	Cockroach	*Blatella asahinai*	*Telchatta*
6.	Fish	-	*Machhlee*
7.	Fly	*Musca domestica*	*Makkhee*
8.	Frog	*Rana catesbeiana* and *Conraua goliath, Xenopus laevis, Rheobatrachus silus,* and *Rhinoderma darwini*	*Meandhak*
9.	Lizard	-	*Chipkalee*
10.	Mosquito	*Culex pipiens*	*Machchar*
11.	Scorpion	-	*Bichchhoo*
12.	Snake	-	*Saanp*
13.	Spider	-	*Makdee*
14.	Tortoise	*Pyxis arachnoides, Geochelone gigantean, Geochelone emys, Gopherus polyphemus,* and *Geochelone elephantopus.*	*Kachhuaa*

Table 6.8: List of common birds

S. No.	English Name of Bird	Scientific Name of Bird	Local Name of Bird
1.	Black raven	*Corvus corax*	*Kala-Kauaa*
2.	Cock	*Gallus gallus*	*Murga*
3.	Crow	*Corvus brachyrhynchos, Corvus caurinus, Corvus ossifragus,* and *Corvus imparatus*	*Kauaa*
4.	Cuckoo	*Cuculus canorus*	*Koyal*

contd...

5.	Dove	*Columba livia* and *Streptopelia risoria*	*Parkee*
6.	Duck	*Anas platyrhynchos*	*Battak*
7.	Eagle	*Haliaeetus leucocephalus* and *Haliaeetus albicilla*	*Garoor*
8.	Hen	*Gallus gallus*	*Murgee*
9.	Nightingale	*Luscinia megarhynchos*	*Bulbul*
10.	Parrot	*Probosciger aterrimus*	*Tota*
11.	Partridge	*Perdix perdix*	*Titar*
12.	Pigeon	*Columba livia*	*Kabootar*
13.	Sparrow	*Melospiza melodia, Spizella passerina,* and *Zonotrichia leucophrys*	*Goraiya*
14.	Teal	*Anas crecca, Anas discors, Anas cyanoptera,* and *Anas querquedula*	*Chaitee*
15.	Vulture	*Vultur gryphus, Cathartes aura, Coragyps atratus, Gymnogyps californianus,* and *Gyps rueppellii*	*Giddh*
16.	White heron	*Ardea herodias, Ardea cinerea, Butorides striatus, Nycticorax nycticorax,* and *Nyctanassa violacea*	*Ujala-Bagula*
17.	Wild goose	*Anser anser* and *Anser cygnoides*	*Jangalee Hans*

NOTES AND REFERENCES

1. Wheat is a member of the family Poaceae (formerly Gramineae). It makes up the genus *Triticum*. Today, the most common and commercially important varieties are common, club, and durum wheat.
2. Nigella is member of a genus of flowering plants of the buttercup family. Its flowers are of white, blue, and yellow colours. Nigella is native to Mediterranean and Western Asia region. It belongs to genus *Nigella*.
3. Grasses is a common name for a large family of flowering plants. The grass family contains about 635 general and 9000 species, making it the fourth largest family. It makes up the family Poaceae (formerly Gramineae).
4. Ants make up the family *Formicidae* in the order *Hymenoptera*.
5. Fishes are classified into more than 100 orders and suborders. The subphylum Vertebrata is divided into two super classes such as Agnatha

and Gnathostomata. With more than 2000 different species, catfish (named for whisker like feelers on their jaws) are a diverse collection of tenacious fish that have adapted to life in a variety of environments. One type of catfish is found in Madhepura, locally called *Siangahee Machlee* (*Clarias batrachus*). It is native to shallow ponds. When droughts cause these ponds to dry up, the walking catfish is capable of traveling across land to move to deeper ponds.

6. Scorpions belong to the order Scorpionida in the class Arachnida.
7. Snakes make up the suborder Serpentes in the lizard and snake order Squamata. It falls in the class Reptilia.
8. The common house spider belongs to the funnelweb spiders in the family Agelenidae and in the suborder Araneomorphae.

APPENDIX-II: VILLAGES OF MADHEPURA DISTRICT

Table 7: C. D. Blocks according to number of villages (from less to more)

SL. NO	BLOCK	NO OF VILLAGES
1.	Shankarpur	09
2.	Gamharia	12
3.	Ghailarh	16
4.	Bihariganj	22
5.	Singheshwar	27
6.	Alamnagar	29
7.	Puraini	31
8.	Chausa	43
9.	Udakishunganj	44
10.	Murliganj	45
11.	Madhepura	49
12.	Gwalpara	51
13.	Kumarkhand	71
TOTAL		449

Table 7.1: Villages in Alamnagar C. D. Block

C. D. BLOCK	VILLAGE CODE	VILLAGE NAME
ALAMNAGAR	1	BASANWARA
ALAMNAGAR	2	KHUMAN MILIK
ALAMNAGAR	3	BISPATTI
ALAMNAGAR	4	MOHIUDDINPUR
ALAMNAGAR	5	KESHOAPUR
ALAMNAGAR	6	LADMA
ALAMNAGAR	7	BARHAUNA
ALAMNAGAR	8	HARU DUMRA
ALAMNAGAR	9	KHURANMAL OR KHURAN
ALAMNAGAR	10	BARGAON
ALAMNAGAR	11	SANOTI CHAK
ALAMNAGAR	12	PARAIL
ALAMNAGAR	13	KAPASIA
ALAMNAGAR	14	KISHUNPUR RATWARA
ALAMNAGAR	15	GANGAPUR
ALAMNAGAR	16	KHAON
ALAMNAGAR	17	ITHARI
ALAMNAGAR	18	HARIHARPUR
ALAMNAGAR	19	PH ULAUT ENGLIS
ALAMNAGAR	20	KUNJAURI
ALAMNAGAR	21	NARTHUA BHAGIPUR
ALAMNAGAR	22	SHANKARPUR MADHAILI
ALAMNAGAR	23	TILAKPUR
ALAMNAGAR	24	MURAUT
ALAMNAGAR	25	ALAMNAGAR
ALAMNAGAR	26	GAUCHI DIH
ALAMNAGAR	27	SINGHAR
ALAMNAGAR	28	AKHA
ALAMNAGAR	29	MUZAFFAR PUR

Table 7.2: Villages in Bihariganj C. D. Block

C. D. BLOCK	VILLAGE CODE	VILLAGE NAME
BIHARIGANJ	1	BIHARIGANJ
BIHARIGANJ	2	BISHUN PUR JAI SINGH
BIHARIGANJ	3	HATHIUNDHA
BIHARIGANJ	4	BARHAYA
BIHARIGANJ	23	RAJGANJ
BIHARIGANJ	5	BABHANGAWAN
BIHARIGANJ	6	FATEHPUR
BIHARIGANJ	7	TULASIA
BIHARIGANJ	8	KALHAUTIA
BIHARIGANJ	9	SHEKHPURA
BIHARIGANJ	10	BAIJNATHPUR
BIHARIGANJ	11	LACHHMIPUR
BIHARIGANJ	12	RAHIJAGATPUR
BIHARIGANJ	13	MADHUKAR CHAK PARMANANDPUR
BIHARIGANJ	14	GAMAIL
BIHARIGANJ	15	GOALPARA
BIHARIGANJ	16	GANGAURA
BIHARIGANJ	17	BETAHI
BIHARIGANJ	18	PARARIA
BIHARIGANJ	19	LACHHMIPUR
BIHARIGANJ	20	MOHANPUR NISF
BIHARIGANJ	21	MOHANPUR CHAUMUKH
BIHARIGANJ	22	KUSTHAN OR KUSHATHAN

Table 7.3: Villages in Chausa C. D. Block

C.D BLOCK	VILLAGE CODE	VILLAGE NAME
CHOUSA	1	PHULAUT
CHOUSA	2	MORSANDA
CHOUSA	3	PACHRASI AMANAT SARKAR
CHOUSA	4	PACHRASI
CHOUSA	5	LAUALAGAON
CHOUSA	6	SARDAR KHAN SIPAHI JAGIR
CHOUSA	7	DAMAR SINGH HAWALDAR JAGIR
CHOUSA	8	BHATGAWAN
CHOUSA	9	ARAJPUR
CHOUSA	10	CHAUSA AMANAT SARKAR
CHOUSA	11	CHAUSA
CHOUSA	12	ENGLISH GHOSAI
CHOUSA	13	GHOSAI
CHOUSA	14	DHANSESHPUR
CHOUSA	15	PAINA
CHOUSA	16	AMANAT MANULLAH
CHOUSA	17	MANULLAH SUBEDAR JAGIR
CHOUSA	18	BHOLA SINGH JAMADAR
CHOUSA	19	AMANAT MANULLAH JAMADAR
CHOUSA	20	ETWARI JAMADAR JAGIR
CHOUSA	21	PAHARI SUBEDAR JAGIR
CHOUSA	22	AMANAT HEDAETULLAH SUBEDAR
CHOUSA	23	HIDAETULLAH JAMADAR JAGIR
CHOUSA	24	SUBHANI SUBEDAR JAGIR
CHOUSA	25	MOHAMAD HANIF KUMEDAN JAGIR
CHOUSA	26	KEWAT RAM SUBEDAR
CHOUSA	27	NIAMATULLAH SIPAHI JAGIR
CHOUSA	28	CHAMRU HAWALDAR JAGIR
CHOUSA	36	AMANAT MURGIKHAN SUBIDAR
CHOUSA	29	ENGLISH GHOSAI
CHOUSA	30	HASAN SHARIF JAMADAR JAGIR
CHOUSA	31	KHANKUMEDAN JAGIR
CHOUSA	32	RASULPUR DHURIA
CHOUSA	33	JIT SINGH SUBEDAR JAGIR
CHOUSA	34	JAMMAN KUMEDAN JAGIR
CHOUSA	35	DIN MOHAMMAD SUBEDAR JAGIR
CHOUSA	37	DIN MOHAMAD SUBIDAR JAGIR
CHOUSA	38	RAMAKANT SUBEDAR JAGIR
CHOUSA	39	GOVINDRAM KUMEDAN JAGIR
CHOUSA	40	LAUALAGAON AMANAT SARKAR
CHOUSA	41	MOHAMAD HYAT KUMEDAN JAGIR
CHOUSA	42	MOHAMMAD JAFAR SUBEDAR JAGIR
CHOUSA	43	MOHMMAD JAFAR SUBEDAR JAGIR

Table 7.4: Villages in Gamharia C. D. Block

C. D. BLOCK	VILLAGE CODE	VILLAGE NAME
GAMHARIYA	1	DAHA
GAMHARIYA	2	BABHANI BHELWA
GAMHARIYA	3	GAMHARIA
GAMHARIYA	4	AURAHI
GAMHARIYA	5	PIPRAHI
GAMHARIYA	6	RUPAULI (PART)
GAMHARIYA	7	JAGBANI
GAMHARIYA	8	PARWAHA
GAMHARIYA	9	TARAWE
GAMHARIYA	10	KAURIHAR
GAMHARIYA	11	CHIKNI
GAMHARIYA	12	JIVACHHPUR

Table 7.5: Villages in Ghailarh C. D. Block

C. D. BLOCK	VILLAGE CODE	VILLAGE NAME
GHAILARH	1	RATANPURA
GHAILARH	2	GHAILARH
GHAILARH	3	SIRINAGAR
GHAILARH	4	CHITTI
GHAILARH	5	BHATRANDHA
GHAILARH	6	GOT BARDAHA
GHAILARH	7	BARDAHA ARAZI RAMANA
GHAILARH	8	BARDAHA
GHAILARH	9	PIPRAHI CHAKLA
GHAILARH	10	PATHRAHA
GHAILARH	11	PATHRAHA
GHAILARH	12	JHITKIA
GHAILARH	13	BASDEWA
GHAILARH	14	BANCHOLHA
GHAILARH	15	BHAWAN TIKTHI
GHAILARH	16	ARRAHA

Table 7.6: Villages in Gwalpara C. D. Block

C. D. BLOCK	VILLAGE CODE	VILLAGE NAME
GWALPARA	1	DEPURA
GWALPARA	2	BISHUNPUR ARAR
GWALPARA	3	RESHASNA
GWALPARA	4	BABHANGAWAN
GWALPARA	5	TEMA
GWALPARA	6	MAHRAJGANJ
GWALPARA	7	RAKHIA PATTI
GWALPARA	8	CHATRA CHAK
GWALPARA	9	BIRGAON
GWALPARA	10	BIRGAON
GWALPARA	11	BIRGOAN
GWALPARA	12	KALOTAHA
GWALPARA	13	JHITKIA HADI
GWALPARA	14	JHITKIA
GWALPARA	15	PARSI
GWALPARA	16	BISHUNPUR KANTAHI
GWALPARA	17	TEMABHELA
GWALPARA	18	PARSAHA
GWALPARA	19	CHAKLA PITAMBAR MISRA
GWALPARA	20	KALYANPATTI
GWALPARA	21	JAGATPUR
GWALPARA	22	PANDUKIA MILIK
GWALPARA	23	SUKHASAN
GWALPARA	24	ARAZI SUKHASAN
GWALPARA	25	SISWAPATTI
GWALPARA	26	SISWAPATTI
GWALPARA	27	CHATRA BADH
GWALPARA	28	CHATRA BADH
GWALPARA	29	MAHRAJGANJ URF PAHI FATEHPUR
GWALPARA	30	MAHRAJGANJ URF PAHI FATEHPUR
GWALPARA	31	PIRNAGAR
GWALPARA	32	KHOKHSI SARANPUR
GWALPARA	33	KHOKSI SARANPUR MILIK
GWALPARA	34	BISHUNPUR AMUANA
GWALPARA	35	AMUAJA
GWALPARA	36	JHALARI
GWALPARA	37	BHALUAHI ARAZI
GWALPARA	38	RAJPUR SARSANDI OR SARSENDI
GWALPARA	39	MOHAMMADPUR
GWALPARA	40	JHAJHARI
GWALPARA	41	BISWARI
GWALPARA	42	GOALPARA
GWALPARA	43	SAHAHPUR CHAUMUKH
GWALPARA	44	LOHAR
GWALPARA	45	BHALUAHI
GWALPARA	46	SARAUNI KALAN
GWALPARA	47	SINDWARI
GWALPARA	48	FAKIRNA
GWALPARA	49	JOTMANOHAR
GWALPARA	50	CHKLA GOPAL JHA
GWALPARA	51	SHYAM

Table 7.7: Villages in Kumarkhand C. D. Block

C. D. BLOCK	VILLAGE CODE	VILLAGE NAME
KUMARKHAND	1	SARHAD
KUMARKHAND	2	KANKAR
KUMARKHAND	3	RAMPATTI
KUMARKHAND	4	PURAINI
KUMARKHAND	5	SARHAD GATTI
KUMARKHAND	6	SARHADGATTI ALIAS KALAN S CHAK
KUMARKHAND	7	SARHADGATTI ALIAS CHAKLA KALAN
KUMARKHAND	8	DATTA SARDAR CHAKLA
KUMARKHAND	9	RAMNAGAR MAHESH
KUMARKHAND	10	GARHIA
KUMARKHAND	11	GARHIA MILIK
KUMARKHAND	12	GARHIA MILIK
KUMARKHAND	13	BELSANDI
KUMARKHAND	14	GURIA
KUMARKHAND	15	GURIA MILIK
KUMARKHAND	16	GURIA MILIK
KUMARKHAND	17	ISRAIN KALAN
KUMARKHAND	18	BELSARH
KUMARKHAND	19	ISRAIN KHURD
KUMARKHAND	20	KEWATGAWAN
KUMARKHAND	21	SIKRAHTI MILIK
KUMARKHAND	22	MAJHAUL
KUMARKHAND	23	SIKRAHTI
KUMARKHAND	24	KUMAR KHAND
KUMARKHAND	25	BISHUNPUR SUNDAR
KUMARKHAND	26	SIRIPUR MILIK
KUMARKHAND	27	SIRIPUR
KUMARKHAND	28	RAM CHAURA
KUMARKHAND	29	SUKHASAN
KUMARKHAND	30	BABHANTOLI
KUMARKHAND	31	BISHUNPUR KORLAHI CHAKLA
KUMARKHAND	32	LACHHMIPUR MILIK
KUMARKHAND	33	LACHHMIPUR CHANDI ASTHAN
KUMARKHAND	34	BHAWANIPUR

contd...

C. D. BLOCK	VILLAGE CODE	VILLAGE NAME
KUMARKHAND	35	BHAWANIPUR JAGIR
KUMARKHAND	36	RAHTA
KUMARKHAND	37	HANUMANNAGAR
KUMARKHAND	38	ZORAWARGANJ
KUMARKHAND	39	ISRAIN KALAN KHAS MAHAL
KUMARKHAND	40	GORIPUR ISRAIN
KUMARKHAND	41	MANGARWARA MILIK
KUMARKHAND	42	GHORDAUL
KUMARKHAND	43	BELSANDI MILIK
KUMARKHAND	44	RANGPATTI
KUMARKHAND	45	RAHTA CHAKLA
KUMARKHAND	46	PARMANANDPUR CHAKLA
KUMARKHAND	47	RAMNAGAR MAHESH
KUMARKHAND	48	PURAINI KARARIA CHAKLA
KUMARKHAND	49	BAGHMARA
KUMARKHAND	50	HANUMANNAGAR
KUMARKHAND	51	NAINPATTI
KUMARKHAND	52	PARMANANDPUR
KUMARKHAND	53	CHAINPUR
KUMARKHAND	54	CHAINPUR MILIK
KUMARKHAND	55	HANUMANNAGAR CHAKLA
KUMARKHAND	56	CHAKLA GULAM ABBAS
KUMARKHAND	57	HIRAPATTI
KUMARKHAND	58	KHUTHARAJAI
KUMARKHAND	59	SAHORIA BALA
KUMARKHAND	60	LACHHMIPUR BHAGWATI
KUMARKHAND	61	BELARI
KUMARKHAND	62	BISHUNPUR KORLAHI CHAKLA URF JAGIR
KUMARKHAND	63	BISHUNPUR KORLAHI RAJI
KUMARKHAND	64	MANGARWARA KHAS MAHAL
KUMARKHAND	65	MANGARWARA
KUMARKHAND	66	NAWAL GANJ
KUMARKHAND	67	GURIA MILIK
KUMARKHAND	68	LACHHMIPUR BHAGWATI
KUMARKHAND	69	LACHHMIPUR BHAGWATI MILIK
KUMARKHAND	70	SIHPUR
KUMARKHAND	71	SIHPUR CHAKLA

Table 7.8: Villages in Madhepura C. D. Block

C. D. BLOCK	VILLAGE CODE	VILLAGE NAME
MADHEPURA	1	BARAHI
MADHEPURA	2	DUBIAHI
MADHEPURA	3	MATIAHI
MADHEPURA	4	BHELWA
MADHEPURA	5	GORHIARI
MADHEPURA	6	SAHUGARH
MADHEPURA	7	MANIKPUR
MADHEPURA	8	MADHUBAN
MADHEPURA	9	MADANPUR
MADHEPURA	10	TUNIAHI UTTARWARI
MADHEPURA	11	LCHHMIRAMPUR UTTARBARI
MADHEPURA	12	LACHHMIRAMPUR DAKHINWARI
MADHEPURA	13	TUNIAHI DAKHINWARI
MADHEPURA	14	HANUMANNAGAR CHAKLA
MADHEPURA	15	MUDWALA DACHHINWARI
MADHEPURA	16	SIRIPAR UTTARWARI
MADHEPURA	17	SIRIPUR DAKHINWARI
MADHEPURA	18	SUKHASAN UTTARBARI
MADHEPURA	19	SUKHASAN DAKHINWARI
MADHEPURA	20	KHOPAITI BADH BAHADUR SINGH
MADHEPURA	21	CHAKLA BAHADUR SINGH UTTARWARI
MADHEPURA	22	DAKHINWARI CHAKLA
MADHEPURA	23	BUNIAD SINGH CHAKLA
MADHEPURA	24	GOTHKHOPAITI
MADHEPURA	25	KHOPAITI
MADHEPURA	26	MUDWALA UTTARWADI
MADHEPURA	27	BALAM
MADHEPURA	28	GARHIA
MADHEPURA	29	MURHO
MADHEPURA	30	MURHO LAKHERAJ
MADHEPURA	31	BUDHMA LAKHERAJ
MADHEPURA	32	BUDHMA
MADHEPURA	33	BHADAUL
MADHEPURA	34	PARARIA
MADHEPURA	35	MACHH BAKHRA
MADHEPURA	36	GORHAILA
MADHEPURA	37	SAKARPURA
MADHEPURA	38	BETAUNA
MADHEPURA	39	MAHESWA
MADHEPURA	40	CHAURA
MADHEPURA	41	BAKHRI
MADHEPURA	42	DHORGAON
MADHEPURA	43	GARTHAN
MADHEPURA	44	AMANAT UTTARWARI
MADHEPURA	45	AMANAT DACHHINWARI
MADHEPURA	46	BHIRAKHI UTTARWARI
MADHEPURA	47	BHIRAKHI DACHHINWARI
MADHEPURA	48	MADH
MADHEPURA	49	PITHAHI

Table 7.9: Villages in Murliganj C. D. Block

C. D. BLOCK	VILLAGE CODE	VILLAGE NAME
MURLIGANJ	1	GANGAPUR
MURLIGANJ	2	BINDRABAN OR BRINDABAN
MURLIGANJ	3	SAKHUA
MURLIGANJ	4	POKHRAM MILIK
MURLIGANJ	5	POKHRAM
MURLIGANJ	6	PARMANANDPUR MILIK
MURLIGANJ	7	GOPALITOLA
MURLIGANJ	8	TIRKONA
MURLIGANJ	9	PARMANPUR
MURLIGANJ	10	KHARI
MURLIGANJ	11	BELO OR BELO GOTH OR BELOGOTH
MURLIGANJ	12	JITAPUR
MURLIGANJ	13	BHAIROPATTI
MURLIGANJ	14	BISHUNPUR
MURLIGANJ	15	LABTOL
MURLIGANJ	16	PARWA
MURLIGANJ	17	NARHA
MURLIGANJ	18	BHATKHORI
MURLIGANJ	19	JITAPUR ARAZI
MURLIGANJ	20	TAMAUTPARSA
MURLIGANJ	21	JORGAWAN
MURLIGANJ	22	MIRGANJ
MURLIGANJ	23	RAMPUR
MURLIGANJ	24	GAMHARIA EKDARA
MURLIGANJ	25	DINAPATTI
MURLIGANJ	26	KHUSROPATTI OR KHUSROOPATTEE
MURLIGANJ	27	PAKILPAR
MURLIGANJ	28	DIGHI
MURLIGANJ	29	RAGHUNATHPUR
MURLIGANJ	30	SAHEBGANJ ITAHARI OR ITAHARI
MURLIGANJ	31	HARPUR
MURLIGANJ	32	GUDAR CHAKLA
MURLIGANJ	33	SINGHIAN
MURLIGANJ	34	RANI PATTI
MURLIGANJ	35	AMARI DHARAHRA
MURLIGANJ	36	RAJNI
MURLIGANJ	37	RAJNIGOT MILIK
MURLIGANJ	38	BISHUNPUR KORLAHI CHAKLA
MURLIGANJ	39	BISHUNPUR KORLAHI MILIK
MURLIGANJ	40	GHAGHA
MURLIGANJ	41	JAIRAM PUR
MURLIGANJ	42	JAIRAM PUR JAGIR
MURLIGANJ	43	MIRGANJ (MURLIGANJ)
MURLIGANJ	44	MURLIGANJ JAGIR
MURLIGANJ	45	PACHGACHHIA

Table 7.10: Villages in Puraini C. D. Block

C. D. BLOCK	VILLAGE CODE	VILLAGE NAME
PURAINI	1	MEGHU SINGH HAWALDAR JAGIR
PURAINI	2	DURGAPUR
PURAINI	3	KALEKHAN NAEK JAGIR
PURAINI	4	GANESHPUR
PURAINI	5	MADAN MILIK
PURAINI	6	PURAINI MILIK
PURAINI	7	PURANI
PURAINI	8	BAGAHRA
PURAINI	9	PURAINI BANSGOPAL
PURAINI	10	NURULLAPUR ALIAS JAGIRDAR
PURAINI	11	DUMRAIL
PURAINI	12	KANWANRAHI
PURAINI	13	MAKHDAMPUR DHAPDHARA
PURAINI	14	NAGAR ALI MILIK
PURAINI	15	DURGAPUR ARAZI
PURAINI	16	NARDEH
PURAINI	17	NAYATOLA URF HAMIDPUR
PURAINI	18	KHERO
PURAINI	19	AURAHI
PURAINI	20	SAPARDA
PURAINI	21	KARAMA
PURAINI	22	MOHAMMADPUR BALIA
PURAINI	23	RAOTA
PURAINI	24	BASDEOPUR
PURAINI	25	KURSANDI
PURAINI	26	AMANAT SARKAR
PURAINI	27	AMANAT SARKAR
PURAINI	28	HARBAN SINGH NAEK JAGIR
PURAINI	29	NARDA
PURAINI	30	NAYATOLA URF HAMIDPUR
PURAINI	31	PARAN SINGH JAMADAR JAGIR

Table 7.11: Villages in Shankarpur C. D. Block

C.D. BLOCK	VILLAGE CODE	VILLAGE NAME
SHANKARPUR	1	KAMARGAON (PART IN SINGHESHWAR)
SHANKARPUR	2	CHAMPA NAGAR
SHANKARPUR	3	RAIBHIR
SHANKARPUR	4	JIRWA
SHANKARPUR	5	GIDHA
SHANKARPUR	6	BEHRARI
SHANKARPUR	7	BARI
SHANKARPUR	8	MAURA
SHANKARPUR	9	BASANTPUR

Table 7.12: Villages in Singheshwar C. D. Block

BLOCK CODE	VILLAGE CODE	VILLAGE NAME
SINGHESWAR	1	KANHUAN GORIARI
SINGHESWAR	2	JALWARA
SINGHESWAR	3	PIPRAHI
SINGHESWAR	4	LATRAHI
SINGHESWAR	5	MANPUR
SINGHESWAR	6	MAHULI
SINGHESWAR	7	GOPALPUR
SINGHESWAR	8	KAMARGAON
SINGHESWAR	9	BARHARI
SINGHESWAR	10	DANDARI
SINGHESWAR	11	BAIRBANA
SINGHESWAR	12	DULARI
SINGHESWAR	13	BEHRI
SINGHESWAR	14	BURHAWE
SINGHESWAR	15	RAMPATTI
SINGHESWAR	16	SINGHESHWAR OR SINGHESWARSTHAN
SINGHESWAR	17	RUPAULI
SINGHESWAR	18	SUKHASAN
SINGHESWAR	19	GOHUMANI
SINGHESWAR	20	JAJHAT
SINGHESWAR	21	MAJARHAT
SINGHESWAR	22	RAMPUR
SINGHESWAR	23	GAURIPUR
SINGHESWAR	24	SAROPATTI
SINGHESWAR	25	PATORI
SINGHESWAR	26	LALPUR
SINGHESWAR	27	GURTARA

Table 7.13: Villages in Udakishunganj C. D. Block

C. D. BLOCK	VILLAGE CODE	VILLAGE NAME
UDAKISHUNGANJ	1	NAYANAGAR ARAZI
UDAKISHUNGANJ	2	SINGAR PUR
UDAKISHUNGANJ	3	KHANARDA
UDAKISHUNGANJ	4	BUDHMA
UDAKISHUNGANJ	5	SHAHIDPUR
UDAKISHUNGANJ	6	JOTAILI
UDAKISHUNGANJ	7	RUHUA URF HARPUR HINGO
UDAKISHUNGANJ	8	MURLI CHANDWA
UDAKISHUNGANJ	9	KUMARPUR
UDAKISHUNGANJ	10	RAMPUR DEHRU
UDAKISHUNGANJ	11	MAJAURA
UDAKISHUNGANJ	12	RAIBHIRA
UDAKISHUNGANJ	13	PARIHARPUR
UDAKISHUNGANJ	14	DEBAIL
UDAKISHUNGANJ	15	BIRI RANPAL
UDAKISHUNGANJ	16	TIRASI
UDAKISHUNGANJ	17	RAGHUNATHPUR PAKARIA
UDAKISHUNGANJ	18	MAHESHUA
UDAKISHUNGANJ	19	TELDIHA
UDAKISHUNGANJ	20	LACHHMIPUR
UDAKISHUNGANJ	21	LACHHMIPUR MILIK
UDAKISHUNGANJ	22	RASULPUR QASIM URF MURLI CHANDWA
UDAKISHUNGANJ	23	LASHKARI
UDAKISHUNGANJ	24	BARATENI
UDAKISHUNGANJ	25	CHAK FAIZULLAH
UDAKISHUNGANJ	26	BHALUAHI
UDAKISHUNGANJ	27	SHEKHPUR CHAMAN
UDAKISHUNGANJ	28	NAYANAGAR
UDAKISHUNGANJ	29	BHAWANANDPUR AIAS KUMARGANGS
UDAKISHUNGANJ	30	PHANHAN
UDAKISHUNGANJ	31	RAHTA
UDAKISHUNGANJ	32	KISANGANJ
UDAKISHUNGANJ	33	RAMPUR KHORA
UDAKISHUNGANJ	34	HARAILI
UDAKISHUNGANJ	35	UDA OR UDAKISHUNGANJ
UDAKISHUNGANJ	36	RAMSAHAI MILIK ALIAS GARIBJHACHAKLA
UDAKISHUNGANJ	37	RAMSAHAI MILIK GARIBJHA CHAKLA
UDAKISHUNGANJ	38	BARAHI
UDAKISHUNGANJ	39	ANANDPURA MILIK
UDAKISHUNGANJ	40	ANANDPUR
UDAKISHUNGANJ	41	MADHUBAN
UDAKISHUNGANJ	42	ALAMNAGAR
UDAKISHUNGANJ	43	MOHAMMAD DANISH ENGLIS
UDAKISHUNGANJ	44	ROSHAN ALI MILIK

Bibliography

PRIMARY SOURCE

List of Informants

SL. NO	NAME OF THE INFORMANTS	AGE	PLACE OF INTERVIEW	CONCERNED SITE
1	Purnanand Pathak	51	Madhukar Chak	Madhukar Chak-I and II
2	Sudhir Kumar Pathak	55	Madhukar Chak	Madhukar Chak-I and II
3	Rajendra Prasad Yadav	69	Kushathan	Kushathan (Jaso Yadav ka Tila)
4	Nageshwar Das	57	Biri Ranpal	Biri Ranpal-I Jagah (Kabeermath)
5	Sahdev Shah	55	Biri Ranpal	Biri Ranpal-II Bhatwa Jamindari
6	Surendar Rai	73	Laxmipur	Laxmipur
7	Tanuklal Yadav	65	Kumharpur	Kumharpur
8	Diwakar Prasad Singh	52	Nayanagar (Bhagwatee Sthan	Nayanagar (Bhagwatee Sthan
9	Ravindra Kumar Singh	65	Nayanagar	Nayanagar (Bhagwatee Sthan

contd...

10	Mohammed Inammudin	50	Madhelee	Madhelee
11	Ramnaresh Sharma	60	Muraut	Muraut
12	Vinodand Jha alias Baua Jha	47	Khuran village	Dakneesthan in Khuran village
13	Bindeshwari Poddar	60	Rohwa	Rohwa (Hasangadh)
14	Jagarnath Das	60	Rohwa	Rohwa (Hasangadh)
15	Naresh Yadav	28	Itahari	Itahari (Itahari Dih)
16	Ashok Kumar Yadav	50	Gohumani	Gohumani (Deeh in Gohumani)
17	Anmol Yadav	43	Pakilpar	Pakilpar (Baba Jatadharee Shivalaya Sthan)
18	Sitaram Yadav	68	Pakilpar	Pakilpar (Baba Jatadharee Shivalaya Sthan)
19	Satrughan Yadav	–	Dumaria (Amari Gudar Chakla-Murliganj Block)	Dumaria (Amari Gudar Chakla)
20	Bilo Yadav	–	Dumaria/Amari Gudar Chakla	Dumaria (Amari Gudar Chakla)
21	Mahant Ramnaryan Das	–	Dumaria/Amari Gudar Chakla	Dumaria (Amari Gudar Chakla)
22	Vijendra Prasad Yadav	–	Kolhaipatti	Kolhaipatti (Baba Chilka Ram)
23	Ramjee Yadav	–	Kolhaipatti	Kolhaipatti (Baba Chilka Ram)
24	Anil Kumar Bhaskar	30	Jorgawan	Jorgawan (Samedh-Murliganj Block)

contd...

25	Joginder Chaurasia	80	Jorgawan	Jorgawan (Samedh)
26	Badal Razak	80	Jorgawan	Jorgawan (Samedh)
27	Shobakant Yadav	52	Khusropatti	Khusropatti (Nawratna Hatta)
28	Nageswar Yadav	80	Rampur	Rampur (Thakurbaree)
29	Sudeshwar Das	65	Brindaban or Bindraban	Brindaban or Bindraban (Ram Jankee Thakurbaree)
30	Ramjee Mandal	61	Belo Goth	Belo Goth (Lukeshawaree Sthan)
31	Munna Singh	47	Belo Goth	Belo Goth (Lukeshawaree Sthan)
32	Vijendra Singh	59	Belo Goth	Belo Goth (Lukeshawaree Sthan)
33	Rameshwari Mandal	11	Belo Goth	Belo Goth (Lukeshawaree Sthan)
34	Jagadish Prashad Yadav	76	Rajni	Rajni (Mangnee Baba Ka Sthan)
35	Naine Lal Mandal	100	Srinagar	Srinagar
36	Pawan Kumar	38	Srinagar	Srinagar
37	Brahmadev Prasad Yadav	57	Rupauli	Rupauli (Itahdeeh)
38	Shiv Narayan Yadav	69	Piprahi	Piprahi (Mahwariya Gadhee)
39	Jagdeesh Yadav	55	Parwaha	Parwaha (Mahwariya Gadhee)
40	Pushuplal Yadav	84	Itahari	Itahari-I

Source: Field visits

BOOKS

Adams, R. M., *Land Behind Baghdad* (Chicago, 1965).

—. *Heartland of Cities* (Chicago, 1981).

Allchin, V. R., *The Archaeology of Early Historic South Asia: The Emergence of Cities and States* (Cambridge, 1995).

Anand, Kumar, *History and Archaeology of Buxar, Bhojpur and Rohtas Regions* (Delhi, 1995).

Belgar, J. D., *Archaeological Survey of India*, Report, vol. 8, Calcutta, 1878.

Bhattacharya, N. N., *The Geographical Dictionary, Ancient and Early Medieval India* (Delhi, 1991).

Bradford, J., *Ancient Landscapes* (London, 1957).

Chakrabarti, Dilip K., *Theoretical Issues in Indian Archaeology* (Delhi, 1988).

—. *Archaeology of Eastern India: Chota Nagpur Plateau and West Bengal* (Delhi, 1993).

—. *Archaeological Geography of the Ganga Plain- The Lower and the Middle Ganga* (Delhi: Permanent Black, 2001).

Chakrabarti, Dilip K., and N. Lahiri, *Copper and Its Alloys in Ancient India* (Delhi, 1996).

Chakrabati, K. K., *The Archaeology of Ancient India Cities* (New Delhi, 1995).

Chang, K. C., ed., *Settlement Archaeology* (Paolo Alto, 1968).

Chattopadhyaya, B. D., *A Survey of Historical Geography of Ancient India* (Delhi, 1984).

Chattopadhyaya, D. P., ed., *Taranatha's History of Buddhism in India* (Simla, 1970).

Chaudhury, A. K., 'Sultanganj: Its Art and Culture', in A. K. Sinha, *Glories of Bhagalpur*, pp. 26-35.

Chaudhury, P. C. Roy, *Bihar District Gazetteer-Bhagalpur* (Patna: Printed by Superintendent Secretariat Press, 1962).

—. *Inside Bihar* (Calcutta: Bookland Private Limited, 1962).

—. *Bihar District Gazetteer- Purnea* (Patna: Printed by Superintendent Secretariat Press, 1963).

—. *Bihar District Gazetteer- Santhal Parganas* (Patna: Printed by Superintendent Secretariat Press, 1965).

—. *Bihar District Gazetteer- Saharsa* (Patna: Printed by Superintendent Secretariat Press).

Chib, Sukhdev Singh, *This Beautiful India- Bihar* (New Delhi: Light and Life Publishers, 1980).

Chopra, N., ed., *Encyclopedia of India* (New Delhi: Rima, 1992).

Crawford, O. G. S., *Archaeology in the Field* (London, 1953).

Cunningham, A., *Report of Tours in the Gangetic Province from Badaon to Bihar in 1875-76 and 1877-78* (Calcutta, Govt. of India).

—. *Archaeological Survey of India*, Report, vol.3 (Calcutta, 1873).

Cunningham, A., and H. B. W. Garrick, *Reports of Tours in North and South Bihar in 1880-81*(Calcutta, Govt. of India).

Cutterell, Arthur, ed., *Encyclopedia of Ancient Civilization* (New York: Mayflower, 1980).

Diwakar, R. R., *Bihar through the Ages* (Calcutta: Orient Longmans, 1958).

East, W. G., *The Geography behind History* (London, 1965).

Erdody, G. *Urbanization in Early Historic India* (Oxford, 1988).

Evans, John G., *An Introduction to Environmental Archaeology*

(London: Paul Elek, 19787).

Febvre, L., *A Geographical Introduction to History* (London, 1925).

Finzi, Claudio Vita, *Archaeological Sites in their Setting* (London: Thames and Hudson, 1978).

Garick, H. B. W., *Report of a Tour through Behar, Central India, Peshawar and Yusufzai* (Calcutta: ASI).

Gosh, A., *An Encyclopedia of Indian Archaeology* (Delhi: Munshiram Manoharlal Publishers Pvt. Ltd, 1989).

—. *The City in Early Historical India* (Shimla, 1973).

Ghosh, N. N., *Early History of Kausambi* (Delhi: Durga Publications, 1985).

Grmbly, Shona, ed., *Encyclopedia of the Ancient World* (London: Fitzroy Dearborn Publisher, 2000).

Hare, E. M., trans., *Anguttara Nikaya,* vols.3 and 4.

Hester, James J. *Introduction to Archaeology* (New York: Holt, Rinehart and Winston, 1976).

Hole, Frank and Heizer, Robert F., *An Introduction to Prehistoric Archaeology* (New York: Holt, Rinehart and Winston, 1965).

Jain, V. K. *Prehistory and Protohistory of India- An Appraisal-Palaeolithic-Non-Harappan Chalcolithic Cultures* (New Delhi: D.K Printworld Pvt. Ltd., 2006).

Jha, D. N. *Ancient India- In Historical Outline* (New Delhi: Manohar Publishers and Distributors, 1999).

Jha, Ugra Nath, *The Genealogies and Genealogists of Mithila* (Varanasi: Kishor Vidya Niketan, 1980).

Kosambi, D. D., *The Culture and Civilization of Ancient India in Historical Outline* (London, 1966) & (New Delhi: Vikas Publishing House, 1981).

Lahiri, Nayanjot, *The Archaeology of Indian Trade Routes* (up to c. 200 BC) (Delhi, 1992).

Lal, M., *Settlement History and Rise of Civilization in the Gang-Yamuna Doab* (Delhi, 1984).

Law, B. C., *Historical Archaeology of Ancient India* (France: Societe Asiatique de Paris, 1967).

—. *Kshtriya Clans in Buddhist India* (Calcutta, 1922).

Legge, J., *Travels of Fa-Hien* (Oxford: Clarendon Press, 1886).

Majumdar, S. N., ed., *Cunningham's Ancient Geography of India* (Calcutta, 1924).

Martin, M., *The History, Antiquities, Topography and Statistics of Eastern India*, vol. II (London, 1838).

Mishra, Yogendra, *An Early History of Vaishali* (Delhi, 1996).

—. *History of Videha* (Patna: Janaki Prakashan, 1981).

Mookerji, R. K., *Ancient Indian Education* (London: Macmillan and Co., 1947).

Mukhopadhay, N., *Kausiki* (Calcutta, 1998).

Oldham, C. E. A. W., ed., *Journal of Francis Buchanan- Kept During the Survey of the District of Bhagalpur in 1810-11* (Patna: Superintendent, Government Printing, Bihar and Orissa, 1930).

Pandey, M. S., *The Historical Geography and Topography of Bihar* (Delhi, 1963).

Patil, D. R., *Antiquarian Remains in Bihar* (Patna: Kashi Prasad Jayaswal Research Institute, 1963).

Prasad, R. C., *Archaeology of Champa and Vikramsila* (Delhi, 1987).

Raychaudhuri, *H. C., Political History of Ancient India* (Delhi: Oxford University Press, 1996).

Roy, T. N., *The Ganges Civilization* (New Delhi: Ramanand Vidya Bhawan, 1983).

Sahai, B., *The Inscriptions of Bihar* (New Delhi: Ramananda Vidya Bhawan, 1983).

Sahu, B. P., *From Hunters to Breeders: Faunal Background of Early India* (New Delhi, 1988).

Saletore, R. N., *Encyclopedia of Indian Culture* (New Delhi: Sterling, 1983).

Sastri, Hirananda, *Archaeology and Ancient Indian History* (Gujarat Vernacular Society Research Series, 21).

Sharma, R. S., *India's Ancient Past* (New Delhi, 2005).

—. *The State and Varna Formation in the Mid-Ganga Plains: An Ethnoarchaeological View* (New Delhi, 1996).

—. *Aspects of Political Ideas and Institutions in Ancient India* (Delhi, 1991).

—. *Origin of the State in India* (Bombay, 1990).

—. *Material Culture and Social Formations in Ancient India* (Delhi, 1983).

Singh, G. P., *Facets of Ancient Indian History and Culture: New Perception* (New Delhi: D.K. Printworld (P) Ltd., India, 2003).

—. *Republics, Kingdoms, Towns and Cities in Ancient India*

(New Delhi: D.K. Printworld (P) Ltd., 2003).

Singh, Purshottam and Ashok Kumar Singh, *The Archaeology of Middle Ganga Plain- New Perspective* (New Delhi: Aryan Books International, 2004).

Singh, R. L., *Indian: A Regional Geography* (Varanasi: National Geographical Society of India, 1971).

—. *India: Regional Studies* (Calcutta: Indian National Committee for Geography, 1968).

Sinha, A. K., *Glories of Bhagalpur* (Bhagalpur, 1984).

Sinha, B. K., *Archaeology of North Bihar* (Delhi, 1999).

Sinha, B. P., *Dynastic History of Magdha cir. 450-1200 A.D* (New Delhi: Abhinav Publications, 1997).

—. *Archaeology and Art of India* (Delhi, 1979).

—. *Potteries in Ancient India* (New Delhi, 1969).

Sinha, B.P., ed., *Comprehensive History of Bihar,* vols i and ii (Patna: K. P. Jayaswal Research Institute, 1974).

Sinha, H. P., *Archaeological and Cultural History of North Bihar* (Delhi, 1994).

Sircar, D. C., *Studies in the Geography of Ancient and Medieval India* (Delhi, 1971).

Thakran, R. C. *Dynamics of Settlement Archaeology- Haryana* (New Delhi: Gyan Publishing House, 2000).

Thakur, U., *History of Mithila* (Darbhanga, 1988).

Thakur, V. K., *Urbanization in Ancient India* (New Delhi, 1981).

Thapar Romila, *From Lineage to State* (Bombay, 1984).

Thomas, D. H., *Archaeology* (New York, 1998).

Tripathi, Ramashankar, *History of Ancient India* (Delhi: Motilal Banarasidass, Reprint 1981).

Triveda, Devasahpya, *The Pre-Mauryan History of Bihar* (Banaras: Motilal Banarasidass, 1953).

Wagstaff, J. M. ed., *Landscape and Culture: Geographical and Archaeological Perspectives* (Oxford, 1987).

Woodward, F. L., trans., *Anguttara Nikaya* vol. i., p. 225.

ARTICLES IN JOURNALS AND PERIODICALS

Agrawala, V. S., 'Ancient Indian Geography', *IHQ*, 28, 1952, pp. 205-14.

Asher, F. M., 'Vikramsila Mahavihara', *Bangladesh Lalitaka*, Dhaka, 1975.

Bairui, N. C., and S. Chanda 'Late Quaternary pollen analysis in relation to palaeoecology, biostratigraphy and dating of Calcutta peat', *Proc. Ind. Nat. Sc. Acad. B.* vol. 58, no. 4, pp. 191-200.

Chakrabarti, Dilip. K., A.K. Prasad, S.K. Jha, K. Anand, and R.K. Chattopadhyay, 'Preliminary observations on the distribution of archaeological sites in the south Bihar plains', *South Asian Studies* 11, 1995, pp.129-147.

Chakrabarti, Dilip K., A.K. Prasad, S.K. Jha, and A. C. Verma, 'From Purnea to Champaran: The Distribution of Archaeological Sites in the North Bihar Plains', *South Asian Studies* 12, 1996, pp.147-58.

Fairservis, W. A., 'Origin, Character, and Decline of an Early Civilization', *American Museum*, Novitates, 2302, American Museum of Natural History, 1967, pp. 1-48.

Frankfort, H., 'Town-planning in ancient Mesopotamia', *Town Planning Review*, 21, 1950, pp-98-115.

Lal, M., 'Summary of Four Seasons Explorations in Kanpur Districts', *ME*, 1984, p 24.

Trigger, B., 'Settlement Archaeology- Its Goals and Promise', AA 32, 1967, pp.149-60.

Waddel, L. A., 'Discovery of Buddhist Remains at Mount Uren in Mungir', *JASB* 61, 1892, pp.1-24.

Willey, Gorden R., 'Settlement Patterns', *Americanist Archaeology.*

Various 'Explorations and Excavations (Bihar)', *Indian Archaeology- A Review,* New Delhi.

JOURNALS AND PERIODICALS

Ancient India-Bulletin of the Archaeological Survey of India.

Annals of the Bhandarkar Oriental Research Institute.

Epigraphia Indica.

Imperial Gazetteer.

Indian Antiquary.

Indian Archaeology - A Review.

Indian Culture.

Indian Historical Quarterly.

Journal Asiatique(French).

Journal of Historical Research, Ranchi University.

Journal of Indian History.

Journal of Oriental Research, Madras.

Journal of U. P. Historical Society.

Journal of the American Oriental Society.

Journal of the Asiatic Society of Bengal.

Journal of the Banaras Hindu University.

Journal of the Bihar Research Society.

Journal of the Department of Letters, Calcutta University.

Journal of the Pali Text Society.

Journal of the Royal Asiatic Society.

Modern Review.

Proceedings of the All-India Oriental Conference.

Proceedings of the Indian History Congress.

Purnima (Nepali).

Sahitya (Hindi).

Sanskrita Sanjivana Patrika (Sanskrit).

The Indian Historical Quarterly.

The Indian Historical Review.

WEBSITES

URL: http://www.angindia.com/angika_anga_tourism.html-59k

URL: http://www.angindia,com/angika_silk_city_bhagalpurhtm/48k

URL: http://www.answerscom/topic/kingdoms_of_ancient_India_67k

URL: http://www.answers.com/topic/vikramshila - 30k

URL: http://www.asi.nic.in/writereaddata/sublinkimages/39.htm - 28k

URL: http://www.asi.nic.in/writereaddata/sublinkimages/148.htm - 875k-

URL: http://www.banglapedia.search.com.bd/HT/V_0046.htm - 10k

URL: http://www.Bhagalpuronline.com/ - 76k

URL: http://www.education.nic.in

URL: http://www.education.nic.in/cd50years/12/8I/62/8I620E01.htm -2

URL: http://www.en.wikipedia.org/wiki;Anga

URL: http://www.en.wikipedia.org/wiki/category:Ancient_Indian

URL: http://www.en.wikipedia.org/wiki/Landscape

URL: http://www.factbites.com/topics/Vikramshila - 50k

URL: http://www.hindubooks.org/temples/bihar/sultanganj/page7.htm -22

URL: http://www.indianngos.com/districts/munger_abouthtm-58k

URL: http://www.island.lk/index.html

URL: http://www.madhepura.nic.in/ - 24k

URL: http://www.madhepura.nic.in/Dist%20Int.htm - 40k

URL:http://www.munger.nic.in/ATMA/Munger/Munger%20district

URL: http://www.purnia.nic.in/aboutpurnia.htm - 24k

UNPUBLISHED SOURCES

Alam, Mohammed Eharar, 'Socio-Economic Profile of Muslims in the Kosi-Mahananda Doab: A Geographical Analysis', unpublished Ph.D. thesis, Department of Geography, Jamia Milia Islamia University, New Delhi, 2002.

Dutt, B., *PGW Settlements in Haryana*, unpublished Ph.D. thesis, Kurushetra University, Kurushetra, 1980.

Index

E

F

G

H

I

J

K

❏ ❏ ❏